BORNE ON THE CARRYING STREAM

BORNE ON THE CARRYING STREAM

THE LEGACY OF
HAMISH HENDERSON

Editor
Eberhard Bort
University of Edinburgh

BORNE ON THE CARRYING STREAM
THE LEGACY OF HAMISH HENDERSON
First published 2010 by Grace Note Publications
in collaboration with the Carrying Stream Festival
Grange of Locherlour, Ochtertyre, PH7 4JS, Scotland

ISBN 978-1-907676-01-7

A catalogue record for this book is available from the British Library

Cover design by Grace Note Publications

Front cover photo by the late Ian MacKenzie, with permission of Talitha MacKenzie and the School of Scottish Studies, University of Edinburgh. First verse of 'The Freedom Come-All-Ye' in Hamish Henderson's own hand-writing, from the collection of Margaret Bennett.

Back cover photo by Gonzalo J Mazzei. Hamish Henderson portrait by Andrew J Ward, Bardic Voyage Project. (www.andrewjward.com).

ACKNOWLEDGEMENTS

Ewan McVicar's chapter is an expanded version of the Carrying Stream Annual Hamish Henderson Lecture of 10 November 2007.

Geordie McIntyre's chapter is a slightly revised and expanded version of his illustrated talk at the fifth Carrying Stream Festival in November 2006—he was vocally assisted by **Alison McMorland**.

Margaret Bennett's chapter is based on her Hamish Henderson Lecture at the third Carrying Stream Festival on 13 November 2004.

Timothy Neat's essay is an expanded version of the Hamish Henderson Lecture given by him as part of the fourth Carrying Stream Festival, delivered on 12 November 2005 in the City Chambers, Edinburgh.

An earlier version of **Donald Smith**'s chapter was published in Geddes and Grosset (eds), *A Sense of Place*, New Lanark: Waverley Books Ltd, in association with Edinburgh UNESCO City of Literature, 2005, and is here published with the kind permission of the editors and publishers.

Mario Relich's chapter is an expanded version of a review published in The Dark Horse (winter 2001-2002), with the kind permission of the journal's editor Gerry Cambridge.

Pino Mereu would like to thank Paddy Bort for inviting him to the Carrying Stream Festival, Margaret Bennett and her husband Gonzalo for organising his trip with love and support, and Alison Adam, the translator of his talk, who unfortunately could not be in Edinburgh. She is a Scottish singer and actress who lives in Rome and appears in Pino's two shows, *Quadernos Iscrittos* and *The Ballad of the D-Day Dodgers*. He would like to dedicate his chapter to Martyn Bennett and Stuart MacGregor.

Sections of **Steve Byrne**'s chapter appeared in his paper 'Scots Song and Tobar an Dualchais/Kist o Riches: a reassessment of current perceptions', given at the Òran 2010 Sang conference at Sabhal Mòr Ostaig, Skye, 3 June 2010, proceedings of which were unpublished at the time of writing.

Joy Hendry's chapter is the edited and slightly expanded transcript of a BBC Radio 3 programme compiled and presented by her and produced by Julian May. *The Sympathetic Imagination: Scottish Poets of the Second World War* was broadcast by BBC Radio 3 on 7 May, 1990 and is here published for the first time, with the kind permission of the Producer.

Gary West's chapter first appeared in Tocher, 58, pp. 41-49 (2005) and is here reproduced with the kind permission of the author.

We thank all who have given permission for work reproduced in this volume. Every effort has been made to trace copyright holders and where this has been unsuccessful and work has been included here, it is with apologies and in the hope that such use in this volume will be welcomed.

FOR KÄTZEL HENDERSON

CONTENTS

HAMISH HENDERSON:
THE DEMOCRATIC MUSE

Eberhard Bort

La fuente y el arroyo
de la canción añeja.

The fountain and the stream
of the ancient song.

Federico García Lorca, 'Balada de la Placeta'[1]

November 1999. We did not know then that it would be the last Edinburgh Folk Festival. We knew it was Hamish Henderson's eightieth birthday. And an illustrous crowd of musicians and singers paid homage to Hamish. A packed house at the Hub. Alison McMorland gave a breathtaking rendering of 'The Flyting o Life and Daith'. Towards the end of a memorable night, 'The Freedom Come-All-Ye' rang out, led by Hamish himself. Coming down from the stage, he stopped at his seat to pick up his trademark hat, donned it and—while the red sea of the audience parted in a standing ovation—made straight for the bar. A gallus moment.

A few hours earlier, David Francis, the director of the Edinburgh Folk Festival, had dispatched me to collect Hamish from his home on the southside of the Meadows. Riding up to the Hub, we chatted about his favourite German poets—Hölderlin, Heine and Rilke—whose poems he had translated into English and who had a profound influence on his own poetry. The following afternoon the cream of Scottish poets and songwriters would come together for a ceilidh in

Hamish's honour, from Eddie Morgan to George Burns, Angus Calder, Joy Hendry, Nancy Nicolson and George Gunn.

The following year, at the Scottish Storytelling Centre, Hamish Henderson's *Collected Poems and Songs* were launched. At long last, thanks to the editorial efforts of Raymond Ross, Hamish's work was made more widely accessible. Hamish, a 'fully paid up member of the oral tradition', had been reluctant to commit his poems and songs to print, rather relying on the 'democratic muse', hoping that others might be inspired to help carrying them along into the tradition. The *Collected Poems and Songs* completed what could loosely be termed a trilogy: a selection of his letters in 1992 and of his critical writings in 1996, both edited by Alec Finlay.[2]

When we learned of Hamish's death in March 2002, the committee of Edinburgh Folk Club decided to organise a festival in his memory, to be held around his birthday in November. We have called it the Carrying Stream Festival, as this best reflects Hamish's concept of folk culture. On the suggestion of our committee member Roddy Macdonald we also commissioned the artist Jan Miller to produce a papermaché bust of Hamish which was revealed at the first Festival, then found a home in Sandy Bell's, Hamish's inofficial office, before we loaned it to the National Museum where it now graces the 'Scotland: A Changing Nation' exhibition.

The Festival has, ever since, celebrated the rich legacy Hamish Henderson has left us with—be it as a collector of folk songs, ballads and stories, as one of Scotland's finest songwriters, as translator from Gaelic, French, German, Latin and Greek, or as political activist. We thus honour and celebrate the father of the Scottish folk revival. Without him, who knows whether there would be an Edinburgh Folk Club? Every autumn we try to bring together singers, musicians, storytellers and poets, established names, tradition bearers of renown, and young talents, both from Scotland and—Hamish was a small 'n' nationalist and a big 'I' Internationalist—from other countries. Thanks are due to all my fellow committee members over the years since we embarked on the Carrying Stream venture: the late Iain MacLennan, Andy May, Roddy Macdonald, John Jessiman, Ian Hardie, David Ferrard, David Vivanco, Heather McKenzie and Allan McMillan.

Hamish's trust in the carrying stream of the tradition is the inspiration behind the Festival, as it has inspired the folk revival for the past sixty years or so. No fear of contamination—let art forms cross-fertilise, have fusions, cross-overs, the well is there, 'the fountain and the stream/ of the ancient song'. It was in that spirit that he endorsed the daring musical explorations—the 'brave new music'—of Martyn Bennett. It was in that spirit that he entered into the flytings with Hugh MacDiarmid about the role of folk song and folk culture as 'resources … of unrivalled beauty and power… resources hardly comprehended as yet, let alone tapped.'[3]

At the Carrying Stream Festival 2009, celebrating what would have been Hamish's ninetieth birthday, and the publication of Timothy Neat's second and final volume of his groundbreaking biography, we organised a panel at the Storytelling Centre, under the auspices of its director, Donald Smith, to discuss the role of Hamish and his work in the twenty-first century. One very interesting remark stuck in my mind. Donald Smith observed that there seemed to be a divide between Hamish's contemporaries, those who knew the man, those with an anecdote to tell that sums the man up, a tale from Sandy Bell's, a reminiscence of encouragement, of time spent in his company—and, on the other hand, those who have come after or never met him in their lives. In the audience was a student from Edinburgh University, engaged in writing a PhD thesis on Hamish Henderson, and he remarked how little he could find in writing about his subject, but that nearly everyone he spoke to had a warm-hearted story to tell. Donald made the point that there seems to be an in-crowd, the initiated, those who speak with great fondness of their idol, and those who are slightly baffled, perhaps feel excluded because they lacked that key to unlock the Hamish phenomenon—divide, as it were, between those who always speak fondly of 'Hamish', and those who would use 'Hamish Henderson'.

Hamish once gave the 'Immortal Memory' at an Edinburgh Folk Club Burns Night which, as Jean Bechhofer recalls,[4] was in danger of becoming the never-ending memory, as it ran for a solid hour or so—that is the stuff legends are made of. Or take Angus Calder's vivid reminiscence of Hamish presiding over a typical 'impromptu colloquium' on an afternoon in Sandy Bell's.[5] 'Everyone, it seems, has a memory of Hamish Henderson,' Mark Wade observed:

> For some, the image is of this gentle giant of a man holding out a microphone, collecting the songs, the poetry, the voices of a thriving folk culture. For others the picture is of a freedom fighter, a socialist

whose songs popularised the heroic achievements of ordinary people. For still more, perhaps, it is a recollection of an inveterate performer, the poet of the public bar, for whom singing and reciting are as important as anything on the printed page.[6]

In the words of Frank Bechhofer (who composed the graduation address when the University of Edinburgh conferred an honorary degree on Hamish): 'It is fitting that a man so committed to the oral transmission of culture should himself have been so memorable a personality', but what about those who never had the privilege to meet that 'slightly shambling figure with the distinctive hat'?[7]

Donald Smith's observation rang a bell. At the Carrying Stream Festivals, we had noticed that those events branded explicitly as celebrations of Hamish drew a different audience than the more general folk nights trying to reflect Hamish's broad church approach to the traditional arts. While the first have often resembled family gatherings, sometimes highly emotional affairs, the latter have been frequented by folk who perhaps did not care too much about the Hamish connection (and certainly the 'in-crowd' has tended to be selective and shown less interest in the latter). It is a gap that needs to be bridged. The Carrying Stream Festival itself, and also this volume, can hopefully play a part in this bridging exercise.

A constant of the Festivals has been the annual Hamish Henderson Memorial Lecture, supported by Edinburgh City Council, and the idea was, from the very beginning, to collect these and make them available in a publication. The inaugural lecture was given by Fred Freeman, followed since by Ted Cowan, Margaret Bennett, Timothy Neat, Geordie McIntyre, Ewan McVicar, Pino Mereu, Michael Russell MSP, and Sheila Stewart. Due to time constraints and other commitments, not all of them can be present in this volume, but six of the lectures are at the core of the following pages, complemented by commissioned pieces and revised versions of previously published essays.

The contributions range from friends and comrades of Hamish's like Geordie McIntyre, George Gunn or Ewan McVicar, from his closest collaborator in the School of Scottish Studies, Margaret Bennett, from Sheila Stewart who first met the burgeoning folk collector in the berry fields of Blair, from his biographer Timothy Neat and his occasional publisher Joy Hendry, to Pino Mereu, Hamish's friend from Rome (and

organiser of the Hamish Henderson Folk Club in the Italian capital),
the poets Tessa Ransford and Tom Hubbard, Rob Gibson MSP, the
former co-organiser of the Highland Traditional Music Festival, the
critic Mario Relich, the singers Steve Byrne and Brian McNeill—and
that PhD student from the panel session at the Storytelling Centre,
Corey Gibson. Some of them have never met Hamish Henderson—
but that is he point: only if people who have not known Hamish
personally can be persuaded to take an interest in his work, will his
legacy matter for the present and the future.

There are three main parts to this book. The first section is
dedicated to song-writing and song-collecting. Hamish
Henderson wrote some songs which have entered he tradition, like
the 'Ballad of the D-Day Dodgers' or 'The 51st Highland Division's
Farewell to Sicily'. The two songs he was most proud of were 'The John
MacLean March' and 'The Freedom Come-All-Ye'. Encountering the
latter was a slow-burning but life-changing event for Brian McNeill,
one of the founders of the Battlefield Band, as he recalls in his brief
but affectionate memoir. 'No Gods and Precious Few Heroes', one of
his most famous and powerful songs is clearly inspired by Hamish
Henderson, using a line from the 'First Elegy' as its title. Geordie
McIntyre, himself a respected collector and writer, approaches his
subject wearing his singer's hat, weaving in and out of Hamish's songs
and associating them with others, among them his own, which were
inspired by them. 'All songs are ghosts/ And long for a living voice',
he quotes the Irish poet Brendan Kennelly; for him, 'Big Hamish was
such a voice: of and for the people.'[8]

Turning to Hamish's role as collector, Ewan McVicar shares some of
his research into children's songs in Scotland with us, on which he has
published an important book,[9] and points out the sometimes under-
rated role Hamish Henderson played in collecting children's songs
and rhymes, showing us some of the 'small gems' of Hamish's harvest.
'As early as 1946, Hamish Henderson was advocating the systematic
collection and study of Scots folksong as part of a radical agenda for
the democratisation of the Scottish literary renaissance.'[10] His role as
a ghillie for Alan Lomax, recording the 'primitive' music of Scotland,
made him the ideal recruit for the newly-founded School of Scottish
Studies at the University of Edinburgh, where these recordings
formed the corner-stones of an ever-growing archive.

In the late 1940s Hamish had helped Joan Littlewood and Ewan MacColl to set up 'fringe shows' during the newly-founded Edinburgh Festival at the Epworth Hall, mildly lampooned by Robert Garioch in 'Embro to the Ploy':

> The Epworth Haa wi wunner did
> behold a pipers' bicker;
> wi *hadarid* and *hindarid*
> the air gat thick and thicker.
> *Cumha na Cloinne* played on strings
> torments a piper quicker
> to get his dander up, by jings,
> than thirty u.p. liquor,
>   Hooch aye!
> in Embro to the ploy.[11]

It is Hamish's claim to have been in at he start of what would become the Edinburgh Fringe. In the early 1950s, Hamish was involved in putting together the Edinburgh People's Festivals, 'In many ways,' he would later state, 'that programme of the '52 People's Festival is my finest work of art.'[12]

Margaret Bennett, Scotland's leading contemporary folklorist, well-kent not just this side of the Atlantic but also in North America, and particularly in Appalachia, Nova Scotia and Newfoundland, reflects on Hamish Henderson's pivotal role in transatlantic folklore studies — all the more noteworthy, given the fact that Hamish never set foot on American or Canadian soil.

In 1953, Hamish had 'discovered' Jeannie Robertson, an 'unknown tinker woman'[13] whom Alan Lomax would soon praise as the finest ballad singer in the world. Hamish himself thought of this 'discovery' as 'the most important, single achievement' of his life.[14] It was the beginning of a long and mutually beneficial relationship between him and the travelling community. Maurice Fleming recalls:

'Go amongst the travellers,' he told me, 'and here are a few songs to ask for.' He scribbled a quick list of titles. At the top was 'The Berryfields o' Blair'... The following week I wrote him: 'You were right! The fields are full of songs. I have found nearly all the ones you asked for – and the woman who wrote 'The Berryfields'.'
Before I knew it a tape recorder from Edinburgh arrived at my door

and all else was forgotten as I filled tape after tape. Belle Stewart, the singer who wrote 'The Berryfields', and her talented family became great friends and their home in Rattray, over the river from Blair, was a collector's dream house... Soon Hamish himself arrived in town and a hectic time was had by all. It was at sessions in and out of doors that summer that some of the best material held by the School of Scottish Studies was collected.[15]

That was in the summer of 1954. Fleming would later reminisce: 'When I invited Hamish to come to Blairgowrie, I had no idea that I was bringing him home.'[16] In more than one way—Hamish had been born here and had spent his early childhood here, but he should also find a home with the Stewart family. Sheila Stewart pays heartfelt homage to Hamish in this volume and has been invited to give the annual Hamish Henderson Memorial Lecture 2010. In the book about her mother, Belle Stewart, she wrote:

> Hamish Henderson opened the door for us to come out of our seclusion and be accepted by society as having something to offer them, but only in the folk scene. My mother and father often said they thanked Hamish for doing this because at least some folk in the world accepted us for what we were.[17]

George Gunn not only claims the bard—or, rather, the *fili*—for the Gunn clan and for Caithness, he also continues the story about Hamish among the travellers—his 'discovery' of the Stewarts of Remarstaig. George is a long-standing associate of Hamish's. In an interview on his publisher's website he says:

> Through Joy [Hendry] I met Hamish Henderson who, probably more than any single person, has both inspired me and taught me so much about literature, politics and art. So it's a continuing thread of experience and influence I have been fortunate enough to be exposed to – what Hamish called 'the carrying stream'.[18]

Another connection to the north-east of Scotland connection is explored by Gary West, the Head of the School of Scottish Studies, and a fine piper to boot: Hamish Henderson's kenspeckle use of pipe tunes from the North-East for some of his songs.

Tom Hubbard, peripatetic academic and poet, looks beyond Scotland, on the parallels between Hamish Henderson and Bela Bartók as collectors of their national folk song tradition. Like Bela Bartók, Pino Mereu remarked to Timothy Neat, Hamish believed that 'folk music is like a human being–it changes minute by minute.'[19] Bartók 'made the attempt of purifying Hungarian folk music, getting rid of additions and deformations, restoring the freshness and strength of the originals.'[20]

Where Bela Bartók and Zoltán Kodaly were researching the folk-music of Hungary, the Scots were contorting their musical heritage into the drawing-room ballads of Marjorie Kennedy-Fraser. It was Henderson and his colleagues from the School of Scottish Studies who, in the 1940s and afterwards, scraped the varnish off, and rediscovered a wealth of music which had remained stuck in the throats of fisherfolk, farm labourers, gypsies and travelling harvesters.[21]

In the second section of the book we turn to Hamish the poet. As Paul Scott wrote in his review of Timothy Neat's first volume of his Hamish biography, 'He is largely ignored in the schools and universities and by writers of literary history and anthology editors.'[22] Indeed, Robert Crawford and Mike Imlah did not find space for any of his poems in their *New Penguin Book of Scottish Verse* (2000). Worse, even an article that specifically addresses Rilke's influence in the English-speaking world, and discusses the likes of C Day Lewis, W H Auden, Stephen Spender and Edith Sitwell, manages to completely ignore Hamish Henderson, and to add insult to shameful negligence for the Cambridge-educated Henderson, it appears in a book published by Cambridge University Press.[23] The MacDiarmid industry seems to bear some grudge against Hamish Henderson, perhaps stemming from the flytings of the 1960s, or from personal animosities—or how is it to be explained that neither Alan Bold's *MacDiarmid*—a 550pp-plus biography—nor Nancy Gish's centenary volume on MacDiarmid ever mention Hamish?[24] Strange, if one reflects on the fact that Hamish was always championing Hugh MacDiarmid's poetry. Robert Crawford's 830 pp history, *Scotland's Books,* devotes a half page to Hamish, mentioning the *Elegies* but then focusing solely on his folk collector role.[25]

We think now may be the time for a reassessment of Hamish Henderson's poetry. Mario Relich and Tessa Ransford bring their own poetic sensitivities and perspectives to Hamish's work, while Timothy Neat holds up the mirror to see how Hamish's poetry is reflected in the work of his peers, nationally and internationally.

The strange neglect of Hamish's poetry is particularly puzzling when it comes to his *Elegies for the Dead in Cyrenaica*[26]—which won him the coveted Somerset Maugham Prize. Although this sequence of poems about the desert war in North Africa make him, for Douglas Gifford, 'the greatest Scottish World War Two poet,'[27] Nigel Alderman and C D Beaton's *Concise Companion to Post-war British and Irish Poetry* (2009) seems to be too concise to have room for Hamish Henderson. And Hamish Whyte discusses George Campbell Hay and Sorley MacLean in his *Modern Scottish Poetry* (2004), but ignores the *Elegies*, despite claiming the 1940s as the key decade for Scottish poetry.

David Kennedy, by contrast, does give space to Hamish's *Elegies* in his recent work and points out how he 'prefigures the late-twentieth-century elegist's refusal to submit to the ultimate end of the genre: detachment from the dead.' He continues:

> Henderson makes this explicit in the final elegy of his sequence when he writes of the dead that 'their sleep's our unrest, we lie bound in their inferno–/ this alliance must be vaunted and affirmed, lest they condemn us!' The poet's job is to 'carry to the living/ blood, fire and red flambeaux of death's proletariat.'[28]

He seems to follow on from Edwin Morgan's perceptive reading of the tenth elegy:

> The tenth and last elegy ('the Frontier') makes clear that Henderson sees how his duty as an elegist must include something more than remembrance, there must be something more active, if the dead are to be appeased, more active even than Wilfred Owen's warnings. The dead will hold us in contempt if we fail to change society, reform government, make freedom and justice efficacious.[29]

Joy Hendry, in her introductory piece to a BBC radio broadcast she put together in 1990, the transcript of which is published here for the first time, brings together that astonishing array of Scottish World War

Two poets, and we can only marvel at the unity of spirit and their 'sympathetic imagination' which is the hallmark not just of Hamish Henderson's *Elegies*, but also of Sorley MacLean's 'Gaor na h-Èorpa/ The Cry of Europe' and the poems of Tom Scott, Robert Garioch, Ian Campbell Hay and Norman MacCaig. They all wrote from their immediate experience. By contrast, it took Edwin Morgan two decades before he could address his war experience in North Africa. But in his poem 'North Africa', he names his fellow war poets from Scotland.[30]

The third section of this volume offers perspectives on Hamish Henderson's politics and his role and influence as a political activist. As Eddie Morgan commented, based on his reading of the tenth elegy, it is not difficult to see 'in passages like that... a carry-forward into Henderson's later work with ballad and folk-song, his involvement with CND and protest politics, his exegesis of Gramsci.'[31] The war experience had a huge influence on Hamish Henderson's thinking. It was 'the most dramatic period of a life-long opposition to fascism and oppression,'[32] and it brought him in close contact with the Italian partisans. That story is movingly told by Hamish's friend Pino Mereu from Rome. A direct result of Henderson's friendship with the partisans was his interest in the Italian Communist thinker Antonio Gramsci which led to him becoming the first to translate Gramsci's *Prison Letters* into English and thus to introduce him to the British Left.[33]

It is all the more astonishing how many British books on Gramsci omit any mention of Henderson's pioneering work. Neither Roger Simon's *Gramsci's Political Thought: An Introduction* (1990), which is introduced by Stuart Hall, who shared an Edinburgh platform with Hamish on Gramsci in 1987, nor Steve Jones's *Gramsci* (2006), nor Anne Showstack Sassoon's *Gramsci and Contemporary Politics: Beyond Pessimism of the Intellect* (2006), nor Nigel M Greaves's *Gramsci's Marxism: Reclaiming a Philosophy of History and Politics* (2010) make mention of Hamish Henderson. Yet, Greaves may have the key to explain Henderson's keen interest in the Sardinian Marxist: 'Gramsci seeks not to destroy the main tenets of Karl Marx's theory of historical materialism, but to humanise and reinvigorate them.'[34]

As Corey Gibson shows, Hamish was drawn to the *Prison Letters* because he was particularly interested in Gramsci's remarks about folk culture. Henderson was aware of the Janus-faced nature of folk culture, embedded in Gramsci's 'creative clash of contradictions'[35] —backward looking, reactionary, on the one hand, but also taking sides in the struggle for emancipation, freedom and equality: 'Scottish folk-song is part of the submerged resistance movement which reacted against the tyranny of John Knox's Kirk at a time when the Kirk was making a bid for absolute rule in Scotland.'[36] Marxists were quick to condemn folklore and folk song to the dustbin of history, and the Hugh MacDiarmid of the famous flytings in 1960 and 1964 is polemically representative of this. Others seem more ambiguous, some closer to Hamish. Walter Benjamin, for example, could express admiration for the power of folk tales—'This story from ancient Egypt is still capable after thousands of years of arousing astonishment and thoughtfulness'[37]—but, in accordance with most of the Frankfurt School thinkers, he was also convinced that the art was firmly of the past:

Familiar though his name may be to us, the storyteller in his living immediacy is by no means a present force. He has already become something remote from us and something that is getting even more distant.[38]

Familiar with German culture and history, Hamish was acutely aware of the abuses of folklore by the Nazis which built on the Romantic notion of the 'Volk'. Critical of this Romantic concept of 'the people' as an 'organically developed, homogeneous entity,'[39] the Austro-Marxist Ernst Fischer's view is more differenciated: 'In folk songs, the tradition of a far distant collective is often mixed with elements which come from the conflict between the "people" and the ruling class.'[40] For José Lemón, capitalist production was 'eliminating the authentic voice and nature of folklore,'—it was no more than 'a historical phenomenon associated with precapitalist modes of production, socially marginal sectors, or children.'[41]

Hamish Henderson put more confidence in the vitality of folk traditions, rejecting the low opinion of folklore that characterised much thinking on the Left: 'If we haven't learned by now that folk-song has enormous resilience, and that after the late-night final there is always a final night edition, and so on into the dawn, we shall never learn.'[42] He emphasised 'the possibilities of a political utilisation of folklore—the fostering of an *alternative* to official bourgeois culture, seeking out the positive and "progressive" aspects of folk culture,'[43] as explored by Italian folklorists in the wake of Gramsci.

And if Hamish's claim that the folk revival was 'Gramsci in action' holds truth, this is, in a narrower sense, certainly the case for the inspiration Hamish's use of folk songs and ballads for political action gave to some of the most poignant political campaigns of the second half of the twentieth century and beyond, from his 'Ballad of the Men of Knoydart' and the campaign for land reform to 'The Freedom Come-All-Ye', dedicated to the Glasgow Peace Marchers in 1960.[44] Rob Gibson dips into the rich tapestry of political activism in the Highlands, encouraged by, and in the spirit of, Seumas Mòr. And the use of political song, of satirical ditties and campaign chants continues. Alistair Hulett spent an entire Wee Folk Club night at the Royal Oak regaling us with songs, mostly grafted onto popular tunes, for the campaign to save the Glasgow Southside Baths;[45] and David Ferrard and Roy Bailey introduced Edinburgh Folk Club audiences to the songs they had collectively written on the Peace March from Faslane to the Scottish Parliament.

Whether 'old Labour'[46] or 'small c communist',[47] Hamish Henderson was a home ruler in the John MacLean tradition. He was a founder-member, frequent visitor and participant in the 'Vigil for a Scottish Parliament' which was maintained for 1997 days, from 1992 to 1997, at the foot of Calton Hill.[48] And it would surely have pleased him to see the lines from 'The Freedom Come-All-Ye'—Scotland's 'Internationale'[49]—inscribed on the Canongate Wall of the Scottish Parliament. Shortly after his death, the Parliament honoured Hamish Henderson with a debate, initiated by Cathy Peattie MSP.[50]

'His memory always we'll revere/ For all he loved and held so dear,'[51] rhymed Bob Bertram—whom Hamish had hailed as an 'excellent folk poet' as early as 1964[52]—on the day of Hamish's funeral. As Timothy Neat notes in this volume, 'a stream of songs and poems' were penned in the wake of Hamish's demise: by Ian and Neil MacDonald, Elizabeth Stewart, Geordie McIntyre, Donald Smith and Donald Meek.[53] His name and legacy is honoured by 'Hands up for Trad', Simon Thoumire's brainchild, which hands out the annual Hamish Henderson award—hitherto, among others, to two founders of Edinburgh Folk Club: Ian Green and John Barrow. Busts of Hamish can be seen in Edinburgh Park, in the National Portrait Gallery, the Scottish Storytelling Centre and—our modest contribution, as already mentioned—in the National Museum. Apart from the Carrying Stream Festival in November, Colin Fox and comrades have revived the idea of the Edinburgh People's Festival in August, complete with a Hamish Henderson lecture.

But there have been disappointments too. Neither Edinburgh University Library nor the National Library, nor the Mitchell in Glasgow showed an interest in Hamish's library—which therefore had to be sold off. Donald Smith pays homage to a lifetime in books. And maybe there is something in it that books assembled over a lifetime then find new homes and new readers, as another aspect of the carrying stream. More worrying, and indeed shameful, has been the lack of interest in Hamish's archive of papers and letters. A Hamish Henderson Trust has been formed recently, on the initiative of Steve Byrne, aiming at the preservation of the archive for the nation and at making it available for researchers. In his concluding chapter of this volume, Steve Byrne gives us a glimpse of the 'kist of riches' the archive at the School of Scottish Studies truly is, and the exhilarating story about its digitising which will help to secure and widen the legacy of Hamish Henderson, whose collecting in the early 1950s provided the foundation for it. One more reason to celebrate the sixtieth anniversary of the School in 2011 and Hamish Henderson's massive contribution to it.

This volume does not set out to make extravagant claims. Hamish was no Scottish messiah. But he definitely deserves more than the one measly mention he gets in Rob Young's *Electric Eden*, a 660-odd pages story of Britain's folk music, a perplexing case of shallow digging and myopic Anglocentrism.[54] Hamish was, and is, an important figure in contemporary Scottish, British and international cultural and political history. He is, Chris Dolan rapturously affirms:

> our Woody Guthrie, our Alan Lomax and Studs Terkel, our William Blake (for writing what should be our national anthem, Freedom Come-All-Ye), and much more besides. Nationalist and internationalist, radical and lover of tradition, peacemongering soldier, family man with gay outbursts, academic and poet with the common touch: Henderson was a man of many parts...[55]

A man of many parts indeed. He was 'at once a practical realist and an emotional visionary, who thought with his heart.'[56] Or, in Dick

Gaughan's words, 'a mass of contradictions'—which leads him to conclude:

> Perhaps the only way to remember and understand Hamish is to embrace the apparent contradictions—poet and polemicist, Internationalist and Nationalist, warrior and pacifist, realist and romantic, traditionalist and modernist, brashness masking shyness, intellectual confidence hiding personal insecurities.[57]

Maybe it is just what you get when you cross the Democratic Intellect with the Democratic Muse? Anyway, 'Hamish's life is with us—his story, his poetry, his songs: the music he collected grows beside us as we grow. If you think about wars, emigration, racism, unemployment, socialism, nationalism—you will find everything in his poetry, in his songs, in the words he spoke. Hamish's ideas are still fermenting in our consciences.'[58]

Hamish—'Gramsci in action'—overcame the pessimism of William Butler Yeats, who saw himself surrounded by 'ghost voices', standing at 'a precipice which marks the imminent and seemingly irrevocable death of the folk tradition.' He believed that the 'ghostly voice' was 'still alive, still renewing itself in the carrying stream.'[59] While both Yeats and Henderson were folk collectors and adapters of folklore and writers of folk songs, they could not have been further apart in the political outlook. The aristocratic elitism of Yeats was something Henderson detected in his flyting partner Hugh MacDiarmid and, given his experience in Germany before the war and during his campaign in North Africa and through Italy, he never dilly-dallied with fascism, as both MacDiarmid and Yeats did. His credo was summed up in a letter during the apartheid protests: 'Freedom is never, but never, a gift from above; it invariably has to be won anew by its own exercises.'[60]

But one thing now connects Hamish Henderson with the Irish national poet. Yeats rests at Drumcliff Churchyard, 'Under Bare Ben Bulben'. That mountain in County Sligo shares the same linguistic root as Gulabeinn, the 'curlew's mountain' in Perthshire to the north-east of the Spittal of Glenshee (Glen of the Fairies) on which Hamish wanted his ashes to be scattered by his long-standing associates George Gunn, Angus Calder and Timothy Neat.

Geordie McIntyre's 'From Gulabeinn', which was first published in the *Carrying Stream Programme* of 2009, has since been recorded[61] and is, in Jim Gilchrist's words, 'a stirring evocation of the Perthshire hill which the late Hamish Henderson, patriarch of the Scottish folk revival, loved—and on which his ashes were scattered.'[62] Geordie was inspired by Timothy Neat's description of this memorable mission, particularly the moment the ashes were released when, 'through fissures in the rocks, plumes of white ash shot up all around us in the heather —as though a family of dragons had woken.'[63]

From Gulabeinn
(for Hamish Henderson, 1919-2002)

From Gulabeinn's bell-heathered slopes
His dust was scattered to the sky
Particles of song unite
With trilling curlew cry.

This mystic hill 'of youth and age'
Towers o'er the Fairy Glen
Banner-bright in May morn light
To welcome Hamish home.

From Glenshee to Sicily
A' the airts the winds do blaw
'Come gies a sang' cried Seamus Mòr
Let the music flow.

A song to cheer a weary heart
Ane to drive away dull care
Tales of comradeship and hope
That we all can share.

Rabbi Burns and Thomas Paine
Gramsci, Lorca, John MacLean
Listen to their clarion call
Let peace and freedom reign.

All the sacrifices made
Do not let them be betrayed
Raise your voices, stand as one
Is the song—from Gulabeinn.

Is it not uncanny that at the foot of this hill, as Ossianic legend has it, Diarmuid and Gráinne found their last resting place?

Beneath thy grey stones, O Ben Gulbein,
The brown-haired chief is laid.
His blue eyes are sleeping forever
Under thy green grassy shade.[64]

Timothy Neat's biographical effort has been a milestone in the ongoing project to give Hamish his due and to show why his work still matters, why his life still inspires. This volume is but a modest further offering which will, we hope, underline Hamish's contemporary relevance. It may be uneven, given the diversity of contributions, but we trust its kaleidoscopic range of angles and perspectives will find favour, both with readers already familiar with Hamish Henderson's life and work, and with those who encounter him for the first time.

Thanks are due to Ian Spring for all the work he has done for this publication; thanks also to all our contributors—and apologies to all who could have contributed but were not asked this time or had to decline. Big thanks to Gonzalo Mazzei for coming to the rescue, ensuring that the book could be launched at Hamish's 91st birthday— in the end it seems very appropriate that this book on Hamish should be published by a Perthshire press. This volume will by no means be the last word on Hamish's legacy. The Carrying Stream Festival will, hopefully, continue, and also the Hamish Henderson Memorial Lectures. So, perhaps, in due time, another volume beckons.

Tomorrow, songs
Will flow free again, and new voices
Be borne on the carrying stream.[65]

References:

1   Frederico García Lorca, *Selected Poems*, translated by J L Gili, (London Anvil Press Poetry, 2010), p. 29.

2   Hamish Henderson, *Collected Poems and Songs*, edited by Raymond Ross, (Edinburgh: Curly Snake Publishing, 2000); Hamish Henderson, *The Armstrong Nose: Selected Letters of Hamish Henderson*, edited by Alec Finlay, (Edinburgh: Polygon, 1992); Hamish Henderson, *Alias MacAlias: Writings on Songs, Folk and Literature*, edited by Alec Finlay, (Edinburgh: Polygon, 1996).

3   Hamish Henderson, letter to the *Scotsman*, 13 January 1960; in *The Armstrong Nose*, p. 96.

4   Jean Bechhofer, 'Nights to Remember: 30 Years of Edinburgh Folk Club', Carrying Stream Programme (Edinburgh: Edinburgh Folk Club, 2003), p. 9.

5   Angus Calder, Introduction', in *Alias MacAlias*, p. xiii.

6   Mike Wade, 'Poet for the People', *Scotsman* (5 October, 2000).

7   Frank Bechhofer, 'Hamish Henderson: A brief personal memoir', Carrying Stream Programme, (Edinburgh: Edinburgh Folk Club, 2002), p. 4.

8   Geordie McIntyre, 'Reflecting on Hamish Henderson', Carrying Stream Programme (Edinburgh: Edinburgh Folk Club, 2002), p. 6.

9   Ewan McVicar, *Doh Ray Me When Ah Wis Wee: Scots Children's Songs and Rhymes* (Edinburgh: Birlinn, 2007).

10 Donald Smith, *Storytelling Scotland: A Nation in Narrative* (Edinburgh: Polygon, 2001), p. 145.

11 Robert Garioch, 'Embro to the Ploy', *Complete Poetical Works*, (Edinburgh: Macdonald Publishers, 1983), p. 15.

12 Geordie McIntyre, 'Resurgimento!—An Interview with Hamish Henderson', *New Edinburgh Review* (Festival Issue, August 1973), reprinted in Carrying Stream Programme, 2006, p. 15.

13 Timothy Neat, *Hamish Henderson: A Biography: Volume 2, Poetry Becomes People* (Edinburgh: Polygon, 2009), p. 16.

14 Geordie McIntyre, (2006), p. 15.

15 Maurice Fleming, 'Hamish of the Songs', *The Scots Magazine*, (May 2002), reprinted in the *Carrying Stream Programme*, 2009.

16 Maurice Fleming, 'The Summer that was a Landmark', *Tocher*, 43 (1991), p. 47.

17 Sheila Stewart, *Queen Amang the Heather: The Life of Belle Stewart* (Edinburgh: Birlinn, 2006), p. 65.

18 See www.tworavenspress.com.

19 Quoted in Timothy Neat (2009), p. 302.

20 Ernst Fischer, *The Necessity of Art: a Marxist approach* (Harmondsworth: Penguin, 1963), p. 76.

21 Christopher Harvie, 'Hamish Henderson: The Grand Old Man of Scottish Folk Culture', Carrying Stream Programme (Edinburgh: Edinburgh Folk Club, 2004), p. 5.

22 Paul H Scott, *Sunday Herald*, (9 December, 2007).

23 Karin Leeder, 'Rilke's Legacy in the English-speaking World', in Karin Leeder and Robert Vitain (ed.), *The Cambridge Companion to Rilke* (Cambridge: Cambridge University Press, 2010), pp. 189-205.

24 Alan Bold, *MacDiarmid* (London: John Murray, 1988); Nancy Gish (ed.), *Hugh MacDiarmid: Man and Poet* (Orono, Maine: The National Poetry Foundation and Edinburgh University Press, 1992).

25 Robert Crawford, *Scotland's Books: The Penguin History of Scottish Literature* (London: Penguin, 2007).

26 Hamish Henderson, *Elegies for the Dead in Cyrenaica* (London: John Lehmann, 1948).

27 Douglas Gifford, 'Literature and World War Two', in Ian Brown and Alan Riach (ed.), *The Edinburgh Companion to Twentieth-century Scottish Literature* (Edinburgh: Edinburgh University Press, 2009), p. 95.

28 David Kennedy, *Elegy* (London: Routledge (New Critical Idiom), 2007), p. 74.

29 Edwin Morgan, 'The Sea, the Desert, the City: Environment and Language in W S Graham, Hamish Henderson, and Tom Leonard', *The Yearbook of English Studies*, special number: *British Poetry since 1945*, Vol. 17 (1987), p. 38.

30 See Roderick Watson, "Death's Proletariat": Scottish Poets of the Second World War', in Tim Kendall (ed.), *The Oxford Handbook of British and Irish War Poetry* (Oxford: Oxford University Press), pp. 315-39.

31 Edwin Morgan (1987), p. 39.

32 Frank Bechhofer (2002), p. 4.

33 See Raymond Ross, 'Hamish Henderson: Folklorist, Poet and Songwriter', *The Scotsman*, (11 March 2002); reprinted in Carrying Stream Programme, 2008, p. 10.

34 Nigel M. Greaves, *Gramsci's Marxism: Reclaiming a Philosophy of History and Politics* (Leicester: Matador, 2010), p. 13.

35 *Alias MacAlias*, p. 356.

36 *Ibid.*, p. 28.

37 Walter Benjamin, 'The Storyteller', in W Benjamin, *Illuminations*, edited by Hannah Arendt, translated by Harry Zohn (Glasgow: Fontana Collins, 1973), p. 90.

38 *Ibid.*, p.83.

39 Fischer (2010), p. 75.

40 *Ibid.*, p. 77.

41 José Lemón, 'Western Marxism and Folklore', quoted in Jack Zipes, 'Folklore Research and Western Marxism: A Critical Replay', *The Journal of American Folklore Studies*, Vol. 97, no. 385 (July-September 1984), pp. 329-37, p. 329. Zipes attempts a critical balancing between the political vitality of folklore and its alleged decline.

42 *Alias MacAlias*, p. 42.

43 *Ibid.*, p. 356.

44 See Ailie Munro, *The Democratic Muse: folk music revival in Scotland*, (Aberdeen: Scottish Cultural Press, 1996), p. 43.

45 See Ewan McVicar, *The Eskimo Republic: Scots Political Song in Action, 1951-1999* (Linlithgow: Gallus Publishing, 2010), pp. 122-24.

46 Raymond Ross (2002), p.16.

47 Angus Calder, 'Introduction', *Alias McAlias*, p. xiii.

48 Ivor Birnie, 'Hamish: At the Vigil', *Carrying Stream Programme*, (Edinburgh: Edinburgh Folk Club, 2004), pp. 9-11.

49 David Stenhouse, 'Scotland's Internationale', *Sunday Herald* (7 November 1999), reprinted in Carrying Stream Programme, 2007, pp. 13-16.

50 Both Cathy Peattie's and Michael Russell's contributions to that debate have been reprinted in the *Carrying Stream Programmes* of 2007 and 2008, respectively.

51 Bob Bertram, 'For Hamish in St Mary's', first published in the Carrying Stream Programme (Edinburgh: Edinburgh Folk Club, 2005), p. 11; subsequently included in Bob Bertram, *Selected Songs and Poems*, (Edinburgh: Norma Allan, 2008), p. 22.

52 *MacAlias*, p. 125.

53 Donald Meek, 'Seumas MaEanraig', Carrying Stream Programme, (Edinburgh: Edinburgh Folk Club, 2003), p. 20.

54 Rob Young, *Electric Eden: Unearthing Britain's Visionary Music* (London: Faber and Faber, 2010), p. 131.

55 Chris Dolan, 'Celebrating a life lived to the full', *The Herald* (17 November 2007).

56 Timothy Neat, 'The unknown soldier', *Scotland on Sunday* (11 November 2007).

57 Dick Gaughan, 'Hamish Henderson (1919-2002): A Personal Appreciation', *The Herald* (2002), reprinted in the *Carrying Stream Programme*, 2005, p. 5.

58 Pino Mereu, quoted in Timothy Neat (2009) p. 302.

59 Alec Finlay, 'A River That Flows On: A critical overview of Hamish Henderson's life and work' (Afterword), *The Armstong Nose*, pp. 332-33.

60 Hamish Henderson and Robert Tait, letter to *The Scotsman* (23 December 1969), in *The Armstrong Nose*, p. 186.

61 Alison McMorland and Geordie McIntyre, *Where Ravens Reel*, Birnam CD, 2010.

62 Jim Gilchrist, 'Honour to the memory of the unsung hero who could forgive but not forget', *The Scotsman* (2 September 2010).

63 Timothy Neat (2009) p. 365.

64 Antony Mackenzie Smith, *Glenshee: Glen of the Fairies* (Phantassie, East Linton: Tuckwell Press, 2000), p. 65.

65 Hamish Henderson 'Under the Earth I Go', *Collected Poems and Songs*, p. 155.

HAMISH HENDERSON: CHAMPION OF THE ORAL TRADITION

Brian McNeill

I met his music (and I use the word advisedly, for to me he was much more than just a man of words) long before I ever met Hamish. It was at one of the Perth festivals, late sixties, early seventies, some time around then. I was a student at Strathclyde University, a good all-round musician not long out of a high school rock band, and a very puzzled newcomer to the folk scene. I had got as far as having my life changed by Dave Swarbrick's fiddle playing, but I remember looking round the festival site on a Saturday morning and wondering how it was all linked up to this ... this chaos. The beards. The politics. The incredible expertise. The total lack of rehearsal.

All of which meant that the hospitable kitchen of Sheila Douglas, where the festival's collection of waifs, strays and recovering hangovers had congregated, was a considerable puzzle to me. What the hell was that weird instrument with the buttons? What were the 'collections' these people were talking about? What was a 'source singer'? And then someone (I think it was Brian Miller) picked up a guitar and began to sing: 'Roch the wind... heelster gowdie ower the bay... gallus, fresh and gay...'

I would love to be able to claim some kind of epiphany, some kind of blinding flash, but the truth is much more prosaic; mesmerised though I was by the nonchalant musicality with which everyone around the big kitchen table joined in, I did not understand the half of it. The tune lodged in my head immediately, but like many another lowlander confronted with a distillation of the language he speaks daily, it took several furtive looks at a Scots dictionary for me to get the best of the words—and it was only fifteen years later, after I had taken the first hesitant steps towards becoming a songwriter in the traditional mould myself, that I realised the importance of what Hamish Henderson had done.

For this song is the most potent of mixes—contemplative, frank, principled in its conclusions about Scotland's part in the world's problems and incendiary in its solutions to them. Yes, 'The Freedom Come-All-Ye' is a call to arms, but it is of the most subtle kind. It builds image upon image, all striking, but it is only in the final verse that you realise what you are endorsing. And if it is a shock to the singer— I will always remember the total silence with which the song was received the first time I sang it in the United States, to an extremely well-heeled, largely Scottish expatriate audience in Oklahoma. The crowd's enthusiasm for freedom died in exactly the amount of time it took to sing the line 'the black boy frae yont Nyanga dings the fell gallows o' the burghers doon'.

So, it is inescapably a song about insurrection, uncomfortable to some even when it is arrived at as a logical conclusion from entirely reasonable premises. What is less obvious is that the song's appeal for insurrection is fuelled by resurrection—by the robust revival of a language which, at the time of the song's writing, was nearly on the scrap heap.

By the middle years of the twentieth century, Scots had become frankly sterile. It was looked down upon, not least by those who used it every day. I remember my mother sending me (in vain) to elocution lessons to try and lessen its grip on my speech. That might have been understandable from her, an Austrian immigrant who had bought into the idea of being British as much as being Scottish, but my father, Falkirk born and bred, was just as enthusiastic. If I wanted to get on in life, etc., etc… (I did not have an opinion, I just hated the lessons).

And when I was old enough to become aware of them, I did not find anything remotely attractive about the language's advocates—possibly acolytes would be a better word—either. They seemed strange, they seemed obsessed, they seemed (whisper it) incredibly middle class, and above all, they seemed determined to garner the kind of suspicion usually reserved for pacifists and vegetarians. Authentic or not, the mither tongue had simply become marginalised, the property of the arcane and obscure. There were exceptions, writers like MacDiarmid with powerful bodies of work, enthusiastic revivalists, but they never did more than scratch the public consciousness, and to my mind as a Scottish working class kid on the lookout for some kind of believable reality, they never existed to any great degree outside the library or the literary journal. Even with my mind opening to new ideas at university, I avoided Scots at all costs. What did this language have to do with my life? Scots was too weird, too self-conscious. Scots was just too damn tweed-suit-and-brogues worthy.

'The Freedom Come-All-Ye' changed that. It redeemed the language. That was Hamish Henderson's greatest gift to me, and I suspect I am not alone in that. The concentration of the song's power on a demonstrably believable overview of Scotland's national life convinced me that it was still possible to reconnect this language with the lives and aspirations of the punters standing beside me in the drizzle of the Falkirk bus queue—and it also showed me that the grafting of it on to a good tune was perhaps the single most important element of the whole process.

In fact, almost as a by-product, this one song taught me the songwriter's most important lesson: song and poetry, no matter how many elements they might share, are not the same animal at all. The dawning of this realisation was a nugget of pure gold to me, a man who at that point had aspirations to write both. It seems obvious, a truism, but it is not; the drawing of the dividing line between the two disciplines is the blackest of arts, and entirely subjective. I think it is completely fitting that this was made manifest to me by a man who was not just one of his nation's best songwriters, but also undoubtedly one of its best poets.

But to stay with song; the only other songwriter who came close to providing a template of similar power for my generation was Hamish's great contemporary, Ewan MacColl. The two of them, both gifted evangelists for traditional song and all of its offshoots, were probably the left's most important mascot figures within what is loosely called the folk revival, but they were very different. Both men's writing has affected me greatly. Of the two, MacColl's body of work is larger, more didactic, more in-your-face. I would also be gently inclined to say that, despite incredible highs, it is patchier. The lyricality with which he told of 'The Shoals of Herring' or 'The Thirty-foot Trailer' has to be balanced against the clumsiness with which he managed to smell apartheid in an Outspan orange pie. (And I've always, frankly, been suspicious of that changed name. What the hell was wrong with Jimmie Miller?) And there is the question of action, the 'making things happen' factor. The urge to it is around in the songs of both writers, but it seems to me to be closer to the surface in MacColl's work. Well-crafted or not, his are songs which appeal to the rabble rouser in me. The *Radio Ballads* apart—and a remarkable piece of work they are—what I learned from him was how best to frame an argument in song, with the payoff of an anticipated result, an impetus towards making a given situation move.

What I am still learning from Hamish Henderson is a subtler gift: how to present the humanity of one man in another's eyes. In 'The John MacLean March', the figure of MacLean is entirely presented to us through the thoughts of friend and admirer: 'Hey, Mac, did ye see him?', 'It's hard work the speakin', 'I'll sleep on the flair, Mac, and gie John the bed'.

Did you see him? not did you read him? Here is your leader, one of communism's great theorists, made of hard, great, immutable political stuff. But the fact that he is a man—seeable, touchable, followable—is what seals his status for working people. Immerse your lyric in the excitement of ordinary folk at their hero's return and you have a unique setting for a story told in four verses. And told comprehensively; this is Hamish the songwriter, not Hamish the poet or Hamish the socialist academic, the translator of Gramsci. The man knew his tradition, the economy it demanded if a song was to live orally—there is not one wasted word.

The great triumvirate of songs, 'The Freedom Come-All-Ye', 'The John MacLean March' and 'The 51st Highland Division's Farewell To Sicily', are shot through with this approach, and they are unforgettable because of it. The atmosphere of the latter is just so remarkable. The conjunction of weather, personality, the perception of music, even military orders, to build the scene of an army getting ready to move, has not ever, I think, been equalled. As a lyric, it could stand as straight reportage, but as a song it stands as one of the great insights into the ordinary Scottish soldier's war.

And, of course, he himself was no ordinary Scottish soldier, no ordinary fighter. The facts of his career were amazing enough, but to anyone who knew him in his later years, it was sometimes hard to connect it all up. Was this tall, argumentative old bloke in the pork pie hat really the man who had prepared the axis surrender in southern Italy? Was this crusty old codger propping up the bar in Sandy Bell's really the guy who had helped the Quakers smuggle Jews out of Berlin in the thirties? My contemporaries and I were fascinated, dazzled by the paradox. But if the man's truth was fantastic enough, what was it about him that so often propelled it even further, into the realms of legend? A nation's need to find a coherent sense of good? Some kind of atavistic desire to elevate principle to the heroic?

If the latter is the answer, he seems such an unlikely figure to personify it, to gather myth, but it undoubtedly happened—so many of the stories were amplified, exaggerated practically to the point of hagiography. Even my father, not a man easily impressed by celebrity, claimed to have seen him, riding a white horse on a Sicilian beach, directing the allied landings. And then, of course, there are the tales about him being royal, a latter-day Stuart. On that one I am with the debunkers who believe the source of this is simply the Scottish political right being unable to come to terms with one of our best intellects being a genuine left wing hero. But the fact that the tales, true or false, gathered round the man at all is proof of a unique status.

Did he court it? Not that I could see. In fact, in many ways the best of his legacy was totally at odds with it—he would have included himself in the line 'No Gods And Precious Few Heroes'. The unglamorous business of collecting song and tradition was his great animus, and without his methodical, backbreaking work in this field, the generations which followed him, the singers and musicians, would have been immeasurably poorer. And then the other half of the collector's work has to be taken into account, for he was not prepared simply to archive and collate, as others had done before him. He publicised the great champions of song he had discovered, figures like Jeannie Robertson and Willie Scott. He brought them on to the folk revival's concert stages along with the younger generation of singers who were following in their wake. He gave the new singers old songs, he encouraged cross-fertilisation at every level and, as a result, he succeeded in presenting Scotland and its traditions as a living and healthy organism of the highest artistic merit, capable of—and indeed insistent upon—being taken seriously on the world's cultural stage.

In the end, I think the finest thing he gave us was his example, his refusal to be stereotyped or pigeonholed. The poet with his ear on the other man's muse as well as his own. The academic who was as at home with travelling people as with literary discourse. The committed man of the left who never trimmed his opinion for political advantage. The collector who believed the new had as much place as the old. And, above all, the songwriter who believed that his own songs had to achieve a life of their own, in the same oral way as the tradition which inspired them.

HAMISH HENDERSON:
A SINGER'S PERSPECTIVE

Geordie McIntyre

In this essay I will attempt to highlight Hamish's work in what was, for me, his central or core activity as a song hunter gatherer, a disseminator of these songs and, not least, a songsmith and a skilful singer in his own right.

'Living Ghosts' by Brendan Kennelly[1] captures so much of the spirit, the magic and the power of song:

Richard Broderick celebrates
This winter's first and only fall of snow
With a midnight rendering
Of *The Bonny Bunch of Roses O*

And Paddy Dineen is rising
With *On Top of the Old Stone Wall*
His closed eyes respect the song.
His mind's a festival.

An now *Romona* lights the lips
Of swaying Davy Shea.
In a world of possibilities
This is the only way.

His face a summer morning
When the sun decides to smile
Tom Kean touches enchantment
With *Charming Carrig Isle*.

I've seen men in their innocence
Untroubled by right and wrong.
I close my eyes and see them
Becoming song.

All the songs are living ghosts
And long for a living voice.
O may another fall of snow
Bid Broderick rejoice!

Hamish was such a living voice. He spent a lifetime, by word and deed, extolling the virtues of this form of self expression and actively encouraged it in others. He spoke and wrote eloquently of the vital oral core or heartbeat of what is, in essence, a democratic muse which, at its best, is populist, non-elitist and inclusive. At one point, he described himself as 'a paid up member of the oral tradition'.[2] However, he fully acknowledged a parallel printed tradition reflected in the plethora of chapbooks, broadsheets and books which circulated widely, in Scotland and beyond, from the nineteenth century onwards. He wrote: 'The evidence of a reverence for the written word co-existing with a strong and resilient oral tradition is abundant in our history.'[3]

He appreciated the fruitful co-existence and inter-action(s) which occurred but nonetheless was also sympathic to the views of Margaret Laidlaw, mother of James Hogg (The Ettrick Shepherd) when Walter Scott presented her with her ballads in print in his *Minstrelsy of the Scottish Border*. In her, much quoted, reproach to Scott she said: 'There was nane o' my sangs prentit till ye printed them yersel and they have lost their charm a' thegither.'

For charm read glamourie or enchantment. Hamish spoke of the 'unnatural captivity of print' and he released these 'prisoners' by the simplest of methods, namely singing them! This may seem obvious today but back in 1951 (a date of significance I will return to) it was much less so. By the late 1940s and early 1950s much of the traditional song repertoire was 'underground'.[4] Hamish, along with such folk song revival luminaries as A L Lloyd and Ewan MacColl in England, helped to bring those songs into the light. Hamish's contribution. however, was first nurtured in his early years.

Hamish was an only son of a one-parent family. His mother Janet exercised a profound and lasting influence. This was a situation in which Hamish developed a lifelong identification with the suffering of others—an empathy and sympathy with the underdog and the marginalised; this was later reflected in his anti-establishment stances. Hamish, like Rabbie Burns and James Hogg before him, was exposed to his mother's singing from the very cradle and he had a receptive ear. He described his mother as 'a fine singer with a big repertoire in Scots, Gaelic and French'. 'Belt wi' Colours Three' was one of this mother's songs, a 'sombre elegiac love lament', to quote Hamish, which 'could scarcely be faulted for tragic eloquence':

> The firsten thing ma laddie gied tae me.
> It was a cap weel lined wi lead.
> And the langer that I wore it
> The heavier grew on ma head
> The heavier grew on ma head.
>
> The neisten thing oh ma laddie gied tae me,
> It was a mantle wi sorrow lined.
> I will wear that black mantle
> Till one to borrow I find, I find,
> Till one to borrow I find.
>
> The thirden thing oh ma laddie gied tae me,
> It was a belt wi colours three.
> The first shame, the next sorrow
> And last of all sad misery,
> And last of all sad misery.
>
> Now I maun climb as high a tree yet,
> And herry a far far richer nest
> And come down without falling.
> And mairry the lad that I loe best,
> And mairry the lad that I loe best.
>
> But why should ye now climb a tree, may?
> Or pu the cherries ere they be ripe?
> For if the gairdner yince does see you,
> He'll throw you owre yon garden dyke,
> He'll throw you owre yon garden dyke.
>
> Then up she rose and gaed on slowly,
> And stately stepped owre yon lea;
> And by the samen, it is weel kennen,
> That mourners crave nae company,
> That mourners crave nae company.

This period was surely Hamish's seed-time and, at the age of eight, he moved to Somerset. His mother died in England four years later. For the following seventeen years Hamish was an exile, either living in England or serving overseas. This turbulent period served to sharpen his Scottish identity: 'Nobody on earth felt more Scottish than I did at Cambridge'.[5] At the same time, his political and philosophic perspectives were firmly socialist and internationalist.

While still a student at Cambridge, immediately prior to the war, he assisted a Quaker organisation in helping Jews escape from Nazi Germany. 'The Peat Bog Soldiers' ('Die Moorsodaten') is a magnificent song which was written in 1933 in Börgermoor Concentration Camp in Emsland, North Germany. It is not difficult to see why its message of hope and ultimate triumph over oppression and injustice was so admired by Hamish (to be echoed later in some of his own compositions such as 'The Flyting o' Life and Daith', where life triumphs in a striking sexual metaphor in its last verse):

> Far and wide as the eye can wander,
> Heath and bog are ev'rywhere.
> Not a bird sings out to cheer us,
> Oaks are standing, gaunt and bare.

> We are the peat-bog soldiers,
> We're marching with our spades
> To the bog. (repeat)

> Up and down the guards are pacing,
> No one, no one can go through;
> Flight would mean a sure death facing,
> Guns and barbed wire greet our view.

> But for us there is no complaining,
> Winter will in time be past;
> One day we shall cry out rejoicing:
> 'Homeland dear, you're mine at last!'

> Then will the peat-bog soldiers
> March no more, with their spades
> To the bog.

During the Spanish Civil War (1936-39) this was a favourite marching song of the International Brigades. Hamish, knowing of my interest in this conflict (a rehearsal for World War Two), gave me, in 1962, a photostat of his 'Canciones de les Brigadas Internationales', published in 1938. This generosity was typical of him. Hamish also encouraged me in song writing—an experience shared by many!

Much later, in 1986, I wrote 'Another Valley', inspired by the reminiscences of a Scots Brigader, the late Eddie Brown. This is the last verse:

> The sun breaks o'er the Golden City,
> Mourning shrouds soon disappear,
> A flower blooms from a darkened corner,
> A laverock rises in the air,
> For iron hearts and fists of steel,
> Cannot smoor the vibrant voice,
> That sings for peace and cries for justice
> Leaving us to make a choice.[6]

Hamish was neither just an antiquarian nor a mere preservationist but always actively encouraged and inspired new song writing. Back in 1973 I asked him, in an extensive interview, whether the explosion in new song writing was a major indicator of the evident success of the folk song revival. His answer was unequivocal:

> Absolutely. The revival will sink or swim by its capacity to throw up new and constantly fresh thinkers and writers who will be open and free to take and adapt anything. The health of the whole set up depends on the musician's freedom of movement.[7]

Ewan MacColl wrote, in relation to Hamish's own songwriting:

> I think as a songwriter he made his greatest contribution. His output of songs is comparatively small but each song he has written is a jewel. He writes in the classic Scots tongue of Dunbar and Henryson with never a hint of the couthie accents of the Kailyard. They are models of their kind and an inspiration to all Scots singers and songwriters.[8]

Hamish was also a fine singer and did more than justice to songs like 'Lang Johnny More', 'Tail Toddle', 'The Spanish Lady' and the classic bothy song, 'Rhynie' — to name but a few. He also made a good job of his own songs!

During his war service, songs loomed large — at all points.[9] In his work for military intelligence as an interrogator he would often ask the prisoners, be they German or Italian, if they knew any songs. And better still, whether they could sing them! Such was his compassion, humanity and vision he would not let himself be 'disfigured by the villainy of hatred' and this is reflected in his superb *Elegies for the Dead in Cyrenica* published in 1948[10] in which he honoured 'the dead, the innocent' of either side.

Hamish collected 'The D-Day Dodgers',[11] his classic, authentic, squaddy song during the Italian campaign. He probably wrote at least one verse of the song himself but, to my knowledge, never owned up to it.

We're the D-Day Dodgers, out in Italy –
Always on the vino, always on the spree,
8th Army scroungers and their tanks
We live in Rome – among the Yanks.
We are the D-Day Dodgers, way out in Italy.

We landed in Salerno, a holiday with pay;
The Jerries brought the bands out to greet us on the way,
Showed us the sights and gave us tea.
We all sang songs the beer was free,
To welcome the D-Day Dodgers, to sunny Italy.
Naples and Cassino were taken in our stride,
We didn't go to fight there – we just went for the ride.
Anzio and Sangro were just names,
We only went to look for dames –
The artful D-Day Dodgers, way out in Italy.

On the way to Florence we had a lovely time,
We ran a bus to Rimini right through the Gothic Line.
Soon to Bologna we will go
And after that we'll cross the Po.
We'll still be D-Day Dodging, way out in Italy.

Once we heard a rumour that we were going home,
Back to dear old Blighty – never more to roam.
Then someone said: 'In France you'll fight!'
We said: 'No fear – we'll just sit tight!'
(The windy D-Day Dodgers, way out in Italy).

Dear Lady Astor, you think you know a lot,
Standing on the platform and talking tommy-rot
You, England's sweetheart and its pride,
We think your mouth's too bleedin wide,
That's from your D-Day Dodgers – in far off Italy.

Look around the mountains, in the mud and rain –
You'll find the scattered crosses –
there's some which have no name.
Heartbreak and toil and suffering gone,
The boys beneath them slumber on.
Those are the D-Day Dodgers who'll stay in Italy.

In 1949, to be precise, Hamish 'saw a tape recorder for the first time', at a party given by the Olivetti family in Italy. In an interview for *Scotland on Sunday* magazine he called it 'a real turning point in my life'. In short, he recognised its capacity and potential as an invaluable collecting tool, and this proved to be the case. Subsequent recordings in the north-east of Scotland with Alan Lomax[12] in 1951 played a major part in the creation of the School of Scottish Studies. At this point the school existed on paper only. Hamish noted: 'The tapes were the very origin of the school, boy they really did shake them.' These recordings, in fact, helped convince the powers-that-be in the University of the wealth of material (in Gaelic and in English/Scots) yet to be tapped. Again, Hamish stressed the (nowadays obvious) value in having 'the living voice—the sounds you need.'

1951 was, in fact, a very significant year. It saw the first of the four consecutive People's Festival ceilidhs in Edinburgh, organised by Hamish and Martin Milligan, et al. This is well documented[13] and indeed was recorded.[14] The ceilidh had three elements: north-east Scottish song, Gaelic song and piping. It exposed an urban audience to a 'masterly group of authentic traditional singers and musicians from rural Scotland' and included Flora MacNeill of Barra, John Strachan of Fyvie, Jimmy McBeath of Portsoy, Jessie Murry of Buckie and the virtuoso piping of John Burgess of Easter Ross. The event was a revelation, and its importance can hardly be overstated. The audiences were deeply impressed by the artistry and importantly they included the poet and songwriter Morris Blythman (aka Thurso Berwick) as well as Norman and Janey Buchan. They became leading movers and shakers in what was to become the Scottish folk song revival—spearheaded by Hamish.

Norman Buchan wrote later:

Looking back that evening was devastatingly new to me… it shouldn't have been. Although I grew up in the Orkney Islands, my folk came from the North-East coast. The Revival didn't really start that night at the ceilidh. Things were going on, it's just that we did not know about it.

Here is a song from that evening, 'Skippin' Barfit Through the Heather' sung by the Buckie fishwife, Jessie Murray:

As I was walkin' doon yon hill
It was in a summer evenin',
It was there I spied a bonny lass
Skippin' barfit through the heather.

Oh but she was neatly dressed,
She neither needed hat nor feather;
She was the queen among them a',
Skippin' barfit through the heather.

'Will ye come wi' me, my bonny lass,
Will ye come wi' me and leave the heather?
It's silks an' satins ye will wear
If ye come wi' me and leave the heather.'

She wore a goon o' the bonnie blue,
Her petticoats were a pheasant colour,
And in between the stripes were seen
Shinin' bells o' bloomin' heather.

'Oh young man your offer's good,
But sae weel I ken ye will deceive me:
But gin ye tak my hert awa'
Better if I had never seen ye.'

Oh but she was neatly dressed,
She neither needed hat nor feather;
She was the Queen among them a',
Skippin' barfit through the heather.

The song 'Rivonia' (to the tune of 'Viva la Quince Brigada') was written after the Rivonia trial of 1964. It was sent to South African freedom-fighters and also reached Nelson Mandela while incarcerated in Robben Island. It was even in the Tanzanian hit parade at one point! On his release, Nelson Mandela came to Glasgow in October 1993 to receive, in person, the freedom of the city. Nelson thanked Hamish for the song, and on that momentous day in George Square they danced together on stage! Indeed, Ian Davison wrote an excellent song as a result.[15]

They have sentenced the men of Rivonia
Rumbala rumbala rumba la
The comrades of Nelson Mandela
Rumbala rumbala rumba la
He is buried alive on an island
Free Mandela Free Mandela
He is buried alive on an island
Free Mandela Free Mandela

Verwoerd feared the mind of Mandela
Rumbala rumbala rumba la
He was stifling the voice of Mandela
Rumbala rumbala rumba la
Free Mbeki, Goldberg, Sisulu
Free Mandela Free Mandela
Free Mbeki, Goldberg, Sisulu
Free Mandela Free Mandela

The crime of the men of Rivonia
Rumbala rumbala rumba la
Was to organise farmer and miner
Rumbala rumbala rumba la
Against baaskap and sjambok and keerie
Free Mandela Free Mandela
Against baaskap and sjambok and keerie
Free Mandela Free Mandela

Set free the men of Rivonia
Rumbala rumbala rumba la
Break down the walls of their prison
Rumbala rumbala rumba la
Freedom and justice Uhuru
Free Mandela Free Mandela
Freedom and justice Uhuru
Free Mandela Free Mandela

Power to the heirs of Luthuli
Rumbala rumbala rumba la
The comrades of Nelson Mandela
Rumbala rumbala rumba la
Spear of the Nation unbroken
Free Mandela Free Mandela
Amandla Umkhonto we Sizwe
Free Mandela Free Mandela

To quote Timothy Neat: 'Hamish believed that music and song can with almost magical force connect past and present: like water they find their level and make their way.'[16]

Hamish strove to make Scotland and the wider world a better place, and he believed our democratic muse contributed (and contributes) mightily to this. A song that exemplifies his spirit (he would ask Alison and I to sing it on many occasions in his final months and weeks) is Ewan MacColl's 'Joy of Living'. This is the last verse:

Take me to some high place
Of heather, rock and ling
Scatter my dust and ashes
Feed me to the wind
So that I may be
Part of all you see
The air you are breathing
I'll be part of the curlew's cry
And the soaring hawk
The blue milkwort
And the sundew hung with diamonds
I'll be riding the gentle wind
That blows through your hair
Reminding you, how we shared
In the joy of living.

References:

1   Brendan Kennelly, *Familiar Strangers: New and Selected Poems (1960-2004)* (Tarset: Bloodaxe Books, 2004), p. 463.

2   Timothy Neat, *Hamish Henderson: A Biography: Vol. 1, The Making of the Poet (1919-1953)* (Edinburgh: Polygon, 2007); *Vol. 2, Poetry Becomes People (1952-2002)* (Edinburgh: Polygon, 2009).

3   Hamish Henderson, 'The Oral Tradition', in Paul H Scott (ed.) *Scotland: A Concise Cultural History* (Edinburgh: Mainstream, 1993).

4   Hamish Henderson, 'The Underground of Song' in *The Scots Magazine* (February 1963), reprinted in Hamish Henderson, *Alias MacAlias*, edited by Alec Finlay (Edinburgh: Polygon, 1992), pp. 31-36.

5   Geordie McIntyre, from '*Resurgimento*. Interview with Hamish Henderson' in the special Festival issue of *New Edinburgh Review* (August 1973). Reprinted verbatim in the programme for the fifth Carrying Stream Festival (Edinburgh: Edinburgh Folk Club, November 2006).

6   Geordie McIntyre, *Inveroran: Songs by Geordie McIntyre* (St Ervan, Wadebridge, Cornwall: Lyngham House, 2005).

7   '*Resurgimento*'

8   *Tocher*, no. 43 (1991), p. 14.

9   Neat (2007) Roughly thirty percent of this weighty volume is, rightly, devoted to the war period.

10   Hamish Henderson: *Collected Poems and Songs*, edited by Raymond Ross (Edinburgh: Curly Snake Publishing, 2000)—which includes the *Elegies*, first published in 1948.

11   *Ibid*, p. 94.

12   Neat (2007); and Ailie Munro, *The Democratic Muse: Folk Song Revival in Scotland* (Aberdeen: Scottish Cultural Press, 1996).

13   See Munro, *Ibid*.

14   Recorded by Alan Lomax, now on a CD from Rounder Records, Cambridge Mass. This is superbly remastered digitally and edited by Ewan McVicar. Thirty-five memorable tracks, including some from Hamish.

15   'Mandela Danced' from the CD *The Best of Ian Davison*, a double CD produced by Clyde Tracks.

16   Neat (2007), p. 276.

17   *The Essential Ewan McColl Songbook* (New York: Oak Publications, 2001).

HAMISH HENDERSON: A TRAVELLER'S TALE

Sheila Stewart

Hamish came into the Travellers' lives in July 1954. My family, the 'Stewarts of Blair', welcomed him with open arms. To meet such a respected man as Hamish changed our lives forever. He was a man who could adapt to any way of life, and I can tell you he was thrown in at the deep end with us. We had the ballads he was looking for, which surprised us because we thought at the time they were too old for any one to be interested in, far less a professor of Hamish's standing. He opened the door for us to be accepted by the non-Traveller.

Hamish put up his tent in our berry field at Essendy among hundreds of Travellers and was readily accepted; my father made sure of that. Then we invited Travellers to our house every night for Hamish to record them with his big massive tape recorder. This went on for about five weeks and, as Hamish said, 'It was like holding a tin can under Niagara Falls.' The oldest ballad he collected from us was our version of 'The Twa Brothers'. His excitement overflowed when we sang our version:

> Two pretty boys were going to the school,
> And one evening coming home,
> Said William to John can you throw a stone
> Or can you play at a ball, or can you play at a ball.
>
> Said William to John I cannot throw a stone
> Nor little can I play at a ball

But if you come down to yon merry green woods
I'll try you a wrestling fall,
I'll try you a wrestling fall.

So they came do on tae yon merry green woods,
Beneath the spreading moon,
And the little pen knife slipped out of William's pocket,
And gave John his deadly wound,
and gave John his deadly wound.

You take off your white Holland shirt
And tear it from gore to gore
And you will bind my deadly wounds,
And they will blood no more,
and they will blood no more.

So he took off his white Holland shirt,
And he tore it from gore to gore
And he did bind his deadly wounds
But they bled ten times more,
and they bled ten times more.

What will I tell to your sister dear
This night when I go home.
You can tell her I'm away to a London school
And the good scholar I'll come home,
and a good scholar I'll come home.

And what will I tell to your sweetheart dear,
This night when I go home,
You can tell her I am dead and in grave laid
And the grass is growing green,
and the grass is growing green.

And what will I tell to your father dear,
This night when I go home
You can tell him I'm dead and in grave laid,
And the grass is growing green,
and the grass is growing green.

And what will I tell to your stepmother dear
This night when I go home,
You can tell her I'm dead and in grave laid
For she prayed I might never come home,
for she prayed I might never come home.

The exciting thing for us about Hamish's visits was when we sang him a ballad. The excitement on his face was a picture, and he said, 'I thought that one was gone long ago, and now you come up with a version of it, wonderful.' Later, when he researched it, Hamish dated 'The Twa Brothers' back to the twelfth century.

I must give all credit to Maurice Fleming. He was the first to introduce us to Hamish. He was looking for the person who wrote 'The Berry Fields of Blair'. Of course, that was my mother. I had known Maurice all my life but never spoken to him. Now, I hope, he is my friend, and has been for many years. His father owned shops in Blairgowrie and was a well respected man in the community.

There is a little story I want to tell about Hamish. One sunny hot day at the berry pickin' we were all up at the top of the field having our hour's break and of course Hamish was with us, and my father had just lit the fire and put the kettle on for our tea, when one of the boys ran across the road into the green field and stripped his shirt off, and started shouting: 'Anyone for a fight or are you too afraid of me?' We all started laughing, because we knew he was a joker. Then his cousin appeared and he challenged him to fight. So he stripped off his shirt, ran across the road and jumped the fence, and they got stuck into the fight. The look on Hamish's face was a picture. He turned to my father and said, 'Is nobody going to stop them, Alex?' 'Oh,' said my father, 'They always let off steam now and again, it's no real.' 'Well, it looks real to me, they are covered in blood.' When the boys saw how upset Hamish was, they stopped and started lickin' the blood off their hands, shouting, 'It's tomato sauce, Hamish!'—and they came over to let him see. 'I'll sing you a song tonight, Hamish, for trickin' you.'

That night around the fire he sang two songs for Hamish, and he was a great singer, and the songs were wonderful. One was a funny one about an Irishman trying to get out of his marriage. The second one was one he composed himself about his brother going into the army and getting shellshocked and how he never was the same again. It was very sad.

There are many things I can say about Hamish, and one song I do not want to miss out. There is only one verse to it, but Hamish loved it.

If you have the toothache, and greetin wi the pain,
Dinny buy bags o' sweeties, for that's a silly game,
Just fill your mouth wi water, and mix wi caster oil,
And put your arse upon the fire, till it begins to boil.

Maybe not a suitable verse for a book on Hamish, but he would not mind. He understood the life of a Traveller, and the way we lived. It was so different from anyone else as he soon found out.

I can only speak for my family and many Travellers who knew him. Yes, he liked a dram, but he never wavered on his job as collector. I have a small story that I will never forget, and that sums Hamish up to the Travellers: One day we were out in the field and I was in charge of the money box to pay the pickers. All was quiet, then Hamish crawled out of his tent after a good night's sleep. It was a bitterly cold day and he was frozen. He came up to me at the weights and said, 'Oh, Sheila, it's a cold day today, isn't it,' just as a small boy came out of the bushes with a small bucket full to the brim with raspberries to be weighed, and he had a big drip hanging from his nose. I looked at Hamish to see his reaction. Then the wee boy took his sleeve across his nose and wiped it off. I looked at Hamish and he also had a drip from his nose. He looked at me smiling, and said, 'Sheila, when in Rome,' and he used his cuff to wipe it off as well. Now that was the real Hamish that the Travellers knew.

Once Hamish settled in and understood the Travellers he became a different man—so relaxed and content with his collecting. One weekend, my father took him up to Banff to meet some Travellers. They met Frank and Ruby—great, great folk—and Ruby's mother. She was a fine singer, in the style of the old Aberdeenshire Travellers. Hamish got a wealth of material from them and old Maggie Kelbie. My father and Hamish had a wonderful time, and William Kelbie was the best mouth organ player Hamish said he ever heard. All this material is in the School of Scottish Studies and should be put on CDs. It would help to keep Hamish's name alive.

Monday night when they came home they were both on a high, and could not stop laughing because of the songs they recorded from auld Maggie. Hamish said they were nearly all bawdy songs she collected from other Travellers, and some she made herself.

There was also another ballad that Hamish said was his favourite, from my singing: 'Where the Moorcocks Crow'. This was a ballad my granny used to sing (my father's mother). In this ballad there is a line that says, 'So gie me your hand', and no matter where he was sitting in a room he would make up to me and stuck out his hand in answer to the song.

It made a bond between Hamish and myself forever. Now I cannot sing it without remembering him, and I go to the nearest person and stick out my hand to them and we shake hands. I do it in memory of Hamish. There are many things we can do in memory of this great man. This is mine, humble as it may be:

With my dog and gun through the bloomin' heather,
For game and pleasure I took my way,
I met a maiden she was tall and slender,
And her eyes enticed me some time to stay.

Says I fair maid do you know I love you,
Tell me your name and your dwelling also,
O' excuse my name sir, I have my dwelling,
By the mountain streams where the moorcocks crow.

Says I fair maid if you wed a fermer,
You'l be tied for life to one plot of land,
But I'm a rovin Johnnie and if you'll gang wi me,
You will have no ties so gie me your hand.

But if my parents knew sir I loved a rover,
Then that I'm sure 'twould be my overthrough,
So I'll stay at home for another season,
By the mountain streams where the moorcocks crow.

So it's fare ye well love another season,
We will meet again in yon woodland vale,
And I will sit you down upon my knee then,
And I will listen to your love sick tale.

Then it's arm in arm we will go together,
Neath the lofty trees into the valley below,

Where the linnets are singing their song sae sweetly,
By the mountain streams where the moorcocks crow.

Hamish met his wife Kätzel in our berry field. She was there picking berries with her sister. My father had put their tent up for them. Hamish was besotted. She was a lovely girl. In due time, they would have two lovely daughters who are a credit to them.

Hamish brought many professors to visit us over the years. That in itself is a wonderful legacy, bringing in people from all over the world. He will never be forgotten in the years to come, ever. I just hope the people who are writing books on Hamish realise he was a people's man. Not an academics' man. I know he lived with all the academics, and was one, but to us he was just Hamish, a Traveller's friend, and saviour.

He had the biggest heart, was good-natured, and knew what he wanted in the collecting world. I miss him so much. I always thought he would always be there. He educated folk without being a teacher, through common sense and knowledge—the Travellers' motto. We have no education, but we could see that he had the three of them—education, knowledge, and common sense—and there's not many men can say they have all three of them.

Then and forever he was a gentleman among men. The legacy he has left behind will continue forever. If it were not for him, Travellers would never have been recognised as having anything to offer society. Not only did he bring to life our culture in music and song, but he fought with us to be accepted by the snobs of this world, and proved to them that we were human beings, and not some kind of animals as they all thought.

I am so glad I can write this to show the other side of Hamish. Yes, the other side, a great people's man. And the friend of the Travellers. I sang 'A man you don't meet every day' at his funeral:

Me name is Jock Stewart, I'm a canny young man,
And a rambling young fellow I have been,
So be easy and free when you're drinking with me,
I'm a man you don't meet every day.

I have acres of land, I have men at command,
I have always a shilling to spare,

So be easy and free when you're drinking with me,
I'm a man you don't meet every day.

So come fill up your glasses, with brandy or wine,
And whatever the cost I will pay,
So be easy and free, when you're drinking with me,
I'm a man you don't meet every day.

I think I have made it clear what Hamish meant to the Travellers. It is hard for me to write this, putting Hamish in the past tense. I am sorry I cannot write any more. Just one thing I would like to mention, I have a son called after him, he is a minister of the cloth, The Reverend Hamish MacGregor, and he and my oldest son Ian carried Hamish's coffin out of the church to the hearse.

When his ashes were scattered in Glenshee, Timothy Neat and Hamish's son-in-law came by my house to let me cuddle the urn and say my final goodbyes to my old pal. Always remember: he was 'a man you won't meet every day'. Hamish, you will be in my heart forever!

WEE GALLUS WEANS: HAMISH HENDERSON AS A COLLECTOR OF CHILDREN'S LORE

Ewan McVicar

Why choose the topic of Hamish Henderson as a collector of Scots children's lore? Hamish Henderson was not known for this. However, on the few occasions he did so between 1954 and 1960, his recordings are always illuminating and at times joyous.

He found some impressive informants and fascinating and unique items, and the recordings illustrate neatly the range of settings in which he could collect lore. His informants included a crowd of over-elated children in a roaring Edinburgh playground, polite young girls at a house ceilidh in Campbeltown, jovial trade union officials caught 'on the fly' in Glasgow, the majestic traveller singer Jeannie Robertson in concert in Aberdeen, and the Leven mother of another famous singer, Jean Redpath, quietly in her own home recalling what she sang when she was wee.

Very few of the items last more than sixty seconds. They are small gems. When some of them became performance material in folk clubs and concerts through the folk revival, new verses would be added, or several short items would be sequenced together.

Children's lore is strongly associated with activity—physical play like ring games or skipping or hand-clapping, or manipulation of a baby's limbs—or social interaction with one or two others—riddles, lullabies, 'nursery songs'. Even word-play and amusement songs are not intended for formal performance before a passive audience, but for sharing with a few playfellows. In Henderson's recordings the listener can at times hear the informants struggle to recall items that are being recorded outwith their usual context, while on the playground 'field recordings' the voices are confident and sure. Even such a consummate professional performer as Jeannie Robertson stumbles over such songs, because they are not from her performance repertoire but part of a presentation directed by Henderson as collector.

Henderson learned the basics of field recording while acting as one of Alan Lomax's guides in a 1951 jaunt round Scotland that garnered astonishing riches of song and music. Alan Lomax was assistant curator of the US Library of Congress, Washington DC, a seminal collector, writer and broadcaster, and the most important single influence on the US folk revival. His 1951 collecting trip round Scotland was crucial to the Scottish folk revival, and copies of his 1951 recordings are the first 25 hours of the sound archives of the School of Scottish Studies. It was not always a comfortable tour. Henderson commented in a 1994 BBC Scotland programme that 'Lomax's tape recorder was called a Magnecorder, and it was a colossal uncouth beast of a thing. It came in two huge halves, I found myself not really so much a guide as a coolie for him.' Henderson was, of course, more a shikari than a coolie, hunting down singers, musicians and other informants for Lomax to record on his wonderful new machine.

One of these was Dr James T R Ritchie of Edinburgh. A major collector of the songs, games, and stories of Edinburgh schoolchildren, 'Docky' Ritchie was a much-loved and respected teacher in Norton Park Secondary School in North East Edinburgh. He was part of the Norton Park Group which, a few months earlier, had made the black and white film, *The Singing Street,* with its astonishingly evocative 1951 scenes of Edinburgh children at play. The film is still much utilised in nostalgia settings by the BBC and museums. Ritchie went on to write two books of children's lore, *The Singing Street* in 1964 and *Golden City* in 1965, which were both republished recently by Mercat Press.

Ritchie and one of his principal young informants, Peggy MacGillivray, who had recently sung on the soundtrack of the 1951 film, were interviewed by Lomax. He asked how Ritchie had begun to collect:

Well, I got started because – eh, one day I had a class. I'm supposed to be a science teacher, you see, and if you teach certain girls science, you find it's very difficult, and they're not interested in scientific explanations of why a blanket keeps you warm. They know it keeps you warm. They don't want to know anything about the conductivity of the air. So I says to them, 'Well, tell me, what are you interested in?' Because I couldn't get their interest aroused. And – eh, of course, no answer. Then I says, 'What do you do?' No answer. 'What do you do during the holidays?' 'We play.' 'Where?' 'In the street.' 'What at?' And then they began to tell me about their games, you see.[1]

Ritchie goes on to ask Peggy MacGillivray for a 'counting-out' rhyme. She responded with:

> Three white horses in a stable
> Pick one out and call it Mabel
> If it's Mabel, set the table
> Three white horses in a stable

Later in the interview she sweetly sings a 'tearjerker' which was surely used as a Halloween guiser piece, yet Lomax recorded it as a bouncing 'two rope' skipping song when he went soon after to collect directly from children at Norton Park School. A neat example of how children adapt their material and reapply its use:

> I'm a little orphan girl
> My mother she is dead
> My father is a drunkard
> And won't buy me my bread
>
> I sit upon the windowsill
> To hear the organ play
> And think of my dear mother
> Who's dead and far away
>
> Ding-dong, my castle bell
> Farewell to my mother
> Bury me in the old churchyard
> Beside my eldest brother
>
> My coffin shall be white
> Six little angels by my side
> Two to sing and two to pray
> And two to carry my soul away

Lomax had some difficulty in transcribing this lyric, and rendered 'And won't buy me my bread' as the startling 'And goes right in my bed'. Henderson, in his wide-ranging 1962 *Scottish Studies* article 'An Aberdeen White Paternoster', reprinted in *Alias MacAlias* in 1992,[2] linked this song to the 'parent charm':

> Matthew, Mark, Luke and John
> Guard the bed that I lie on

Alan Lomax's 1951 recordings of children's song and rhyme were in 2004 issued on CD by the US label Rounder Records.[3]

Hamish Henderson had also taken Lomax to meet jovial bothy ballad singer John Mearns in Cedar Place, Aberdeen, who duetted with his wife the old courting ballad 'Pennyworth O Preens', which is considered by Iona and Peter Opie to be a 'singing game'. John's son Jackie and daughter Kathleen then gathered their street playpals. In polite tones they shared a host of 'het'-selecting rhymes, skipping, ball-bouncing and round game lyrics. Their small performance songs included 'My Girl's A Corker', comic verses about Harry Lauder and Mussolini, and

> An angel said to me, would you like a cup of tea?
> I said oh, no, I like cocoa better than tea

This small squib was warbled to the tune of the very popular sickly-sweet song 'Down In The Glen'. Jackie, now John Mearns, still vividly recalls Lomax's visit, and his enthusiastic account of Alan Lomax playing guitar and stomping on the floor is one highlight of the DVD by filmmaker Rogier Kappers that retraces Lomax's European recording jaunts, *Lomax The Songhunter*.[4] In the ball-bouncing song

> One two three aleerie
> I spy Bella Peerie
> Sitting on her basket chairie / bumbaleerie
> Eating chocolate babies

John Mearns Junior recalled that the children had been instructed by his father to sing the polite 'basket chairie' but some of them persisted in carolling the 'rude' version. Henderson recorded for Lomax on the

1951 tapes an authoritative account of the development of the widely known children's song 'Wha Saw The Forty-Second', which he had found in Robert Ford's *Children's Rhymes, Game Songs and Stories*.[5]

By November 1954 Henderson was himself recording children's songs, for the School of Scottish Studies. The 1954 recordings[6] were made in the playground of Craigmillar Primary, a large depressed local authority housing estate on the southern edge of Edinburgh. The recording sound quality is at times so poor it proved not possible to use any of them in the Scottish Tradition CD 'Chokit On A Tattie'. The problem is not tape quality or microphone placement, but sound overload and distortion caused by the sheer volume of exuberant and excited singing. I speculate that Henderson was trying out a new recording machine, and had not given full attention to the flickering needle that indicates volume input suddenly being jammed against the right-hand restraining post, since he at times records at a grossly distorted level.

He recorded 32 separate items, some of them versions of well known pieces like 'The wind the wind', 'Are you going to golf, sir?', 'There came a girl from France' and 'The big ship sails on the Illy Ally oh'. Others are further to seek, and are only found in print in

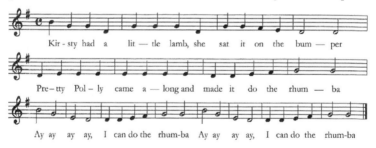

Kir - sty had a lit — tle lamb, she sat it on the bum — per

Pre — tty Pol — ly came a — long and made it do the rhum — ba

Ay ay ay ay, I can do the rhum-ba Ay ay ay ay, I can do the rhum-ba

Ritchie's books. Some are chants or rhymes, some game songs, some are amusement or insult songs. Where Ritchie tells us the texts and uses, Henderson's recordings tell us what tunes were applied to them, and let us hear the joyous spirit that performance imparted to them. In the following song we can hear the skipping feet of the dancing ring described by Ritchie, but also the conga-like tune employed.

This is a very early sound recording of such material, particularly in a field setting, and the impossibility of fully deciphering lyrics is more frustrating because to my knowledge a couple of the items have not been noted, let alone recorded, elsewhere. However, the tunes are clear, and nearly all the problem lyrics can be understood through reference to Ritchie's books, and to Lomax's 1951 recordings at Norton Park School.

It has been suggested to me that Lomax's playground recordings were to some extent staged, with the jumprope being turned so the sound of it hitting the ground is heard, while the singers are closer to the microphone and giving their full attention to song. These singers were already versed in performance, they had only a few months earlier been recorded in BBC Scotland's Edinburgh studio, singing for the soundtrack of the Norton Park Group's *Singing Street* film.

In contrast, the Craigmillar kids are clearly out in the large playground before the school. The girls are fluent in the words and tunes of the game songs, but boys are so determined to be part of the very unusual event they contribute shrill whistling and participative yells that further muddy the recordings. One other problem is that Henderson switches on the recorder just as the children launch themselves, so the machine cannot get up to full speed in time.

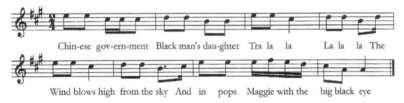

Chin-ese gov-ern-ment Black man's dau-ghter Tra la la La la la The
Wind blows high from the sky And in pops Maggie with the big black eye

For example, the recording of 'Chinese Government' starts with a squeal and gross distortion, with the children already in wild action, then settles down to merely a high overload, and at last a good recording level. At the end of a well-recorded verse Henderson says politely and efficiently, as addressing equals, 'That'll do fine, thank you,' but the kids charge on with more 'Chinese government, black man's…' and he must halt them, conserving expensive tape.

He seems to have already auditioned the children, because he can sometimes be heard calling for a named next piece. And a female voice, a teacher probably, is assisting him. At one point a peremptory small male voice announces what in some Scottish schools was known as a 'yuvtae' —'Yuv tae go up for drill.' Hamish says 'Go on, sing it,' and a woman says 'Hurry up'. A small boy then sings a rushed solo version of the three verses of 'I've a sweetheart in America'. This is followed by a more measured group female version of the same song.

At the end of the loudly chanted 'Are you going to golf, sir?' ecstatic small boys yell incomprehensibly. Henderson records the piece again, perhaps hoping for a clearer version, but the volume is such that the distortion increases and the yelling by small males at the end is even more concerted. Ritchie tells us this pandemonium level chant was also used for a solo ball game, the ball bouncing on the word 'sir'.

The latter part of the recording of 'Monday is my washing day' is quite undecipherable.

> Monday is my washing day
> Tuesday I am done
> Wednesday is my ironing day
> Thursday I am done
> Friday is my (incomprehensible) day
> Saturday I am done
> Sunday is my (incomprehensible)

Repeated playings to the audience during my November 2007 lecture in Edinburgh elicited some possible but not fully convincing readings. Then a thorough rescouring of Ritchie's two books provided the answer. Ritchie gives a skipping game in *The Singing Street* titled 'Mary Kelly & Harry Brown'. The last eight lines of this show that the Craigmillar kids are singing the surprisingly literary:

In the Craigmillar recording there follows a suggestion of child abuse involving two 1930s film stars! The children also tag this item on to the end of two other self-contained pieces.

> One two three aleerie
> I saw Wallace Beery

Sitting on his bumaleerie
Kissing Shirley Temple

The tune for 'Monday is my washing day' is a variant of the first half of the old popular song 'Where did you get that hat'. That for 'One two three aleerie' is the tune usually employed for it in Scotland, 'Chan 'eil mo leannan ann a' seo'.

Two years later, some of the same songs are among fifteen items recorded by Henderson from a small group of bright-voiced Campbeltown schoolgirls at 'Willie Mitchell's ceilidh, December 1956, Campbeltown'.[8] Half the pieces are performed before an appreciative small audience, with ripples of applause, murmured 'hurrays' from Hamish and appreciative proprietorial chuckles from, I think, Willie Mitchell himself. The rest are recorded more quietly, closer to the microphone in a room with little echo.

I was certain the informants would have been Willie's daughters, Agnes, Mary and Catherine, who during the 1960s folk revival performed widely around Kintyre as The Mitchells. In a 2007 telephone conversation Agnes assured me it had not been them, but Henderson's description of the Mitchell family in his 1979 *Tocher* article about Willie where he describes his first meeting with them all in December 1956, made it hard to think who else these girls would have been.[9]

However, the song lyrics offer pointers to their identity. The singers insert the names Margaret and Flora into 'Chinese Government', spell out the name Flora Henderson at the end of 'Dr Brown was a very good man', and one nervous solo singer names Evelyn Lang in 'The wind the wind'. It is seldom in collecting folklore that one gets clues to the informant's identity from the lyrics employed.

Songs held in common, though in varying versions, in Campbeltown and Craigmillar and recorded by Henderson were 'The wind the wind the wind blows high', 'There came a girl from France', 'Chinese Government', 'One two three aleerie' and 'Knees up Mother Brown'. Another from Campbeltown is still in use by Scots children today.

Henderson knows what some of their repertoire will be. He asks, 'What about 'Teddy bear'?' There is a chorus of affirmation, and they launch into the rhyme.

Teddy bear, teddy bear, touch the ground
Teddy bear, teddy bear, turn around

Show your shoe / That will do
Run up stairs / Say night prayers
Switch off the light

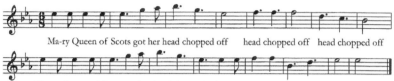

Ma-ry Queen of Scots got her head chopped off   head chopped off   head chopped off

Ma - ry Queen of Scots got her head chopped off On the four-teenth of Nov - em - ber

They end with 'Teddy bear, teddy bear, say goodnight', and a consciously cute spoken final 'Goodnight teddy bear', followed by self-amused giggles.

The Campbeltown girls also shared at the ceilidh two songs with ancient connections, 'Three gypsies came ariding' and 'Mary Queen of

Three gyp – sies came   a   ri — ding   a   ri — ding   a   ri — ding   Three

gyp – sies came   a   ri — ding   Y   O   U

Scots got her head chopped off'. Ritchie (*Golden City*) tells us the latter is usually chanted when 'ye wheech the head off a yellow dandelion or dandelion clock'. But when Henderson asks, 'And is that a game?', he is told 'It's a ball and you've a string on it. Holes in it, and you've got a string with […] on the other side. You keep on bouncing it.'

The Opies, in *The Singing Game*,[10] give many pages over to 'Three gypsies came a-riding', with variants from all around Europe and the Americas, yet none feature the suitor that was successful in Campbeltown.

The verses proceed with interrogation and defiant response.

What are you riding here for?
We're riding here to marry
Will you marry me, sir?
You're all black and dirty

Just as clean as you, sir
You're all as straight as pokers
Can bend as well as you, sir

The girl finally settles for a royal wooer of practical bent.

I think we'll just take you, sir
Now we've got the Prince of Wales
To help us with the washing

Henderson tries with limited success to learn how this game is played:

'Wait a minute, tell us, what are you doing when you're playing that game?' [There is a babble of response.] 'One [second], one at a time.'

'...some people on this side, and there's one person there, and at the end, when I em you say, 'I think I'll just take you, sir', you take somebody, you dance round and round, then you start all over again, till you get everybody over to this side.'

'Uh huh.'

'It can go on for ages.'

Henderson sounds doubtful that he has understood. 'Right.'

The tunes for both 'Three gypsies' and 'Mary Queen of Scots' are

variants of one of the most widely employed tunes by Scots children. Best known as 'Here we go round the mulberry bush', it has a fine Scottish pedigree, as 'The merry matanzie' or 'Ma wee ring'.

Hamish also found in Campbeltown another celebrity with practical work skills, this time based on a then very popular US folk hero.

Born on a dustbin in Park Square
Davie Crockett did not care
He swept the lums for half a crown
The best chimney sweep in Campbeltown
Davie, Davie Crockett
King of the chimney sweeps

Parodies on the theme song of the 1950s Davie Crockett TV series multiplied and swept the country. One of Henderson's Campbeltown informants gave him another, beginning 'Born in a monkey cage in London Zoo'. Glasgow children preferred Davie Crewcut, 'Born in a tenement at Partick Cross'.

Only a mile or so from Partick Cross is Peel Street, where in November 1957 Henderson was, I have been told, attending a party in the upstairs flat of folk revival stalwarts and organisers Norman and Janey Buchan. An argument arose as to how easily folklore could be found, and Hamish took his recorder to the downstairs kitchen, where the Buchans' friend and neighbour was entertaining some trade union officials. Hamish proceeded to garner a few child lore gems from them,[11] intermingled with adult pieces like 'The smashing of the van' and the ribald 'Sammy Ha' who 'only had one ba, still it was better than nane at aa'. Now, the tale of how the recording was instigated is rather too neat to be swallowed whole, and I cannot recall who told me about it, but that does not make it untrue, in spirit if not in unvarnished fact.

One informant, Alec Ross, offered Hamish a verse in which the surprising use of the word 'bonny' gives alliterative force to an explosion.

Mrs Maclean had a wee wean
She didny know how tae nurse it
She gied it tae me, ah gied it some tea
And its bonny wee belly burstit

Ross also had a version of the counting out rhyme that Peggy MacGillivray had given Alan Lomax in 1951 that, if overheard in the playground by a passing teacher, would have led to a visit to the chair outside the heidie's door.

Two white horses in a stable
Take one out and skin its navel
If another says a word
Hit it wi a horse's turd
Eerie orie eerie orie
You are out

Another informant downstairs in Peel Street was the senior trade unionist Josh Shaw, himself known for writing and singing songs at union meetings. That evening Shaw first recalled a baby-dandling song from the area where Glenlivet whisky is distilled, then gave Henderson a song that became a standard piece for the folk revival. Shaw explained, 'Noo Stevie MacDougall, he's in Rhodesia noo, but he came from the Gorbals. But this is a wee song that he gave us.'

Oh, yir ma wee gallus bloke nae mair
Oh, yir ma wee gallus bloke nae mair
Wi yir bell-blue strides an yer bunnet tae the side
Oh, yir ma wee gallus bloke nae mair

When I went by the sweetie works, ma hert begun tae beat
Saw aa the herry pie walkin doon the street
Wi their flashy, dashy petticoats, flashy, dashy shawls
Their five an tanner gutty boots, oh we're big gallus molls

At the end Shaw says, 'An it's been done very much better than that, but that's as good as you're gonny get the noo.'

The song was popularised in the Scottish folk revival in the 1960s, and was printed by Norman Buchan in *101 Scottish Songs*[12]. But there Shaw's syncopated phrasing was ironed out, the impolite 'hairy pie' was replaced by 'factory lassies', and a new verse added about a mink coat.[13]

After finding Shaw's song, Henderson asked famed Aberdonian singer Jeannie Robertson if she knew it. She recalled the following, to a different tune, and Henderson got her to sing it, along with a few other children's songs, in a 1960 Aberdeen ceilidh:

> For we are three wee Glesga molls, we kin let you see
> An if you hit the one wee moll, ye'll hae tae hit the three
> Flashy dashy petticoats, flashy dashy shawls
> Twelve an a tanner's worth o boots, an we're the gallus molls

The usually majestic Robertson is at times hesitant about her texts, this is in no way her usual concert material, and she comments: 'It's beginnin to leave ma mind now.' Writing about vagueness of mind recalls an event I was present at in Glasgow about 1960, in the basement of the Iona Community building in Clyde Street. Hamish was lecturing on recordings he had made, but had partaken of a dram or four, and teetotaller Janey Buchan had to assist him in disentangling tapes. Hamish was unabashed, and in the midst of this he played delightedly a new recording of a children's song, introducing it as a true discovery:

> Last night there was a murder in the chip shop,
> a wee dog stole a haddie bone.
> A big dog tried tae take it aff him
> so ah hit it wi a tattie scone.
> Ah went round tae see ma Aunty Sarah,
> but ma Aunty Sarah wisny in.
> So ah peeked through a hole in the windae,
> and ah shouted 'Aunty Sarah, are ye in?'
> Her false teeth were lyin on the table,
> her curly wig wis lyin on the bed.
> An ah nearly split ma sides wi laughin,
> when ah saw her screwin aff her wudden leg.

Hamish smiled in anticipation of an enthusiastic response, but the hearers sat puzzled. Janey voiced the general surprise—all the audience knew it well from childhood, because they were from Glasgow, Hamish was from Edinburgh.

Several of the young singers who attended that 1960 talk in the Iona Community were active in the newly formed Glasgow Folk Club, and also participated in reciprocal visits with the Edinburgh University Folk Song Society, instigated in 1958 with Hamish's energetic involvement. Jean Redpath, a shining light in the EUF Club who later became one of Scotland's most famous folk singers, took Henderson to see her mother in Leven. Mrs Isabella Redpath sang Hamish twelve children's items rich in melody and text,[14] several of them marked by the assembly of elements from differing songs.

The following unites a verse of 'Down in yonder meadow' with one that tells quite a different story, of a dead baby who is attended by the undertaker in his tall black silk hat reminiscent of the tubular shape of a piece of sweet liquorice, and she includes her daughter's name in this and other songs:

> Down in the meadow where the green grass grows
> There Jeannie Redpath bleaches her clothes
> She sang and she sang and she sang so sweet
> She sang her true love across the street
> He kissed her, he cuddled her, he put her tae bed
> He sent for the doctor before she was dead
> In came the doctor and out went the cat
> And in came the man wi the sugarelly hat

In another children's game song, 'The bonnie bunch of roses', Mrs Redpath's version begins with a ball-bouncing instruction, moves to a courting verse, then three stanzas about crime and retribution, ending with a typical Scots threat of ritual violence when the offender is caught:

> Up against the wall, the London ball
> An a bonnie bunch o roses
> Ah met ma lad in the bramble law
> Wi a bonnie bunch o roses

Ha ha ha, ye needna rin
Wi a bonnie bunch o roses

Ma faither bocht a new top-coat
An Jeannie tore the lining
Ha ha ha, ye needna rin
For ye'll get yer licks in the mornin

A third attractive item has elements of the very well known 'Spanish Lady' song which is set in Dublin. The last two lines of verse two seem a pleasant 'nonsense' filling in of a memory gap, and verse three conjures an image of a soldier lad sporting his beloved's ribboned favour.

As I gaed up by London Castle
Ten o'clock on a summer's night
There ah spied a bonny lassie
Washin her face in the candlelight

She had boots of patent leather
And her stockings lined with silk
Ma dar aye the red red rosie
Halliloo for Jeannie oh

Jeannie I shall wear your ribbons
Jeannie I shall wear them braw
Jeannie I shall wear your ribbons
Till your laddie gangs awa

Mrs Redpath also records for Hamish a sweet version of another widely popular little song, 'Queen Mary Queen Mary', which is a fragment of an eighteenth-century fifteen-verse ballad, written by a Falkirk farmer, re-cycled by children for a friendship game, or for solo performance. But Mrs Redpath's version has a happy ending, usually absent:

Queen Mary, Queen Mary, her age is sixteen
Her father's a farmer in yonder green
He's got plenty o money to dress her up braw
But nae bonny laddie'll tak her awa

One mornin she rose an she looked in the glass
An said she tae hersel 'What a handsome young lass'
Her hands by her side an she gave a 'ha ha'
An some bonny laddie he took her awa

Mrs Redpath recalled another courting song 'The lad that canna kiss a lass is no the lad for me, For my ain bonny laddie's kissed twa or three', sung to the tune 'Brochan Lom'. This in turn reminded her of another that she also sings to that tune, though it is generally sung to the tune 'Castles in the air'.

Oh, the Ball the Ball the Ball the Ball, the Ball of Kirriemeer
Fower an twenty auld wives, they were aa there
They sat them on the cabbages, they sat them on the peas
But ye couldny see the cabbages for hairy legs and knees

Hamish's lifelong interest in bawdy song is aroused. He asks, 'Do you know any more verses?' She is a little embarrassed at the slightly indelicate nature of what she has just sung, and answers, 'No, I'm afraid that's plenty.' He mistakenly thinks she knows other verses, and delicately presses her for 'Just one more,' but neither she nor daughter Jean know of the bawdy version he has in mind, and he gently and tactfully turns to seeking more game songs. Mrs Redpath was not, however, prudish. She recorded three 'bawdy songs' for Hamish, and a number of local sayings that include 'Yer arse an parsley an green herbs are ae colour.'

One other rich item of Scots child lore collected by Hamish in 1960[15] is discussed by him in his 1973 *Tocher* obituary piece on entertainer and street singer of cornkisters and ballads, Jimmy MacBeath.[16]

Mary Annie, sugar cannie
Bumbee bedlar
Saxteen saidler.
A mannie in a hairy caipie
Rowin at the fairy boatie
Fairy boatie ow'r dear
Ten pounds in the year
Jock Fite had a coo

Black and white aboot the moo.
Hit can jump the Brig o Dee
Singin Cock-a-linkie.

Jimmy had learned these lines in about 1902 in 'the playground of
Portsoy School, from a boy called Muir who became a farmservant'.
Hamish labels this small sub-category of 'rigmarole' disjointed
couplets as 'dreg songs', describing these as 'nonsense verses forming
a lengthy version of the half-traditional, half-improvised rowing song
of the oyster fishers of the Firth of Forth'. There are several others
of similar ilk to Jimmy's in Volume 8 of the *Greig-Duncan Folk Song
Collection*.[17]

In 1776 David Herd printed 64 lines bumper full of puzzling
references to character and location that put a higher priority on
rhythm and rhyme than on rhyme and reason.[18] Herd titled that piece
'Dreg Song', but only 12 lines of that variant relate to working on the
water and dredging for oysters in the Firth of Forth, the rest are a
jumble and rumple of non sequitur. Loath though I am to question any
assessment of Hamish Henderson's about Scots song, it seems to me
that this genre is created as a children's feat of memory, incorporating
pieces of—or references to—other rhymes and songs of place or about
characters.

The last four lines of Jimmy MacBeath's piece mash together
elements of three Scots children's pieces, including 'Katie Bairdie'.
Henderson makes an ingenious connection between the 'mannie
in the hairy caipie' couplet and the Horseman's Word. For me, the
reference in Jimmy's piece to a ferry boat, plus the appearance in some
Greig-Duncan variants of other references to water-based activity and
to fishermen's quarry (skate, eel, haddock), do make a link of sorts to
Herd's title, but none of the North-East sources make any use of the 12
Herd lines that seem to refer directly to dredging.

Fragments of 'dreg song' have been found in the Forth fishing ports
now encompassed by Edinburgh. Francis Collinson devotes 17 pages
to the topic of 'The Oyster dredging songs of the Firth of Forth'.[19] At
Hamish tells us of two of these in 'Folk-singing in Auld Reekie'.[20] At
other times, he found and recorded a few more such items for the
School of Scottish Studies sound archive. But none of the texts quoted
by Collinson and Henderson is a lengthy assembly of 'nonsense'
couplets, they are nearly all short and to the point regarding dredging

and associated work.

It seems to me likely that if Forth shore children cobbled such memory testing pieces together, they naturally wove in threads of local rhyme and phrase. Their North-East colleagues certainly did. Along the Forth, bits of 'dreg song' were used, but not in the North-East. Some common elements do turn up—for example, elements of 'Katie Bairdie'. And Henderson in 1965 quotes with regard to the blinking Newhaven lighthouse: 'There's an auld carle sits by the sea, Wi' a white caun'le on his knee'. Greig-Duncan text 1644A begins 'The carle sits upo' the sea, A' his can'les on his knee'. 36 lines more follow, ending with 'Happiky and Hulzie, Rotten geese and almond waters'. Gavin Greig comments: 'It is a problem how these rhymes originated: and it is equally remarkable that, albeit whimsical, disconnected, and illogical to a degree, they should inhere in the memory for a lifetime.'

I have ended with a small disagreement on terminology, but I am greatly indebted to Hamish Henderson. He recorded remarkably little children's lore in quantity, and I am unclear on the level of his interest. Adam MacNaughtan has pointed out to me that Hamish usually asked informants for children's rhymes, but I have not found that he ever transcribed these items, though they are salted through the School of Scottish Studies tapes. For example, just two tapes away from the Campbeltown ceilidh recording, on SA1956/1969, he recorded 15 children's rhymes and songs from Catherine McElhatton, an adult. And on tape SA1960/242, numerically immediately after his visit to Mrs Redpath in Leven, are recordings made in Rutherglen of 'Mary Annie, sugar cannie' from Jimmy MacBeath, two versions of 'There's an auld carle sits by the sea' from Jack Milne of Aberdeen and Dunbar, and four more children's pieces from Mrs Redpath.

I have discussed in detail what Hamish recorded on a few occasions between 1951 and 1960, but what he recorded is rich indeed in quality. He found the full range of children's lore—dandling, ball-bouncing, 'counting out' and rigmaroles, games, amusement songs and rhymes, rude versions, and very rude versions.

The versions he found were 'unique' because the texts and uses of children's songs and chants tend to change, evolve and mutate quickly where the oral process is involved, though texts can become rigid when they are taught by adults in formal settings rather than passed on in the playground from ten-year-olds to eight-year-olds. There is a general dearth in print or archives of notated versions of tunes used by Scots children for their songs, and a like lack of field recordings, so those Henderson had a hand in are invaluable to those of us who find that the printed words give less than half the picture. As Donald Smith points out, 'So often with children's songs and rhymes, [verbal and musical issues] are playing off each other and only the two in combination make sense of what is happening.'[21]

I have detailed a few problems in the Henderson recordings I discuss, but these are inherent in the nature of the hunt. When you sit a solitary adult down in a quiet supportive surrounding and ask them to sing, they may be nervous initially, but should soon give of their best, though of course the performance style will not be quite that employed in a group social setting. A child in a one-to-one setting or indoor performance situation will often struggle to recall words that are usually the accompaniment for group activity or social interaction. Collectors' tape recordings of lore from children are often marked by repeated stops and pauses as they coax small people to recall another item that is outwith its usual outdoor context.

I have now and then heard anecdotes critical of the attitude of some collectors towards those they are recording, particularly regarding lack of respect, bordering on rudeness, for informants, and demands for specific kinds of songs. But I have never heard such tales about Hamish Henderson. For example, immediately after recording 'Wee gallus bloke', Josh Shaw tentatively offers a sentimental 'cowboy' ditty called 'Twilight on the trail'. Many, if not most, collectors would have refused the offer. Not Hamish. He records it.

Hamish Henderson always showed his appreciation for what he was being given. The chuckle and enthusiasm in his voice, the murmurs of recognition and encouragement that are there on the 1951 Lomax recordings, the courteous request for material addressed to equals, all these appear on his recordings of children's lore, and throughout his recording career.

References:

1   Alan Lomax Archive, New York.

2   Hamish Henderson, *Alias MacAlias: Writings on Songs, Folk and Literature*, edited by Alec Finlay (Edinburgh: Polygon, 1992), pp. 110-114.

3   Alan Lomax, 'Singing in the Streets', Rounder Records, CD 1795, 2004.

4   *Lomax The Songhunter*, directed by Rogier Kappers, Amsterdam: MM Film Produkties, 2005.

5   Robert Ford, *Children's Rhymes, Game Songs and Stories* (Paisley: Alexander Gardner, 1903).

6   School of Scottish Studies archive, SA1954/139-142

7   Greentrax, CDTRAX 9022, 2006.

8   School of Scottish Studies archive, SA1956/171-2.

9   Hamish Henderson, 'Willie Mitchell', in *Tocher*, 31 (Summer, 1979), reprinted in *Alias MacAlias*, pp. 181-89.

10 Iona and Peter Opie, *The Singing Game*, Oxford: Oxford University Press, 1985.

11 School of Scottish Studies archive, SA1957/99.

12 Norman Buchan, *101 Scottish Songs* (Glasgow: Collins, 1962).

13 In *Tocher*, 5 (1972), p. 440, there is a careful notation of the original tune.

14 School of Scottish Studies archive, SA1960/241.

15 School of Scottish Studies archive, SA1960/242.

16 Patrick Shuldham-Shaw, Emily B Lyle and Katherine Campbell (eds), *The Greig-Duncan Folk Song Collection*, Vol. 8 (Edinburgh: Mercat Press, 2002).

17 David Herd, *Ancient & Modern Scottish Songs*, first published 1776 (Edinburgh: Scottish Academic Press, 1973).

18 *Scottish Studies*, Vol 5, Pt 1 (1961).

19 First published in *Folk Scene* (1965), reprinted in *Alias MacAlias*, pp. 5-15.

20 Donald Smith, review of Ewan McVicar, *Doh Ray Me, When Ah Wis Wee: Scots Children's Songs and Rhymes* (Edinburgh: Birlinn, 2007), in *Scottish Affairs*, no. 65 (Autumn, 2008), pp. 132-37.

FROM PERTHSHIRE TO PENNSYLVANIA: THE INFLUENCE OF HAMISH HENDERSON ON TRANSATLANTIC FOLKLORE STUDIES

Margaret Bennett

Following his demobilisation after World War Two, Hamish Henderson wrote: 'The collector-folklorist should never, in the heat of the chase, forget his humanist role.'[1]

Of course, collecting and documenting traditional folk culture goes back centuries, though the word 'folklore' dates only to 1846, when a collector of 'popular antiquities' suggested his interest could more aptly be described as *folk-lore*.[2] The term was rapidly adopted in most European countries as well as in North and South America, Asia and beyond. Common interest groups sprang up, such as the Folk-Lore Society (1878) and the American Folklore Society (1888), both attracting members from far and wide. Though based in London, the Folklore Society encouraged members all over Britain to collect traditions in their own neighbourhoods or localities—songs, stories, tunes, games, dances, customs, weather-lore, 'sayings', medical lore and domestic, farming, fishing and hunting practices. In Scotland, the majority were parish ministers, schoolteachers, policemen and doctors, whose collections in Scots and Gaelic were published by the Society.[3]

With such a broad range, not surprisingly, other societies followed, notably the Folk-Song Society,[4] co-founded by Cecil Sharp in 1898. His groundbreaking research, capturing the sound of the singer's voice on wax cylinders, marked the beginning of a new era not only for collectors but also for singers.[5] In Scotland, one of the first to use the new device was the Perth singer Marjory Kennedy Fraser (1857–1930), who set out in 1905 to record Gaelic songs in the Hebrides.[6] From boyhood, Hamish was familiar with her collection as his mother sang some of the songs, such as the 'Eriskay Love Lilt'. He also read and absorbed any collection of Scottish folklore he could lay hands on, unaware that these very books were to become essential references for his own work.

From the outset, the world of folklore scholarship was an international scene, with British participants such as Maud Karpeles, the Opies, F Marian McNeill, John Lorne Campbell and Francis Collinson and well-known Americans such as Mark Twain, George Lyman Kittredge,[7] Bertrand H Bronson,[8] Charles Seeger[9] and John Lomax.[10] Folklore collections evoked international interest in culture and tradition and, following the lead of Scandinavian countries,[11] issues of language and identity were increasingly debated in political arenas.

In 1935, the Irish Government set up the Irish Folklore Commission to record and document every aspect of traditional culture. The director, Séamus Delargy, was rigorous in training folklore collectors and he appointed an archivist with a passion for poetry, language, culture and politics, Seán Ó Suilleabhain (1903-1996).[12] Among his renowned associates were Douglas Hyde (poet, language activist and founder of the Gaelic League) and Kenneth H Jackson, who later became professor of Celtic at Harvard in 1948 and, in 1950, was appointed to the chair of Celtic Languages, History and Antiquities at Edinburgh University. This was the 'Dublin scene' when Hamish, still in his teens, visited Ireland in 1936 to seek out poets, singers, storytellers and a way of life that would lure him back again in 1948.

In 1951, when the University of Edinburgh established the School of Scottish Studies, the two collectors appointed both had experience of Ireland's formidable folklore collections—Hamish and Calum MacLean (brother of Sorley, from Raasay). Calum had been trained by the Irish Folklore Commission and had spent several years as one of their collectors and transcribers and had also spent a year at Uppsala. And so, this essay proper begins with the 'Folklorist's Prayer':

> May there always be folklorists.
> May there always be professionals concerned that the folk
>   and their traditional arts
>   are not marginalised
>   disregarded,
>   or dismissed.

May they also have the courage
    to take a public stand
    on issues affecting traditional cultures
    of all races
    and creeds.
May there always be cultural activists!

Though it is unlikely that the earlier 'greats' ever heard these words, the 'prayer' sums up the essence of Henderson and MacLean. Transatlantic visitors to Scotland find it curious, however, that the archive housing their collection does not use the word folklore, (common currency in Ireland, Scandinavia as well as North America, with world-class collections such as those held at the Smithsonian and the Library of Congress.) Be that as it may, there are innumerable American folklorists and singers who shared, and share, Hamish's passion not only for songs and stories, but also for human rights, social justice and civil liberties.

Being a folklorist is not (as I once thought) just 'going on recording trips and collecting songs'—but, like the songs, the work touches every aspect of life and can heighten the nation's awareness of social issues, or keep a cause alive among ordinary folk. Without Hamish, for example, it is doubtful if the names of Mandela or Gramsci, or John MacLean, would be burned into our collective Scottish conscience; we might even wonder what they stood for or why they should be immortalised.

As Hamish reflected, however, it is often with the songs that the passion for folklore begins. I recall when I first realised that folklorists record the stuff that we often take for granted until it is too late: I was about twelve when my mother bought the first record ever produced by the School of Scottish Studies—Gaelic on one side and Scots, or Lallans, on the other—a description that equally fitted my sisters and me: Gaelic on the one side, and Scots on the other. From then on, Radio Luxemburg hardly had a look in as I played and played Hamish Henderson's recordings of Jeannie Robertson singing 'The Braes o Balquhidder' and Willie Scott 'The Keilder Hunt' or (Side B) Duncan Beaton, a formidable old singer who lived opposite my grandparents in Uig. I was forever hooked, though knew little of the man from Perthshire who recorded many of the songs. My mother, however, who had been recorded for the School in 1956 by John MacInnes, knew well who Hamish Henderson was—'And there was another time a man with a big tape recorder who came here—an awfully nice man—Séamus Ennis was his name.' Even at that early age, I sensed that the world of folklore collecting was a tightly knit one, though it would be some years before I fully appreciated how well Hamish's scholarly reputation and recordings were known in North America.

This essay might easily have been called 'The Influence of Hamish Henderson on *International* Folklore Scholarship'. Rooted in Highland Perthshire, as a child Hamish was (to borrow Walter Scott's Borders phrase) 'fed with the legendary lore… as with a mother's milk…' In his mother's day, Perthshire Gaelic was still commonly spoken,[13] and so Hamish was raised with both Gaelic and Scots traditions, totally at ease with the whole gamut of Scottish folklore.

Moving with his mother from Perthshire to the south of England may have increased Hamish's appreciation for the traditions he loved. At that distance he would save newspaper articles and handwritten notes, which today might well occupy a notable place in any archive. As any keen student of folklore would discover, these papers would make an ideal topic for studying childhood collections and would also fit perfectly into the childlore section of any folklore conference.

One of the aspects that still lures me to folklore conferences is that, unlike other academic gatherings, hobbyists and professionals share all levels of discussion across a range of topics. This approach goes back at least to the first International Folk-Lore Congress held in Chicago in 1893 when anthropologists, literature scholars, historians, theologians, biographers, scientists from many fields as well as non-professionals recognised that traditional knowledge—*Folklore*—sits at the crossroads of the arts, humanities and social sciences. Such was the arena in which Hamish's work was to attain widespread recognition on a par with the finest folklore scholars in the world.

The key figure introducing Hamish to the North American scene was folklorist Alan Lomax (1915-2002), son of the famous song collector, John A Lomax, and former folksong archivist at the Library of Congress. Just as in Scotland where Hamish's name and that of Jeannie Robertson have been inextricably linked since 1951, so, in America, the Lomaxes are linked to their 1930s recordings of Leadbelly and Muddy Waters.[14] As well as being an avid collector, Lomax was also a singer, political activist and scholar of note. Throughout his life he attended and spoke at prestigious conferences, and (more regularly than many full-time academics) he published widely. In 1942 he gave a paper at the American Council of Learned Societies where, it was reported, he was one of the two young folklorists singled out from the assembled scholars for the outstanding impression they made; the other one was Herbert Halpert.[15] Within a decade, both were to become key figures in Hamish's life as a folklorist.

Hamish takes up the story:

> The present flourishing folk-song revival in Scotland has its roots in a number of different historical events and accidents: one of the latter was the decisions in 1947 to found a large-scale International Festival of the Arts in Edinburgh... and the second 'accident' was that [the festival]... coincided with the appearance in Britain of the distinguished American collector Alan Lomax... [he] had been a member during the Second World War of a Music Committee formed under the auspices of various US left-wing groupings. This committee had fostered and encouraged the work of Woody Guthrie, Pete Seeger and the Weavers, but with the advent of the Cold War its activities had become more and more suspect in the eyes of authorities. Finally, when full-scale McCarthyishm came into operation, many of its members felt that the US was becoming too hot to hold them... It was this ugly right-wing reaction to the 'liberalism' of the war years which led Alan Lomax to accept a job which would keep him out of the States for several years – namely, a commission from Columbia Records to edit a series of LPs covering the 'folk and primitive music' of the world... Scotland was to be vol. VI in the series. And so it came about that when [we] organized the first People's Festival (1951) Alan Lomax was there to record it on tape.[16]

Earlier in the year Hamish had received a letter from Ewan MacColl:

Cheshire, Feb. 1951

Dear Hamish,

Just a brief note – there is a character wandering around this sceptred isle at the moment... Alan Lomax. He is a Texan and none the worse of that, he is also just about the most important name in

American folksong circles. He is over here with a super recording unit... Columbia Records are financing his trip... he has already covered Africa, America the West Indies, the Central European countries)... he's not interested in trained singers or refined versions of the folksongs.[17]

Clearly, Lomax knew how to get the best out of any field trip by having all the right contacts in place, and, as he did not know them himself, he planned to bring the right people with him at every stage of the journey. Hamish fitted the bill perfectly and so did the other hand-picked fieldworkers Calum MacLean (as well his brothers Sorley and Alasdair) and William Montgomerie.[18]

Lomax's field-notes from June 1951 sum up the impressive ground they covered, not only in miles but, more importantly, in whom and what they recorded. While Hamish was to accompany him to the North-East and Calum to the Uists and Barra, there were also house ceilidhs in Edinburgh and Glasgow with John Burgess, Flora MacNeil, Calum Johnston, Kitty MacLeod, Norman MacCaig, and, later on, the better known People's Festival Ceilidhs.

Lomax was truly blown away by the vast richness of the Scottish tradition—the 'flower of Western Europe', as he called it. But despite his persuasive letters to Hugh McPhee, Head of BBC's Gaelic Department, Lomax's offer of high-quality recordings for broadcast was turned down.[19] Nevertheless, on returning to America, he was eventually to achieve a much wider and more lasting audience as he threw himself into his project with Columbia Records, the World Library of Folk and Primitive Music. His volume on Scotland was launched in 1953 and there was an immediate buzz in the folk world reaching singers and scholars alike. Among them was an up and coming folklore student at the University of Pennsylvania, Kenneth S Goldstein, whose enthusiasm for the Scottish ballad seemed unlimited.

In 1958, while working towards a PhD, Goldstein was awarded a Fulbright Scholarship to go to Scotland, where he hoped to record ballad singers of the calibre of John Strachan, Willie Mathieson or the great Jeannie Robertson. His academic base was to be the University of Edinburgh's School of Scottish Studies where he would have access to the Archive as well as mentorship from senior colleagues, especially Hamish.

As Kätzel Henderson recalls, she and Hamish travelled to the North-East with him, saw him settled and introduced him to key contacts. Goldstein was to make extensive recordings of the Stewarts of Fetterangus, particularly Lucy, whose solo album he produced. Though he had hoped to study ballads for his PhD, his 'internship' with the School of Scottish Studies turned up 'another agenda' — to write a guidebook for collectors. And so he did, gaining the PhD and, more importantly, publishing the book *A Guide for Field Workers in Folklore*. For decades this one book was to be the Bible for every folklore class, not only in the United States and Canada, but right across the world as it had been widely published in translation; there is even a Turkish translation (Ankara, 1977) and a Chinese version (Taiwan, 1982). While Goldstein's ideas on fieldwork changed over the years (as does technology), Hamish's introduction to the book is timeless: 'The collector-folklorist should never, in the heat of the chase, forget his humanist role.'[20]

Goldstein himself produced one of the most prolific collections in the world, covering virtually every genre of the subject. The School of Scottish Studies archive holds the Scottish tapes, which include songs, stories, riddles, proverbs, monologues, descriptions of material culture and folk art. Most of his career was spent as Director of the Folklore Department at the University of Philadelphia, though he also spent sabbaticals in Australia and Canada. His Newfoundland and Labrador song collection alone is on a par with the Greig–Duncan collection, as it amounts to over 4,000 songs. Goldstein produced over 500 LPs, including many 'classics' such as *The English and Scottish Popular Ballads* (9 volumes., Riverside Records,1956), *The Singing Street: Children's Songs and Rhymes from Scotland and Ireland* (Folkways Records,1959), *Lucy Stewart: Traditional Singer from Aberdeenshire* (Folkways Records, 1961), and *Joe Heaney: Come All Ye Gallant Irishmen* (Philo Records, 1975). Along with Arthur Argo he wrote the introduction to, and was a key figure in, the publication of Gavin Greig's *Folk-Songs of the North-East*.[21] Other publications include seven books, including *Folklore: Performance and Communication* (co-edited with Dan Ben-Amos, 1975) and many articles.

All of these folklorists, including some world-class scholars, have, to a greater or lesser extent, benefited from Hamish's work. From my own perspective, however, the closest influence of all concerned the previously mentioned Herbert Halpert. For many years a friend and correspondent of Hamish's, Halpert was also a fellow soldier and comrade who, like Hamish, recorded folklore during his years of military service during World War Two: 'it saved my sanity during my army days.' Also, like Hamish, he was a singer (and, like Lomax, Halpert played guitar), he was also an intellectual, a book-lover with a seemingly encyclopaedic memory. And they both shared the same initials: H H. Halpert's background, however, could scarcely have been more different to Hamish's. He grew up in New York and enjoyed the music 'scene' there as well as the street-songs of the city; he studied anthropology at University, graduating during the Great Depression, when there was virtually no chance of a job, particularly in academia. And so, like millions of Americans, Halpert got a job with the WPA,[22] initially as a folksong research worker with the Federal Arts Project in New York and then with the Federal Theatre Project[23] before being transferred to collect folksongs in the American South. Being ideally suited in both enthusiasm and work ethic, he set off in an old ambulance, converted into a recording studio-cum-camper van. By 1943, when US Army call-up papers put an end to his project, Halpert had recorded over eight hundred 12-inch discs, now housed in the Archive of Folksong in the Library of Congress, all meticulously catalogued.[24] Little wonder he carried on collecting when, as a lieutenant in the North Atlantic Air Transport Command, he was posted to Alaska and Newfoundland.

After the war, Halpert resumed university studies, branching out from anthropology into folklore at a time when it was more fashionable to go to Samoa than to study the folksong traditions among children in the streets of New York. As he later wrote, folklore 'is officially on friendly terms with literature, music, and anthropology, [though] its position is only that of a tolerated stepchild.' Halpert's aim was to change all that so, while Lomax headed back to the 'field', Halpert resumed a PhD programme under the direction of two world-class scholars: Lyman Kittredge, who was a student of (and later son-in-law of) the great ballad scholar Frances James Child and the formidable Stith Thompson, to this day probably the most influential scholar of folk narrative in the world. (His earlier mentors had included the great Franz Boas, then over 90, and Ruth Benedict who had encouraged Halpert to record childlore in the thirties.)

Halpert's opportunity to teach folklore as a 'real discipline' had to wait, however, until 1962 when he moved to Canada to take up the challenge of creating a new department of folklore in Newfoundland. Not only did he set up a folklore archive but also a folklore programme which would produce some of the most rigorously trained folklorists in the world. (This is the same department that the late David Buchan took over after Halpert's retirement.)

Studying with Halpert was both inspiring and challenging. Like Hamish, he was no 'name-dropper', though at times his students sensed they were a mere hand-shake from the great Professor Child. Unlike Hamish, who had endless patience with students, Halpert tended to be more formal, was certainly more strict and had little time for those who did not measure up to his standards. From the very outset, however, Hamish featured prominently in his teaching as Halpert had all the commercially available recordings that included any of Hamish's fieldwork as well as publications such as *Tocher*, the brain-child of Hamish's colleague, Alan Bruford, lecturer and archivist at the School of Scottish Studies as well as editor-compiler of *Tocher* till his untimely death in 1995. It was quite normal, for instance, for Halpert to begin his folksong and ballad class with a version of a ballad recorded by Hamish, have us discuss the ballad, then listen to versions recorded in North America. In one memorable class on broadside ballads[25] that began with Hamish's 1952 recording of Willie Mathieson singing 'I'm a Young Man Cut Down in my Prime' ('The Streets of Laredo'), Halpert played some of his own recordings of the song, ending up with a twelve-bar blues collected by Lomax around the Mississippi Delta. Halpert was an inspiring teacher with a staggeringly wide bibliographic knowledge of Scotland, both Scots and Gaelic: it was he, not my Scottish teachers, who introduced me to the work of Campbell of Islay, Martin Martin, and Gavin Greig. Halpert also shared Hamish's appreciation of Walter Scott and Robert Burns as song collectors and composers, as well as more recent song-makers with their radical songs of social change or protest. Forty years on, I occasionally meet Halpert's folklore graduates who mention Hamish in the same way as we do—first name terms (thought they may never have met the man), as a kind of fixed reference point in all aspects of folksong.

Among those who visited Scotland, some made a point of visiting the School of Scottish Studies hoping to meet the man himself—and many succeeded, as Hamish's vast correspondence shows. Among the visitors were several folklore 'greats' such as Professor Richard Dorson, long-time Director of Indiana University's very prestigious folklore department. One of the great American gurus of folklore scholarship, (generally more famous for his impressive bibliography than for his personality or wit), Dorson wrote to Hamish after a visit in 1965: 'For an itinerant folklorist, the School of Scottish Studies is surely a paradise. All kinds of resources abound: valuable files, indexes, books, journals, tapes... When one becomes intoxicated with folklore, he can sober up at Sandy Bell's around the corner.'

Some of America's best-loved and best-known folksingers, such as Pete Seeger and Tom Paxton, benefited from discussions with Hamish, as did the song-collector-record producers Sandy and Caroline Paton. The great song scholar Bertrand H Bronson also beat a path to Hamish's door and, having successfully trawled the archive for ballad tunes, he later summed up his eternal gratitude in a letter to Hamish: 'Posterity's debt to you is incalculable...'

There was also the warm-hearted Sandy Ives (more formally known as Professor Edward D Ives[26] who, after retirement, became an annual visitor with his wife Bobby. He too was a singer, which, on reflection, seems to be the feature of Folklore scholars that makes them stand out as 'people's folklorists'—like Hamish, they would go to festivals, gigs, sing at sessions (and in class), tell a good story, fit into company of any kind without any need to display or refer to their own academic prowess. Sandy was generally 'drip feeding' a new book or paper and then (like so many visitors who would spend time with Hamish) would return to America with fresh enthusiasm and inspiration.

It is not merely intellectual capacity or knowledge that marks the greatness of any scholar, but more an enormously generous spirit and huge heart. No matter how enjoyable the 'buzz' of those visits or discussions may be, it can also be stressful and frustrating and few appreciate the time, energy and indeed personal cost that goes into any such 'folklore consultation'. As the subject matter, folklore, is so alluring, it rarely occurs to the enthusiastic visitor that this 'cost' often extends to the folklorist's family, as my son Martyn would doubtlessly have told you. (He liked to begin his stories with, 'You'll never believe this...!', to which Kätzel could laughingly reply, 'Yes I would!')

Among those who seemed to make an annual visit was one of Canada's prolific writers of folksong books, Edith Fowke.[27] She would time her visit to take in the Auchtermuchty Festival and Whitby, as well as the Edinburgh Festival—and always, if at all possible, not one but several visits to Hamish, preferably combining any of the above. ('You'll never believe this—she nearly made me miss my plane once!') An unlikely-looking 'folkie', especially at festivals—she seemed to have a repertoire of neat pink suits and always used a long cigarette holder—Edith was in her element listening to Hamish's field recordings or, better still, accompanying him to sessions in pubs or even song competitions. Back home in Ontario, Edith had had her own 'Jeannie Robertson experience' in some of the singers she had recorded, such as LaRena Clark, about whom she wrote a book. And in teaching her folklore students at the University of Toronto, Professor Fowke introduced them to the work of the great Scottish folksong authority, Hamish Henderson.

Among the visitors (and later correspondents) from other walks of life was a famous American calligrapher-artist with a passion for Scots and Gaelic song, Howard Glasser. As a student, he used to do his artwork listening to recordings of Scots ballads, and recalls being fascinated by the way the words looked as well as how they sounded. When he first visited Scotland in 1960, he went to one of the events Hamish had organised during the Edinburgh Festival where, in the course of that one night, he met not only Hamish but also Jeannie Robertson, Jimmie MacBeath and Arthur Argo: 'all these folk I had already met on the Lomax records – I was in heaven!' Howard is now over eighty and his own life-story is worth telling—he and Hamish became lifelong friends, from the days when Hamish helped Howard plan a trip to the west coast and out to Barra to listen to singers, introduced him to the word 'ceilidh' (which was later to become one of Howard's works of art) and recited his poetry, which (later) was also to appear among Howard's best known work—'The Flytin o' Life and Daith'. In 1970, with a career and formidable reputation in art and calligraphy, Howard started an annual folk festival, the Eisteddfod, based in the University of Dartmouth, or 'U Mass', as it is usually called. While the title Eisteddfod may suggest 'only Wales', it nevertheless embraces the Anglo-Celtic world, chosen because it implies a gathering of bards and musicians (which it is) but more significantly because Howard needed an alluring (even obscure) title to secure funding. Forty years on, it is still running, with singers from both sides of the Atlantic such as the Fishers, Norman Kennedy, Lou Killen, Martyn Wyndham Reid and other British Isles singers. In recent years, Alison McMorland and Geordie McIntyre have been invited, as have Shepheard, Speirs and Watson (and I too have appeared at a few). There is, therefore, no festival that is not influenced by Hamish, for not only does Howard regularly mention him or feature his songs, but so also do these singers.

Among festival-goers from all over the States and Canada, there are some who hear about Hamish for the first time—usually through song introductions, made all the more memorable by anecdotes which always speak of the man himself, using his first name. Audiences begin to feel they too know this Hamish, as it was very evident in 2003, the year after Hamish's death, when audiences flocked to special events celebrating Hamish Henderson, as they wanted to participate in tributes to a great man.

Aside from singers who gigged in the States, there were also a number who were resident in the USA, including Jean Redpath, the late Tony Cuffe, and Ed Miller, all of whom kept folk informed about Hamish as they sing his songs or songs he collected. Hamish himself never did make it across the Atlantic—there were good reasons—but he liked to hear transatlantic versions of his own songs, such as the late John Allan Cameron of Cape Breton whose recording of 'Banks of Sicily' was something of a hit across Canada. Hamish did not flinch when he heard slight adjustments to the words he had written—that is the folk process. That is not to say, however, that 'anything goes'; far from it. The integrity and the spirit of the song is what counts. Even when it came to pushing the boundaries far beyond anything that he himself imagined, Hamish had an open mind—perhaps the most unusual 'versions' of his collected songs and stories that were to travel to America and beyond in a new form were those by Martyn Bennett—on his album, *Grit* (produced by Peter Gabriel). For most of his life Martyn knew Hamish, had travelled with him (and me) to folk festivals and had shared many a discussion with him. Before finalising his 're-make' of songs sung by Sheila Stewart and Lizzie Higgins, as well as Hamish's recording of Davie Stewart's story, Martyn brought the final cut to Hamish—he had to hear it first. After a few days when Hamish had listened several times, he wrote a short letter, possibly the last he ever wrote:

19 Dec. 2001

Dear Martyn,

I am delighted to hear about your new music. Brave new music!! Davie Stewart would be proud to know his voice will be heard the world over. I give you my blessing to use my recordings.

Love, Hamish.

Songs recorded years ago by Hamish now travel the world in all sorts of ways, some reaching far beyond the other side of the Atlantic. Recently, as I reflected on the magnitude of Hamish's influence in the world of folklore scholarship, I reached for an article he wrote for one of the Edinburgh Festival lunchtime talks series in the late 1970s (jointly run by the WEA and the University). Ted Cowan published the talks in *The People's Past*, opening the book with Hamish's essay, 'It Was In You That It A' Began.'[28] It had been years since I had read it and I had quite forgotten why Hamish chose that title. I am totally convinced, however, that were we to ask folklorists on both sides of the Atlantic what kindled their passion for the subject, they could truthfully reply: 'It was in you, Hamish, that it a' began.'

References:

1   Hamish Henderson, 'Introduction' to Kenneth S Goldstein, *A Guide for Field Workers in Folklore* (Hatboro, Pennsylvania: Gale, 1964) p. x.

2   William Thoms, in a letter to *The Athenium*, 22 August 1846.

3   Collectors included the Reverend Walter Gregor from the North-East, the Reverend James Napier from Paisley, the Reverend John Gregorson Campbell from Argyllshire and Edinburgh-based Dr Robert Craig Maclagan who himself recruited a team of helpers and correspondents.

4   In 1931 it ceased to exist as such, merging into a new society, The English Folk Dance and Song Society, which, despite its title, has significant interest in Scotland. See Ian Olson, 'The Influence of the Folk Song Society on the Greig-Duncan Folk Song Collection', *Folk Music Journal*, Vol. 5, no. 2 (1986), pp. 176-201.

5   Sharp was not, however, the first to use wax cylinder as a field-recording device, as earlier examples include Zuni and Passamaquoddy voices recorded by American anthropologist J W Fewkes in 1890— archived in the collection of the Center for Folklife and Cultural Heritage at the Smithsonian Institution, Washington. Examples are available on the CD *Anthology of American Folk Music*, edited by Harry Smith, Smithsonian Folkways 40539, (2006).

6   Marjory Kennedy-Fraser, *Songs of the Hebrides*, arranged with piano and clarsach accompaniment, 4 vols, (London: Boosey & Co, 1909-21 and 1928).

7   Kittredge (1860-1941) studied at Harvard with Francis James Child (whose daughter he later married). After Child's death in 1896, Kittredge wrote the introduction to the massive ballad collection as well as many of the comparative notes, and finally saw it through to first publication in 1898.

8   Bertrand H Bronson (1902-1986) was professor of folklore at Berkeley, California when he made Hamish's acquaintance during the compilation of his magnum opus, *The Traditional Tunes of the Child Ballads*; with their texts, according to the extant records of Great Britain and America (Princeton NJ: Princeton University Press, 1959-72).

9   Musician and folklorist Charles Seeger (1886-1979) was the father of three very influential folksingers and activists: Pete, Mike and Peggy.

10 President of the American Folklore Society for several years, John Lomax, his son Alan and daughter Bess Lomax Hawes have all had an enormous impact on the world of folklore and folksong (not to mention their individual roles in several political issues).

11 The Finnish Academy of Science and Letters founded in 1908 established a folklore department in 1910, which is still 'home' to the prestigious Fellows International.

12 Ó Suilleabháin's book, *A Handbook of Irish Folklore* (Dublin: Educational Company of Ireland, Ltd, 1942), became the international bible of 'how and what to collect', 'what to ask' and what to do with it all when you collected it.

13 By the time Hamish began to work at the School of Scottish Studies there had been a drastic decline, though the archives have a significant number of recordings in Perthshire Gaelic from the fifties and sixties.

14 Their actual names were Huddie Ledbetter and McKinley Morganfield. After the Lomaxes recorded Leadbelly singing 'Irene, Goodnight Irene' and 'The Midnight Special' in 1933 the songs spread like wildfire. They published them in *Negro Folk Songs as sung by Lead Belly* (New York: Macmillan, 1936).

15 A summary of the conference report appears in Robert Baron's article, 'Multi-Paradigm Discipline, Interdisciplinary Field, Peering through and around the Interstices', *Western Folklore*, 52, (1993), pp. 227-245.

16 From Hamish's article, 'Scottish Folk-Song and the Labour Movement', first published in *The Scottish Trade Union Review*, No. 41, (Spring 1989), and later in Hamish Henderson, *Alias MacAlias: Writings on Songs, Folk and Literature*, edited by Alec Finlay (Edinburgh: Polygon, 1992), pp. 16-18.

17 Hamish Henderson, *The Armstrong Nose: Selected Letters of Hamish Henderson*, edited by Alec Finlay (Edinburgh: Polygon, 1996), p. 46.

18 Glasgow born and bred, William Montgomerie (then a school teacher in Dundee) had been recording songs and ballads on a 'Wirex' machine since the early 1940s. Ballad scholar, poet, and ardent supporter of the Scots language, Mongomerie believed that the essence of language and culture is captured in childhood, thus 'these rhymes should precede the pleasure derived from the more mature folksongs and ballads. Indeed, their fundamental quality

attunes young ears to all poetry.' The Lomax collection is unprecedented in its acknowledgment of this philosophy.

19 Alan Lomax *A Ballad Hunter Looks at Britain*, BBC script from Programme 6 (of 8), 'Songs from the Highlands and Islands of Scotland', rec. 22 November 1957, transmitted on BBC Home Service, 6 December 1957, 7-7.30 pm.

20 Goldstein (1964), p.x. In making this statement, Hamish cautioned that the folklore fieldworker's 'informants' should never be treated 'purely as sources of information, to be taken up and discarded as occasion demands...' As a result, personal friendships formed in the course of fieldwork are likely to be as close as any formed throughout life.

21 Gavin Greig, *Folk-song in Buchan and folk-song of the North-east*, foreword by Kenneth S Goldstein and Arthur Argo (Hatboro, Pennsylvania: Folklore Associates, 1963).

22 The Work Projects Administration (WPA) was set up by President Roosevelt and funded by Congress following the Emergency Relief Act of 1935.

23 Like Hamish, he had a strong interest in theatre. Modern theatre productions and film (such as *Brother Where Art Thou?*) owe much to Halpert's pioneering ideas of the mid-1930s. He rejected the stage version of the Negro—a white person painted black—and he insisted on the right songs and music for the production. For example, in the 1936 production of *Power*, a play akin to Scottish productions about Scottish hydro-electric dams, Halpert insisted on using songs composed by the men who had actually worked on the hydro dams in Tennessee or who had experienced the trauma of watching a family homestead flooded to create the dam.

24 Halpert's work ethic was legendary. The Library of Congress catalogue notes, for example, that after one recording foray, March -June 1939, Halpert deposited 'four hundred and nineteen 12-inch discs of instrumentals, monologs [sic], prayers, sermons, songs, and stories recorded in Alabama, Florida, Louisiana, Mississippi, North Carolina, South Carolina, Tennessee, and Virginia, along with articles, contact sheets, correspondence, descriptions, interviews, lists, photographs, reports, and song texts.' See Herbert Halpert, 'Folklore: An Emerging Discipline' in *Selected Essays of Herbert Halpert*, edited by Martin Lovelace, Paul Smith & J D A Widdowson (St. John's, Newfoundland: Memorial University of Newfoundland, Folklore and Language Publication, 2002).

25 This rich seam of comparative broadside ballads is well documented in G Malcolm Laws, *American Balladry from British Broadsides*, (Philadelphia: American Folklore Society, 1957).

26 Author of 'The Tape-Recorded Interview: A Manual for Field Workers in Folklore and Oral History' (Knoxville: University of Tennessee Press, 1995), first published 1974, as well as several books about singers (including *The Man Who Made the Songs*).

27 Her books included *Traditional Singers and Songs from Ontario* (1965), *Folksongs of Canada II* (with Richard Johnston, 1967), *Lumbering Songs from the Northern Woods* (1970, reprinted 1985), *The Penguin Book of Canadian Folksongs* (1973), *Ring Around the Moon* (1977), and *Sea Songs and Ballads from Nineteenth-Century Nova Scotia* (1981).

28 Edward J Cowan (ed.), *The People's Past: Scottish Folk –Scottish History*, (Edinburgh: Polygon, 1980), pp. 4-15.

A FILI FROM THE PROVINCE OF THE CAT: HAMISH HENDERSON AND CAITHNESS

George Gunn

Caithness is the shore on which two historic realities meet. The very name highlights this duality: cait—the Gaelic for cat; and ness—the Norse for headland. Emerging from an obscure pre-Pictish world of tribal totems to a practical Viking navigational aid, Caithness is the land where these Norse and Celtic cultures meld; its name a hybrid of both. Thirty per cent of all the place names in Scotland's most northerly county are Norse; the rest are Gaelic. In many other regards Caithness is the most southerly of the Orkney Islands, joined to the archipelago by the stormy Pentland Firth and separated from its landlocked neighbour, Sutherland, by a sea of peat-bog. Sutherland itself is 'soother-laander', defining the southern extent of the Earldom of Orkney. This, then, is a land of dualities, bi-lingualism and shared cultural identities; where exclusivity and singularity are historically impossible. In short, Caithness is a melting pot of Pict, Norse and Gael where nothing is fixed or definite. Just the sort of place, you might imagine, a poet would be glad to claim as their own, and Hamish Henderson did exactly that.

Hamish's grandfather, Alexander Henderson, was certain of this connection and, sometime after 1903 when he had retired to Blairgowrie, he wrote in his occasional diary for the *Dundee Advertiser*:

My family originates from Caithness. 'Gunn' is the name for Henderson. We are descended from the third son of the Princess of Norway, daughter of the King of Norway…[1]

Such a claim, while not entirely unfounded, is the result of the usual Victorian romanticism that insists upon adding bells and whistles to everything. While it is true that the Hendersons are indeed part of that family of names associated with the Gunns, and Henderson is a very common Caithness surname, the actual origins of the Clan Gunn are even more beguiling than the best of the Balmorality brigade could conjure up.

There are, essentially, two myths. The first is that the progenitor of the clan is Svein Asliefarson, the 'last of the Vikings', whose grandson Gunni married Ragnhild, the grand-daughter of Rognvald, Jarl of Orkney who famously built St Magnus Cathedral; this Ragnhild inherited 'estates' in Caithness around 1198 upon the death of her brother Ungi, who had inherited the Orkney Jarldom. The second myth is that the Gunns took their name from a certain 'Guin', son of Olave, King of the Isle of Man. The name 'Henderson' is said to have originated as the result of an on-going feud between the Gunns and the Keiths which came to a head in 1464 when it was mutually decided that the killing had to stop and a meeting was agreed between twelve representatives of each side to take place at the Chapel of St Tears, somewhere on the north coast between Ackergill Tower and Sinclair and Girnigoe castles. Legend has it that on the appointed day the Gunns arrived early, dismounted the agreed 'twelve horse' and entered the chapel to pray. The 'twelve horse' of the Keiths duly arrived but with two clansmen on each mount. The twenty four fell upon the unsuspecting twelve and all but three of the Gunns were murdered. Licking their wounds they retired to the hills to plot their revenge. The boldest of the chief's remaining sons, Henry, proposed a counter attack on the Keiths' stronghold at Dirlot. Wearied of bloodshed, or perhaps too wounded to move, the two other sons declined, so Henry declared, 'Then I am no longer a Gunn' — although this did not stop him and a few of his bold followers ambushing the Keiths in their keep. Henry supposedly fired an arrow through a window killing the chief of the Keiths instantly and let out the cry, 'Iomach gar n'Guinach gu Kaigh!', which means, 'The Gunns' compliments to the Keiths!' From this Henry Gunn we get the surname Henderson.

There are, as is normal in the interpretation of such myths, countless variations on these themes, all striving to give significance to both name and place. Yet the origin of Clan Gunn, the Hendersons and all the septs thereof, is much more logical and ancient than any of these Viking fancies. While it is true that in Norse 'gunnr' does mean war, the word 'Gunn' may, as Ian Grimble suggests, come from a pre-Celtic language whose remnants reside in such place-names as that of Strathnaver, the strath which runs next to Kildonan and the Scarbens, the remote heartland of the Gunns. In his book *Clans and Chiefs*, Grimble offers this as an alternative reality:

> What seems more likely is that the Gunns were a Pictish tribe, especially in view of the inveterate hostility that continued for so many centuries between them and the Mackays (and the Keiths) who were of Gaelic origin and had almost certainly invaded their neighbourhood in large numbers. Anyway, Picts must be looked for somewhere. They had been a more numerous people than the Gaels, a formidable power in the eyes of the Romans, and modern methods of genocide did not exist in those days. The Gunns' territory (along the Caithness-Sutherland border) is exactly where one would expect to find the survivors of so many centuries of misfortune. That incomparable Highland novelist Neil Gunn felt in his bones that his people were Picts: it influenced his work deeply, and it seems very probable that he was right.[2]

This is what Hamish always had in his mind when he would say to me, somewhat mischievously, 'We come from an ancient people'. Whatever their origins, the Clan Gunn evolved, despite early and subsequent pressure, into a fully developed Gaelic society at whose helm sat the Chief, Mac Seamus Cataich (Son of James of Caithness) who as well as being head of the clan also held the hereditary office of Crowner of Caithness, or Am Braisdeach Mor (Wearer of the Big Brooch). As well as their famous martial prowess—in the seventeenth century both William Gunn and Sir Lachlan Gunn of Braemore served with great distinction fighting for the Protestant cause in the army of King Gustavus Adolphus of Sweden in the Thirty Years War— the Gunns have always been noted, down through the ages, for their pipers, who have been prominent tradition bearers. This was ratcheted up a notch in the nineteenth century with the militarisation of the Highlands. Whether the Gunns produced poets, history does not record, but it would be inconceivable that such an old society did not possess and give due respect to the title and function of the bard.

I offer all this in order to claim Hamish Henderson, as he claimed himself, for the Clan Gunn and the 'Province of the Cat', those lands which lie north of Strath Fleet and east of Assynt, but I also wish to claim for him the title of 'fili'—not in opposition to bard, but in clarification of that historic function and the difference between the two.

In his essay 'The Bard Through History', John MacInnes attempts to clarify this 'difference':

> The earliest evidence for the role and status of Gaelic bards comes from Ireland. Here we have two main categories of verse makers. The first is the 'fili', plural 'filidh', whose name is constructed with the verb 'to see'. According to Irish tradition of the ninth century, the 'fili' could achieve mystic vision and engage in divination. The other category is that of 'bard'. Juristic descriptions, which establish a variety of grades within each of the categories of 'bard' and 'fili' (so that we have, for example, 'free bards' and 'unfree bards', each of these containing eight sub-classes) are absolutely clear in making bards the lower of the two.[3]

It is difficult, at the beginning of the twenty-first century, to attribute to one who lived his life so fully in the twentieth century a demi-druidic definition emanating from the tenth century and yet, out of all of Scotland's post-World War Two generation of poets, who fits the bill more comprehensively than Hamish Henderson? His interest in what MacInnes calls 'high mythological and historical lore'[4] and his ability to live on his wits and within what those bardic gifts could materially bring in, coupled with his life-long interest in the culture of ordinary, working people, does indicate that tagging Hamish Henderson with anything is going to be a slippery business. But I will persevere. For example the Irish folk-scholar, Osborn Bergin, in 1912 wrote of the 'fili':

> He was, in fact, a professor of literature and a man of letters, highly trained in the use of a published literary medium, belonging to a hereditary caste in the aristocratic society, holding an official position therein by virtue of his training, his learning, his knowledge of the history and tradition of his country and his clan. He discharged... the function of the modern journalist. He was not a song writer. He was often a public figure, a chronicler, a political

essayist, a keen and satirical observer of his fellow countrymen. At an earlier period he had been regarded as a dealer in magic, a weaver of spells and incantations, who would blast his enemies by the venom of his verse...[5]

Other than 'he was not a song writer', that is one of the best descriptions of Hamish Henderson's life and work that I have ever come across. What is the 'D-Day Dodgers' if not a 'blast' to 'his enemies'? I also think that the key to understanding Hamish in the role of the 'fili' is in what MacInnes alluded to in the meaning of the word in the verb 'to see'. He was, as the Irish traditionally had it, of the 'Aos-dana', which is a collective name meaning 'folk poetry, the learned'. Anyone who ever conversed with Hamish Henderson for more than a minute quickly understood that here was a man who was deeply 'learned'. Very few poets have this ability 'to see' in the way that Hamish possessed it. In many ways the tragedy of his literary career was that the apex of his achievement came early in *Elegies for the Dead in Cyrenaica* in which he saw with his own eyes the horror and futility of modern warfare. This experience of the African desert, the 'sodding desert', the 'brutish desert', the 'rough bounds of the desert', the 'African deadland' where the 51st Highland Division, as part of the British Eighth Army, heroically and at great cost, stopped the advance of the German Afrika Korps and eventually defeated it entirely, this vital life and death struggle, stayed with Hamish all his remaining life and fashioned his cultural outlook, forged it into the hard reality of what was possible, so different from the somewhat romantic notions of the young student who waited on in Cambridge after his graduation to receive his call- up papers. Hamish saw in the lot of the common squaddie, many of them Highlanders and many of them Gaelic speakers, the core of the cultural task which had to be undertaken after the war and, moreover, that which had to be undertaken by him. Whatever quest he was on, whatever it was he was unconsciously looking for, whether he liked it or not, he found it in the North African desert. As he puts it at the end of the 'Sixth Elegy (Acroma)',

So the words that I have looked for, and must go on looking for,
are words of whole love, which can slowly gain power
to reconcile and heal. Other words would be pointless.[6]

That he looked, that he saw and that he reported back is, as the bardic records attest, the function of the 'fili'. Like Ian Lom, the bard of Keppoch, who informed the MacDonald warriors before the Battle of Inverlochy in 1645 'You fight and I will tell,' he performed his cultural duty as was his privilege in the clan system, both real and imagined. Unlike Ian Lom's poem 'The Battle of Inverlochy', which is a triumphalist celebration of the bloody defeat of the Campbells, Hamish's *Elegies* are an erudite lyric epic of great humanity and compassion where pity is shown to the dead of both sides.

In as much as Hamish was proud to declare the Caithness origin of his appellation of 'Henderson'—and in true 'fili' fashion, it was to become a familiar name in Scottish cultural and political affairs after World War Two—it was to that other airt of 'The Province of the Cat' that Hamish was to find, perhaps, a deeper meaning to, and a more joyful chapter in, the legend of his own life. It is in Sutherland, with the Stewart travellers, that I believe Hamish began to 'heal' from the scars the desert war had inflicted upon his psyche. In 1955, ten years after victory in Europe, Hamish Henderson met Ailidh Dall— Blind Alec Stewart of Lairg—and a kind of happiness came upon him that he had not known before.

Much has been written of this encounter and the second, more organised, field trip in 1957, in Timothy Neat's book *The Summer Walkers*—but in order to further my claim for Hamish as a 'fili' and his own claim to be of the Clan Gunn I think it bears a further re-emphasis on just how significant this encounter in the heartland of 'The Province of the Cat' was psychologically to the man, as well as professionally in his role as a folk collector for the School of Scottish Studies at Edinburgh University.

As in most things, for Hamish to actually arrive in north-west Sutherland had taken a mixture of scrounging, luck and inspiration. He had cadged a lift with Peter and Tommy Kennedy who were not even going to go to Sutherland but were bound for Orkney, but once Hamish was aboard, of course, he had other ideas and their plan changed. This is how he describes their approach to the Kyle of Tongue and his 'discovery' of the Stewarts of Remarstaig,

It was late, it was drizzling, but the clouds were lifting and the light was just strong enough, there on the waters below, for us to see 'the pale sands yonder'. And the tensions began to slip away.

The shallow tidal waters of the Kyle can make the Caribbean look very much second best and next morning was perfect. I rose from my tent and walked over the brow of the hill to look south over one of the great landscapes of Scotland: Ben Hope and Ben Loyal silhouetted above the small illumined fields of the croft lands. Suddenly my heart went cold: there just below me, was a half circle of tents with chimneys smoking – bow tents – the domed, grey-green galleys of the Stewarts of Remarstaig. A small remnant of a people I would soon know as 'The Summer Walkers'. I might have been in Mongolia. I might have stood there any summer in the last eight thousand years and seen a similar sight. I know no more beautiful landscape in the world, no grander campsite under the stars. The Stewarts call Brae Tongue the King of Campsites. It remained Ailidh Dall's favourite camping place, long after he went blind, until he died. No wonder.[7]

The first song Hamish recorded from Ailidh Dall was 'Am Bron Binn' (The Sweet Sorrow), which turned out to be one of the oldest in Europe. As he told me many years later, 'Seoras (he rarely called me George), I knew it was going to be old but I didn't expect it to come from the beginning of time!' As he told Timothy Neat, 'To start at the beginning is always good! But to get started in 500AD was the stuff of dreams…' He then goes on to describe a spontaneous ceilidh-dance which happened on a 'milky white night' on a plateau looking north across the Pentland Firth. There was an ever expanding eightsome reel in progress with Ailidh Dall on the pipes:

> The tents were humped round in a semi-circle and at a short distance the horses watched us. With the heather in bloom, the perfume – coming off 'the flower of the mountain' (Ben Loyal) – seemed to become substantial nectar as the dew came down. I went back to my small ridge-pole tent thinking, 'Life is good – life is very good like this'.[8]

He later added, of his second period of two months with the Stewarts wandering the summer strath roads of Sutherland: 'It was the cream of my life, the top of my life.' What I feel is important to understand here is that something deep and profound clicked home in the psycho-drama of Hamish's life as he stood on the high shore-side of Mackay's

Kintail, looking down upon the small half moon which was the bow tent camp of the Stewarts of Remarstaig. Gone were the long short war years of battle and death, gone was the constant struggle of banging his head off the brick wall of, at best, a reluctant academia—for once and once only he had, on his second trip, funds a-plenty to do his work. Before him lay unknown but expected treasure which, almost more than anything else, would give valediction to his heartfelt belief in the 'carrying stream' of culture which was alive and well and dancing before his eyes. As a 'fili' he knew, instinctively and from learning, what he was looking at.

This 'knowing what you are looking at' worked both ways. The Stewarts, as Sutherland's native travelling people, had not survived these many centuries by being easily taken in. They knew fine what they had when they looked at and spoke to Hamish Henderson. As Essie Stewart told me at a ceilidh held in her honour in Armadale, 'Hamish was always a gentleman.' And she stressed 'always'. They knew by instinct—history had taught them—that they had one of the 'Aos-Dana' among them, that somehow Hamish was more than a 'bard', that indeed he was a 'fili'. If it were not so I do not believe they would have said one word, other than in common courtesy, to him. They certainly would not have trusted him in the way they did, and the respect was mutual.

In many ways the Stewarts of Remarstaig Pass, although their life was a hard one, were the recipients of whatever small luck history dispenses. They were, as Irish tradition has it, the last of the 'free bards'. The land these 'Summer Walkers' traversed—the straths of Naver, Kildonan and Halladale—had been emptied of its native population, the very people the Stewarts traded with. Not for them were the ties of clan to chief to prove so fatal. Other than ignorance and prejudice, of which they had grown used, there was for them no cultural and political betrayal as experienced by the vast majority of the people of the Province of the Cat.

Caithness and Sutherland have always enjoyed their comparative remoteness as a double-edged sword. Other than by sea the sheer difficulty of reaching these Pictlands when there were few roads and no maps meant that the far north Highlands were left pretty much to their own devises. The Clan Gunn and the Mackays had been some of the first of the Highland clans to adopt Protestantism as their faith. This did not mean that they took the government side in the endless wrangles each successive Stewart monarch manufactured from Edinburgh to thwart the power of Clan Donald. Up to 1707 they were marginal in Scotland's main narrative and any fighting they were involved in was usually amongst themselves in that age old Celtic fashion. They played no part in any of the successive Jacobite uprisings and in the main showed no favour to the Hanoverians when they replaced the Stewarts. Little good it did them. The history of the late eighteenth and early nineteenth centuries for Sutherland and west Caithness was one of dispossession, poverty and exile. The story of the Highland Clearances is well enough known these days, but the sense of on-going injustice which harbours still in the people who cling onto Scotland by their fingernails along the west and northern shores of Sutherland is perhaps not so well understood by the historians and academics who research who did what to whom and where.

With the lawyer-hungry, land-grabbing Gordons in Dunrobin to the south and the various families of pseudo-laird Sinclairs in the east, all keen to transport the natives to Canada, it is a wonder that any real civilisation was left in the north. I know through having had many conversations with him about it that Hamish felt this tragedy deeply, almost personally. To experience the sheer emptiness of the Flow Country of Caithness and Sutherland is to realise the spiritual dimension as well as the physical and the spatial: it is like looking at the topography of the soul. To go up Kildonan and then along Strathnaver to the coast is to feel the 'caoineadh' (weeping) of so much Gaelic song. It is almost unexplainable but it still chills my blood to this day when I make that journey. As Hamish travelled these ancient routes with the Stewarts in the summers of 1955 and 1957 he was, in his own way, trying to do something about it, to both show and capture the resilience of this 'cante jondo', this 'deep song'.

One of our shared passions (as well as that for Federico Garcia Lorca) was for the poetry of Rob Donn Mackay, the bard of Strathnaver. Why this should be so can be qualified and illustrated by Ian Grimble, who captures the remoteness and the cultural politics of the matter when he writes,

On 1st August 1714 Queen Anne, the last sovereign of the house of Stewart to reign in the British Isles, died and was succeeded by George I, of the dynasty of Hanover that has occupied the throne ever since. The following winter there was born in the most distant corner of the kingdom a child who, like his monarch, did not speak the English language. On the other hand, his native tongue was one that had been spoken in the British Isles long, long before English had been heard here, and during the Dark Ages it had been the speech of men who had brought Christian civilisation to the savage tribes of King George's native Germany. The child's name was Robert Mackay, known throughout his life and ever after as Rob Donn.[9]

The Province of the Cat is crammed, more than any other part of Scotland, with standing stones, brochs, burial mounds and Iron Age forts, yet in many ways these fade into the background when one considers the bardachd of Rob Donn. His work is often looked down upon by many classically inclined Gaelic scholars, as Rob Donn's Gaelic was of the Sutherland variety and has often been viewed as 'uncouth' in certain quarters. However that may be, Rob Donn was certainly more than a 'bard baile', or 'poet of a township'. It is true that the majority of his output was concerned with the people and places he knew best, but not all. Rob Donn was a cattle drover and as such was one of the few to venture firth of the hills and bogs to the trysts at Falkirk, Crieff and other places and to hear of the events of the day at first hand. In the eighteenth century this was how 'news' travelled. This broader subjectivity gives his poetry a far wider canvas than is usually the case of a true 'bard baile' And here it is worth noting that the surviving body of poems and song (some 400) far outweighs the production of any of his contemporaries in the Gaidhealtachd and is only matched by Burns, his contemporary bard in a sister language.

But this is not a quantitive appraisal. The reason we know any of Rob Donn's songs is that the people remembered them. As well as not being able to speak English, Rob Donn could not read or write in his own language. His poems were composed to tunes he either made up or ones he knew already and, mostly, they would have been pipe tunes. What is truly astonishing, and this again validates and is a testament to Hamish's idea of 'the carrying stream', is the sheer collective act of memory by the Mackays which the continuing existence of Rob Donn's poetry represents. It is hard to think of another instance of cultural love by any society, especially one which was battling for its own survival. Crofting is not a pastoral idyll: it is a system engineered by estate owners and government to keep people poor, to have just enough land to keep them from starving but not enough for them to earn a decent wage. On the one hand we have the resilience of a culture which can preserve the work of Rob Donn and keep it current; that can nurture the travelling people of which the Stewarts of Remarstaig were the last; and on the other we have the pornography of vast sporting estates owned by individuals who by their love of wealth keep poverty as their deerhound, and progress just over the horizon.

This dichotomy was not lost on Hamish Henderson. The cause of crofters was always close to his heart. The struggle to reclaim the land for the people has never left the consciousness of the north, and Hamish gave this full vent in the 'Ballad of the Men of Knoydart' of 1948. He was as delighted as anyone when the Assynt Crofters historically took title to the North Lochinver estate in February 1993. It is, sadly, yet another shade in the tragic shadow which hangs over the north that there are still the likes of Lord Brocket (the subject of his Knoydart ballad) and the Vestys (who still own vast swathes of west Sutherland) who continue to hold the Province of The Cat under the suffocating surface of the nineteenth century. While the Scottish Parliament, which reconvened in 1999, is to be congratulated in bringing in progressive land legislation, the 'community buy out' initiative, which allowed the Assynt Crofters to buy their land, has stalled somewhat and needs re-encouraging. It is when you consider such matters you realise the value of Hamish Henderson. His presence is felt by his absence.

When I poured Hamish's ashes into that craggy granite enclave on the top of Ben Gulabhain, in the place he had described to me, in Glenshee in 2002, I knew, as did the three others who were with me, that I was taking him home. Below us we could see the peedie but and ben in which he spent his bairntime. All around us was the world he saw as he peeked out of that little window. So the metaphysical question arises: just what is 'home'? What I am attempting here is to claim Hamish Henderson as a 'fili', as one of the 'Aos-dana', as one of the 'learned ones', because, as is obvious, he was more than a 'bard'. I am also trying to justify his grandfather Alexander's claim that the Hendersons came from Caithness and to prove, as I have tried to, that this claim is far from fallacious. Indeed I am claiming him back as one of our own for Caithness and Sutherland: the Province of the Cat was, for many more reasons than cited above, home to Hamish Henderson. On a broader front it is not too glib to suggest that the whole of Scotland was Hamish's home. That he had to reinvent it in order to live in it is just part of the poet's task. I doubt if he would have had it any other way.

To paraphrase that Canadian media-wizard, Marshall McLuhan, with regard to Hamish, the 'medium was the message'. In the theatre—a world I know—one of the basic unwritten laws is that 'all action comes from character' and that all 'characters' embark upon an 'emotional journey'; that is, they change because of the necessity for 'action'. Characters, when they are off stage, are in the past, in memory. When they enter they are in the here and now world of the present, a place jam packed with subjective emotions. They do this, they say that and then they exit. When they exit they go into the future, which is imagination. I believe that is where Hamish Henderson has gone—into our imagination, because even in death he cannot be still.

In his *Memorabilia Domestica*, published in 1899, the Reverend Donald Sage of the parish of Reay wrote of Rob Donn Mackay:

He stood alone. His poetry is history – a history of everyone and everything he came into contact in the country in which he lived. His descriptions do not merely let us know what these things or persons were, but as things that are.[10]

Hamish Henderson would never claim that he 'stood alone' but he helped us all understand 'things that are'. In this ever increasingly technological age the tendency is to go inwards—computerisation is the cartography of inner-space. Hamish's method was to go out into the world and into people's lives and his primary medium was poetry; that was his language; it is what he was always after. When he found it —whether it came from Ailidh Dall, or whoever, it physically brought him to life. It filled him with joy. As he said himself in 1964, in an interview with Peter Orr, published in *Alias MacAlias*, (he is speaking here about poetry): 'One shouldn't divide it between the moment of creation and the created completed thing. Its joy is the joy of itself, to feel itself in being.'[11] His grand notion was to make poetry become people and he knew all along, as the history of this nation has proven, that people are poetry. He knew fine what he was looking at. So, in the flow country of eternity, 'across her snows', the Clan Gunn embrace their son.

References:

1   Timothy Neat, *Hamish Henderson: A Biography, Volume 1, The Making of the Poet (1919-1953)* (Edinburgh: Polygon, 2007), p.7.

2   Ian Grimble, *Clans and Chiefs* (London: Blond and Briggs, 1980; Edinburgh: Birlinn, 2000), p.71.

3   John MacInnes, 'The Bard Through History', in Timothy Neat & John MacInnes, *The Voice of The Bard: Living Poets and Ancient Tradition in the Highlands and Islands of Scotland* (Edinburgh: Canongate, 1999) pp. 321-52, p.320.

4   *Ibid.*, p. 323.

5   Osborn Bergin, *Irish Bardic Poetry*, (Dublin: Dublin Institute for Advanced Studies, 1970).

6   Hamish Henderson, *Elegies for the Dead in Cyrenaica*, first published 1948 (Edinburgh: Polygon, 2008), p. 38.

7   Timothy Neat, *The Summer Walkers: Travelling People and Pearl-fishers in the Highlands of Scotland* (Edinburgh: Canongate, 1996) pp. 69-70.

8   *Ibid.*, p.75.

9   Ian Grimble, *The World of Rob Donn* (Edinburgh: The Edina Press, 1979; Edinburgh: Saltire Society, 1999), p. 1.

10   Donald Sage, *Memorabilia Domestica: or, Parish Life in the North of Scotland*, first published 1899 (Whitefish, MT: Kessinger Publishing, 2008).

11   Hamish Henderson, *Alias MacAlias: Writings on Songs, Folk and Literature*, edited by Alec Finlay (Edinburgh: Polygon, 1992), p. 325.

HAMISH HENDERSON AND THE PIPING TRADITION OF THE NORTH EAST

Gary West

While the bulk of his collecting concentrated on folksong and oral narrative, Hamish Henderson also held a great affection for the piping tradition, and indeed his knowledge of it was both discerning and deep. He clearly viewed piping as wholly integral to the folk music tradition to which he was so committed, a viewpoint that was by no means always shared by many within the piping establishment itself who seemed to prefer to think of bagpipe music as an art form somewhat 'set apart'.

His inclusion on the programme of the inaugural Edinburgh People's Festival Ceilidh in August 1951 of the seventeen-year-old piper John Burgess was highly symbolic, for in doing so Hamish was making a strong statement of his view that in both the Scots and Gaelic traditions piping and song emerged from the same well-spring. In recent years, this symbiosis has been receiving fairly close attention within the Gaelic tradition, but as yet little notice has been taken of this inter-relationship within the Scots-speaking regions. This short essay is offered as a first step towards addressing this theme.

Farewell to the Creeks

In this first extract, Hamish Henderson talks with Pipe Major James Robertson of Banff, former pipe major of the 1st Battalion Gordon Highlanders. James Robertson (1886-1961) was born at Scotsmill of Boyne, Banff, although his family moved to Coatbridge when he was seven years old. He was taught to play the pipes by Willie Sutherland of Clarkston, and joined the 1st Battalion Gordon Highlanders in 1905, serving with the regiment until 1926. Captured at the Battle of Mons in August 1914, he became a prisoner of war, and it was during that period that he composed some of his most famous tunes. On leaving the army, he was employed as janitor at Banff Academy, a post he retained until his retiral in 1952.[1]

This interview, which took place in his retiral year, is highly significant in that it celebrates the relationship between two major cultural creations of the twentieth-century traditional music landscape of Scotland: the pipe tune, 'Farewell to the Creeks', composed by Pipe Major Robertson, which remains to this day one of the most popular marches in the entire piping canon, and the song composed by Hamish and which was set to that same melody, 'The 51st Highland Division's Farewell to Sicily'. This quickly became one of the songs which helped to define the essence of the folk revival in Scotland in the 1950s and '60s, and it remains a standard part of many folk singers' repertoires today. Also present at this interview was Pipe Major George Hepburn of the Turriff and District Pipe Band.

Hamish Henderson: When did you compose 'Farewell to the Creeks' now?

Pipe Major James Robertson: Oh, I think I composed it about 1915.

HH: Oh aye? During the war itself?

JR: Yes. As a matter of fact it was composed on a piece of yellow blotting paper. I have got the original bit yet.

HH: Oh, have you still got it? Whereabouts did you compose it?

JR: Oh, I think it was in Germany. I was a prisoner of war at the time.

HH: Oh I see, oh aye. And what were you thinking of when you made the title, 'Farewell to the Creeks'?

JR: Well, I was thinking about the Creeks of Portknockie as a matter of fact. I remember my uncle stayed in an old house there, and when I was a boy I went on holiday once. And the place was called the Creeks. I saw it recently as a matter of fact. The first time for many years. And this particular locality was called the Creeks. I remember it was pretty stormy and the waves were washin' hard up against this other wall outside the house. It's known in Portknockie as the Creeks, this particular part.

HH: And are there wee inlets in it?

JR: Yes, yes. Well, all over the Morayshire coast, of course.

HH: Do you know, when I first heard that tune, I didn't know who had composed it, but I was sure that it related to this north-east coast, you know? It seems to me to spring just as naturally out of it as the bothy ballads spring from the soil inland, you know? I heard it played for the first time—to my remembering it anyway—when I was in Sicily, in Linguaglossa. The square of Linguaglossa. The massed pipe band of 153 Brigade played it over.

JR: Aye, but Robbie Reid—Pipe Major Robbie Reid—he put it in one of his books, you know.[2] That's the reason it became so popular. He put a book on the market with not too difficult tunes—more so for pipe bands and the young element, you see? It's not too difficult.

HH: Oh no, it's also one of the few modern pipe tunes that I know that's a properly original tune. It's as original as any of the grand old marches, you know? I think there are very few modern pipe marches of which you can properly say that.

JR: Well, you can't get away very far from the stereotypical tunes in 6/8, you see. You haven't got so much to go on – on the pipe chanter compass you see. You cannot get away – they're so similar to each other. But there have been a few in recent years quite good, you know …'Ballochyle' was one. Oh, 'Dovecote Park' was a fine tune. I have one …Douglas Haig. 'Earl Haig of Bemersyde'. A 6/8 march with an accentuated beat. And George McLennan[3] had one for an uncle of his, John McLennan. 'Major John McLennan', yes …I like George McLennan's one better. It's more musical. I mind showin' George this tune[4], and I pointed out how I sing the lead on the beat, you see, and he says to me, 'Well, Robbie,' he says, 'It's more clever than musical,' he says! (Laughs).

Later in the interview the conversation returns to the relationship between pipe music and song.

HH: I've been listening to a lot of the bothy ballads, as you know, Pipe Major, and it seems to me that a lot of them are in the pipe scale. Do you think that the piping tradition has anything to do with those bothy ballads?

JR: Oh yes, of course, …the fact they speak in one octave, you know. And a good many of the tunes …are just the one octave.

HH: And it is the pentatonic scale—the scale of the old folk song, that is also the scale of the pipes of course. But take for example some of these tunes like the 'Barnyards o Delgaty'—'lintin addie toorin addie'—you could play that on the pipes… And the same with these old 'Rhynie' tunes, or the tunes associated with Rhynie, that Willie Mathieson was singing to me, 'At Rhynie I sheared ma first Hairst'. Well it seems to me that that is just the pipe scale, more or less.

JR: Well a lot of the old tunes, you see, some of the airs, are just real pipe tunes, you know. The songs were put to them, I think. You hear a lot of these cornkisters like the 'Bonnie Country Garden'. And old things like that. 'The Muckin o Geordie's Byre', 'The Barren Rocks of Aden', of course, all these things are played on the melodeon now. The melodeon and the fiddle. The average fiddler roon aboot the north-east, here, he didn't go in for any fancy technique, or anything. He just played the melody.

HH: Oh, no, he just stuck wi' the old melodies, that's right… Then of course some of yer own marches I think, too, Pipe Major—the thing I like most about them, such as 'Farewell to the Creeks', for example, is that they seem to me to link up with this folk song of the north-east in some way or other that I can't quite define. But I think they share a common musical experience. They seem to me to come out of the same sort of tradition as a lot of the bothy songs. Do you think they do?

JR: Oh, well there probably were ideas… just like that. The old folk songs ideas, you see. Melody.

HH: Would you sing over 'Farewell to the Creeks'?

JR: Aye.

The following rendition of the tune by its composer, Pipe Major Robertson, is fascinating as it is sung in a system of vocables that combines elements of piping canntaireachd and north east 'diddling'.

Hi hri om ha di dae hae didee hirom, bim ha didre hum didre hae didee hirum… Hi hri om ha di dae hac didee hirom, he ha didee bee didum hiree, dum.

He hirae hoe hac hi dee, chin tae haree hae didum, an dirin diree, hee hae ohae hirum… Ti hirae ho hae didee, tin tae ha ree hae didum, ha didee hac didum hireem urn.

Hi hira, hiree, he hiree dum de hirom, hiree di dirum di di hirae dirum... Hi him, hiree, de hiree hin de didum. ha didee hae didum hiree dum.

Hi hiree, do hirae di, hac de he hioram, hiree dae hiree dae hi didum hirum... De hiree, do hirae di hae de he diram, ha didae hee didum hirae hum.

HH: My God! That's a fine tune.
Pipe Major George Hepburn: You put words tae that, did ye?
HH: I put words to it, aye. But did I sing you over the words I put to it?

JR: No, what were the words?

HH: Och well, I composed this when the Highland Division were leaving Sicily, you know. And it was the time that the units were going out to Augusta to embark and there was the sense of leaving, you know? And I heard this—the massed pipe band of 153 Brigade play yer tune then. And so the two ideas just sort o came together in my head and I made this ballad which I sang at that time. It goes:

The Pipie is dosey, the Pipie is fey,
He wilna come roon for his vino the day;
The sky oer Messina is unco an grey,
And all the bricht chaulmers are eerie.

An Fareweel, ye banks o Sicily,
Fare ye weel ye valley and shaw;
There's nae Jock will mourn the kyles o ye,
Puir bloody bastards[5] are weary.
Fareweel, ye banks o Sicily,
Fare ye weel ye valley and shaw;
There's nae hame can smoor the wiles o ye,
Puir bloody bastards are weary.

Then doon the stair and line the waterside,
Wait yer tum, the ferry's awa;
Then doon the stair, and line the waterside,
A the bricht chaulmers are eerie.

The Drummie is polished, the Drummie is braw,
He canna be seen for his webbin ava,
He's beezed himself up for a photo an a
Tae leave wi his Lola, his dearie.

Then fareweel ye dives o Sicily,
Fare ye weel ye shielin and ha;
We'll a mind shebeens and bothies
Where kind signorinas were cheery.
Fareweel ye dives o Sicily,
Fare ye weel ye shielin and ha;
We'll a mind shebeens and bothies,
Where Jock made a date wi his dearie.

Then tune the pipes and drub the tenor drum,
Leave yer kit this side of the wa;
Then tune the pipes and drub the tenor drum,
A the bricht chaulmers are eerie.[6]

The Pi - pie is do - sey, the Pi - pie is fey, He wil - na come roon for his vi - no the day; The sky oer Mes - si - na is un - co an grey, And all the bricht chaul - mers are ee - rie. An Fare - weel, ye banks o Si - ci - ly, Fare ye weel ye val - ley and shaw; There's nae Jock will mourn the kyles o ye, Puir bloo - dy bas - tards are wea - ry. Fare - well, ye banks o Si - ci - ly, Fare ye weel ye val - ley and shaw; There's nae hame can smoor the wiles o ye, Puir bloo - dy bas - tards are wea - ry.

HH: Well that was it, anyway.
GB: Damn good that! Yes, very good.

Cauld Wind Pipes

While the north-east of Scotland has for long supported a very strong Highland piping community, it also served as one of the last retainers of the old bellows-based Lowland piping tradition which was current there as well as in the borders and central belt for several hundred years, but which began to go into a lasting decline in the early nineteenth century. By the turn of the twentieth century there appear to have been few players of the lowland form of the instrument remaining, and its very existence seems to have been wiped very quickly from the collective folk memory throughout the country. This is clearly shown in the two interview extracts below: Hamish refers to the instrument as 'Irish Pipes' while the second informant, Dr John Hunter, regarded the bellows as an ingenious alternative for players short of breath, rather than as a separate instrument in its own right.

One of the last known representatives of the original lowland tradition was Francis Jamieson, better known as Francie Markis (1823-1904). The 'Markis' epithet was first applied to his father, William Jamieson, who had the lease on Balthangie farm, Middlehill in the parish of Marquhitter, and who was reputed to be as handsome as the Marquis of Huntly. Francie grew up to be a fine figure of a man himself, earning a reputation as a great athlete, runner and strongman as well as a skilled player of fiddle, cello and 'cauld wind' pipes. Musicianship was certainly in his family, for his nephew, Joseph Sim, nicknamed 'The Wonderful Boy', became renowned as one of the best fiddlers in the north east during the late nineteenth century.

Francie features in the fInal two verses of a bothy ballad, 'Wester Badenteer':

> Aboot the middle of the nicht, tay is handit roon,
> Nae fancy tables, jist a joug an biscuits white and broon.
> Syne Lordie wi the aul Scots sangs nae heard in music hall,
> An Francie Markis gars us lach wi 'Billy Johnston's Ball'.
>
> Syne up an tae the dancing for twa'r three oors an mair,
> An morning is nae faur awa fin we gan doon the stair.
> Lang may aul Francie play an sing, lang may he fill the fleer!
> Lang may the fairmer hae the hairst at Wester Badenteer![7]

The full song was published in *Tocher* 43, along with an interview with Willie Mathieson in which he relates various stories about Francie Markis. However, Willie knew him as a fiddler and cello player, but had never heard him play the bellows pipes. The following conversations between Hamish and Geordie Robertson of Aberdeen and Dr John Hunter of Turriff provide an account of Markis' piping abilities:

Hamish Henderson: Did you ever see Francie Markis?
Geordie Robertson: Oh aye, mony a time.
HH: Did you?
GR: Aye.

HH: He used to play the Irish pipes, didn't he?

GR: Aye, exactly, aye.

HH: And what was this other name you gave them?

GR: Eh, the cauld wind pipes, they ca'd them. Cauld wind pipes. Twa bags, you see… He squeezed his twa airms. He held his airrns like this you see. And I'm telling, he had them in tune.

HH: Had he?

GR: Aye. Some of them was just into one stock, a the three drones. And… different – different styles o them. Davy has some o them oot there – Davy hid that old pipes oot there yet… That's cauld wind pipes in a box. They're awfie auld fashioned thingies, you ken? Kept them. Aye.

HH: And when did he to come down to see you?

GR: Oh, we used tae ca it Skippie Fair, and the June market. That wis the two markets in the year. He used tae aye come roon there and play. Play at the market, you see, for money. Played for money.

HH: And was he a fine performer on the – on the pipes?

GR: Oh he could play. By faith he could play. He could play the fiddle too, richt. Aye, awfie musical folk… He wanted his sister doon tae Gight games tae get a breed o Donald Dinnie.[8] Aye, that was true. Aye. Wanted her doon tae Gight tae get a breed o Donald Dinnie. He was a great man. That was true enough. (Laughs)

HH: A super athlete and he'd put her to the breedin? (Laughs).

GR: …Aye that was true enough. Onybody will tell you roon aboot thon place. That wis his idea… He wis a queer trebbler, mon. He always wore white moleskin breeks. Awfu strides he took. Strides.

John Hunter: There was two characters in Porter Fair when I was a boy. One played the bagpipes. Eh, what's his name? The Wonderful Boy played the violin. The Wonderful Boy – he came from New Byth. He was a marvellously good player of strathspeys. He was a very beautiful player, I believe. And then, eh, Francie Markis.

HH: Oh, Francie Markis?

JH: Francie Markis played the bagpipes. Being rather short on breath, he had an ingenious set o bagpipes. He pumped the air into the bag by means of a bellows with one arm and then he compressed the bag with the other arm, and that gave him his music. (Laughs) He sat … on a small low dyke there down beside the Commercial Bank and played his pipes there. I can remember him quite clearly. He used to be a very famous runner in his young day. He won many prizes at races at the games... He was an extraordinarily good runner. But unfortunately his legs had gone down with him and he was reduced to playing the bagpipes. But he was a very good player on the cello. I believe he played the cello. But I never heard him play the cello. But I believe he was very good at that.

A major revival of bellows piping began in Scotland in the early 1980s, an initiative of which Hamish Henderson was very supportive. The information regarding the old players provided by his fieldwork in the 1950s is of crucial value to the modem players and enthusiasts, for it has provided them with an invaluable link between the survival and revival of the cauld wind pipe traditions of Scotland.[9]

References

1   Hamish Henderson wrote an obituary for Pipe Major Robertson, published in the magazine *Sing* in May 1962. It was reproduced in Hamish Henderson's *Alias MacAlias: Writings on Songs, Folk and Literature*, edited by Alec Finlay (Edinburgh: Polygon 1992), pp. 155-156.

2   Robert Reid, *The Piper's Delight* (Edinburgh: Paterson's Publications, 1933).

3   This was Pipe Major G S McLennan, prolific composer and widely recognised as one of the most skilled pipers of the modem era. He was pipe major of the 1st Battalion Gordon Highlanders when James Robertson first joined up.

4   He is referring here to his own composition, 'Earl Haig of Bemersyde'.

5   In later versions of the song, 'bastards' was replaced by 'swaddies'.

6   Verses 1 and 3 are sung to part 1 of the tune. Verses 2 and 4 are sung to part 4 of the tune. Part 3 is used for the refrain. Part 2 is not used at all in the song.

7   As recorded from Willie Mathieson, Ellon, SA1952.12.

8   Donald Dinnie was a well-known competitor in the heavy events at Highland Games.

9   This essay is based on the following School of Scottish Studies archive recordings: SA1952.23: Pipe Major James Robertson and Pipe Major George Hepburn, Banff, recorded by Hamish Henderson; SA1954.94: Geordie Robertson, Aberdeen, recorded by Hamish Henderson; SA1952.09: Dr John Hunter, Turriff, recorded by Hamish Henderson.

HAMISH HENDERSON AND BÉLA BARTÓK: 'BRIDGEABLE CHASMS'

Tom Hubbard

First, some personal observations over the years. When I was a student in Aberdeen during the 1970s, a tall gangling fellow was kenspeckle equally at gigs for anti-apartheid or like causes, and in the English department looking for 'Dr Crawford'—Thomas Crawford—author of a pioneering study of the poetry of Burns. There you have the two worlds of the long fellow; I was told that his name was Hamish Henderson.

In the early years of the next decade, my academic base was Edinburgh, where I worked for a couple of years in the University library. Viewed from the staff-room during the coffee break, there was the long fellow again, en route from Sandy Bell's to the School of Scottish Studies. You'd see Hamish at the hinder-end of a dog lead, tugged by his reliable if roguish companion, that first-namesake of the howff which they'd just (for a while) vacated; out of six legs, four at least were determinedly functional.

A few years on, and we had people coming into the new Scottish Poetry Library, looking for Hamish's poems. Help! We held several copies of EUSPB's 1977 reprint of the *Elegies for the Dead in Cyrenaica*, and I knew there was much else: in these pre-index days, I had to gather up other pieces which were constellated throughout back numbers of magazines. Fortunately, Joy Hendry brought out a special Hamish issue of *Chapman* (42, Winter 1985), and that was to prove hugely popular with our readers. I still had to direct folk down to Willie Haynes's traditional music shop in Blackfriars Street. Willie's premises were tiny but what a wealth was there!

My feeling at the time was: here are the writings that are clearly 'poems', there in a printed book and in the magazines. There, though, round the corner, are the LPs and cassettes of the songs. Just around the corner, I say, but I wondered about two cultural worlds, both inhabited by Hamish, but which did not seem to meet much.

I should have known that was a mistaken assumption. However, in the process, I was receiving what I believe was a healthy message: in the Poetry Library, while we held audio materials, we were surrounded mainly by texts. Poetry does not reside entirely in print, and I was becoming increasingly interested in its performance dimension, as theatre, as sister-art of music (at that time, I would tend to put it more fustily than I would now). As someone devoted to the oral tradition, Hamish would have felt no strong compulsion to collect his poems into a single volume. That said, the bibliographical situation 'improved' when he shared a three-man selected poems with Sorley MacLean and Tom Scott, *Pervigilium Scotiae (Scotland's Vigil)*.[1] It was great that he was substantially present with such poet-colleagues: that would serve to situate him in the minds of a new generation of readers coming to twentieth-century Scottish poetry. Above all and at last, thanks to editor Raymond Ross, we were soon to welcome a Hamish Henderson *Collected Poems and Songs*.[2] Back in 1992, Polygon had already published Alec Finlay's collection of Hamish's prose, *Alias MacAlias: Writings on Songs, Folk and Literature*, and, in 1996, his letters, *The Armstrong Nose: Selected Letters of Hamish Henderson*. More recently, we have had the two volumes of Timothy Neat's biography of Hamish.

Sadly, I never got to know Hamish Henderson personally. I recall vividly his eloquence in the pub at Langholm, celebrating the unveiling of the MacDiarmid memorial sculpture. He was somewhat fou—and his laughter as he was helped, stumbling, down the step, added to the sense of human warmth and fellowship. Early in 1996, at a Burns conference at Strathclyde University, we chatted amiably in a foyer. And that was it.

A bridgeable chasm

Mario Relich has written that if there is a 'chasm' between the *Elegies for the Dead in Cyrenaica* and Hamish's 'more popular poems and ballads in the folk idiom' it is yet a 'bridgeable' chasm.[3] Unlike his friend and adversary MacDiarmid, Hamish Henderson saw no contradiction between being 'intellectual' and being 'folkish' (if one may describe these seeming polarities in such crude terms). There is an assumption that Rilke is a difficult poet, and there is much resonance from the Austro-German's *Duino Elegies* in Hamish's *Elegies for the Dead in Cyrenaica*.[4] Hamish was, after all, steeped in German poetry: Goethe and Hölderlin are at hand for him. Perhaps the strongest links between Rilke and Henderson are to be found in the former's seventh elegy and the latter's eighth; indeed Hamish makes explicit reference to the earlier work. In both poems, ancient monuments (in particular, Karnak in Egypt) are evoked in terms of a dialectic of timelessness and transience. Not all poets of a left-wing, progressive tendency have warmed to Rilke: Pablo Neruda, for instance, inveighs against the 'rilkistas' and 'falsos brujos existenciales' (false existential magicians) who live off the rot of capitalism. Neruda's sensibility is of a noble, expansive, bardic nature that would surely accord with that of Hamish Henderson, but such a denunciation (in 'Los poetas celestes'/ 'The poets celestial') smacks of a dogmatism that has an unfortunately long pedigree.[5] In his polemic *Chto takoye isskustvo?/ What is Art?* of 1898, Leo Tolstoy growled at Baudelaire, Mallarmé, Verlaine and their associates, condemning them as élitist decadents who pandered to the jaded tastes of the upper classes and whose work meant nothing to the 'people'. George Orwell, in turn, countered by accusing the ageing Tolstoy of seeking 'to narrow the range of human consciousness'.[6] Of Rilke one might say, above all, that his poetry seeks to expand the range of human consciousness, taking language into those interstices of meaning which it has not previously explored. As a poetic heir to Rilke, if also ideological heir to Marx and Gramsci, Hamish Henderson was not going to fall for the purportedly progressive, but actually deeply reactionary, notion that demanding art is not for the 'folk'.

Hamish's old sparring-partner MacDiarmid, for all his own brand of élitism, could try to bring together the world of Rilke and that of industrial workers, as in his 'The Seamless Garment', even if the tone of that poem comes across as a tad patronising. There is no little absurdity in the flyting of MacDiarmid and Henderson: each approaches a similar destination, if from different points of departure. As Thomas Crawford has observed, 'If traces of folk influence can be found in MacDiarmid's "poetry of intellect", then the opposite is true of Henderson: the "high" literary tradition has set its own stamp on his popular and political songs.'[7]

A supposed antithesis between the popular and the refined appears to afflict Scotland more than other European countries. It is odd that this should be the case, as it has often been remarked that the gap between 'art' and 'folk' song is narrower here than elsewhere. It could be argued that in the poetry of Hamish's neglected contemporary T S Law (1916-1997) there is no 'bridgeable chasm' because there is not any chasm in the first place: he moves easily between echoes of traditional bairn rhymes and intricate philosophical speculation.[8] MacDiarmid resorted to Scotland's most demotic language, Scots, as integral to his sophisticated modernist ambition to delve into a rich store of buried meaning, 'a Dostoevskian debris of ideas'.[9] And yet, just wander into any traditional/folk CD store and where are the 'classical' albums? Francis George Scott, Erik Chisholm? Savourna Stevenson is there, but what of her father Ronald? Why do we persist in such cultural apartheid?

Such neurosis has not been suffered by mainland Europe, particularly east and central, at least not since the beginning of the twentieth century. The Romanian composer George Enescu (1881-1955) drew on the spiritual depths of his country's folk tradition for his orchestral, instrumental and vocal works. The Pole Karol Szymanowski (1882-1937), a quintessentially European sophisticate, found in the music of the Tatra Highlands a rich resource for his later works, such as the ballet *Harnasie* (1935/36): he declared that 'each man must go back to the earth from which he derives.'[10] 'Folk', then, was not at odds with the avant-garde: it provided the latter with its very materials, the rawer the better.[11]

Above all, there was the Hungarian Béla Bartók (1881-1945), whose song-collecting field work so anticipates that of Hamish Henderson. According to his host in Glasgow, the Scottish composer Erik Chisholm, Bartók expressed 'his disappointment on learning that no authoritative or basic collection of Scottish folk music existed in print (a defect more recently remedied).'[12]

Scottish music in Europe

It was the mission of Erik Chisholm (1904-65) to counter the provincialisation of Scottish music and to reposition it within the European avant-garde—not unlike MacDiarmid's ambition for a modernist deployment of the Scots language. Chisholm's father-in-law was Francis George Scott (1880-1958), MacDiarmid's former schoolteacher, who made song-settings of his pupil's poetry. Scott did not so much 'arrange' existing folksongs as write original works in a folk idiom. Chisholm effectively inherited that practice in his own compositions, and it is significant that he wrote a monograph (Oxford: Pergamon, 1971) on the operas of the Czech composer Leoš Janáček (1854-1928). Janáček was certainly attracted to actual folk song, but again was primarily an 'original' composer who worked in a 'folkish' manner—indeed he went further: his vocal lines follow the contours of actual *speech* in his native Moravia.

Erik Chisholm was both composer and cultural activist. During the 1930s, the paintings of the Norwegian Edvard Munch were exhibited in Edinburgh; at this time Chisholm worked for a musical equivalent of such activism, in his efforts for the Glasgow-based Active Society for the Propagation of Contemporary Music. The high points include the Society's invitations to Bartók and Szymanowski to perform their music in Scotland.

Bartók twice visited Scotland, in February 1932 and November 1933, staying at Chisholm's house in Glasgow. Swapping notes, as it were, Bartók confessed to Chisholm that he had never had the opportunity to study the folk music of Scotland. Chisholm lost no time in rectifying this, placing scores and gramophone records at the disposal of his Hungarian confrère. Around this time, Chisholm was making a special study of piobaireachd (pibroch), the intricate music of the Highland pipes. He shared his knowledge with Bartók, who went on a Glasgow shopping trip, equipping himself with a chanter and, according to Chisholm's first wife, 'all the piobaireachd music he could lay his hands on.'[13]

In late 2004, when I was invited to give a talk in Budapest on the history of Scottish-Hungarian cultural links,[14] I consulted both Dr John Purser, then working on his biography of Chisholm, and Dr Morag Chisholm, the composer's daughter.[15] I met up with Morag again, in St Andrews at the beginning of May 2010. Bartók had met her, as an infant, in the Chisholm family home. Morag spoke of how, according to her father's account (she herself had been too young for the memory to remain), their guest had made a great fuss of her. Bartók loved children, and indeed was the composer of many piano pieces for them to play. The man's various qualities—his shyness, intensity of purpose, sense of mischief, kindness—were all on display during his time in Glasgow.

During my 2006 stint as a visiting professor at the Eötvös Loránd University of Budapest, Paddy Bort stayed with me for a few days. My rented flat was in a block overlooking a square which had witnessed some of the most horrifying events of October/November 1956. Paddy and I headed up to the Castle Quarter where we visited an exhibition on Bartók and his work in the field, his lugging of heavy recording equipment across south-eastern Europe, Turkey and North Africa. We turned to each other and one name was on our lips: Hamish.

Physically—but in no other sense—Bartók was a small man, with finely chiselled features which a superficial observer might assume to be those of an effete aesthete. Nothing could be further from the truth. Péter Bartók, son of the composer, informs us of a telling detail in the family home at Csalán Street: 'To find my father, the visitor had to walk up a staircase covered by rag-rugs. Many of the rugs in our home were the kind woven out of old rags; these make a colourful, neat covering, of a primitive quality, without a mechanical, factory-controlled pattern as the rags used by their makers had been collected at random; and they were easily washable.'[16] In the run-up to his engagement with the folk music of Hungary and points east and south, Bartók followed a trajectory not altogether dissimilar to other east/central European composers of his time. His early works were late-romantic, in the Wagner-Richard Strauss idiom, all lush orchestral surge and climax. His *Kossuth* symphonic poem of 1903, for all its patriotic subject matter, continues the Austro-German notion of Hungarian music; in this regard, at least, there is no significant departure from Liszt. Szymanowski took somewhat longer to emerge beyond late-romanticism: his first (and unsuccessful) opera *Hagith* (1913) was composed in Vienna and tends to be compared to Strauss's *Salomé*, though in its far wilder, expressionistic passages it would seem, in retrospect, closer to Schoenberg's *Erwartung* of 1909. Eventually Szymanowski drew on his native Polish sources as had Bartók on his Hungarian, even if, inevitably, they were consulting different road-maps.

Bartók, together with his composer colleague Zoltán Kodály and the poet Endre Ady (1877-1919), were central to the Hungarian cultural revival of the early years of the twentieth century. Ady's poetry was set to music by both composers. The three followed a common pattern of bypassing Austro-German cultural hegemony in looking to France: there was much to learn from such as Debussy and his challenge to established tonality. By grafting this influence on to the Hungarian folk idiom, Bartók and Kodály made possible a wealth of new sounds. Ady, a provincial journalist formerly based in Transylvania, had been whisked from there by his sophisticated, worldly mistress to Paris, where he enthused over the poetry of Baudelaire and Verlaine, those *bêtes-verdâtres/jaunâtres* of Tolstoy's—much too sickly, etiolated stuff, surely, for a young hillbilly such as Ady, steeped as he was in the virile imagery of Calvinist Old Testament culture?[17] That question, however, begs many others; besides, Ady also discovered Jehan-Rictus, the poet of working-class Paris, who wrote in *argot* and provided material for the Chat Noir cabaret—as did also Verlaine and Debussy: again, the cultural lines of demarcation are much more blurred than we might assume.[18]

Such supposedly high-art movements as symbolism and expressionism, then, which Tolstoy-influenced commentators would dismiss as merely the epicene, hysterical diversions of a decadent ruling class, could actually be synthesised with the heritage of popular culture: Bartók's opera *Bluebeard's Castle* (1911) is a, if not *the*, supreme example. After all, there's inherent symbolism and expressionism in the traditional ballads of both Scotland and Hungary. Hamish

Henderson knew this instinctively when he composed his 'Flyting o' Life and Daith'. *Bluebeard's Castle* is a ballad-opera: the audience is lured into a highly-charged scenario which proceeds more by moody mise-en-scène than by explicit narrative (think 'The king sits in Dunfermline toun/ Drinkan the bluid-reid wine'—the opening of 'Sir Patrick Spens' is more atmospheric than explanatory). The number of doors in the sinister castle is the ballad-number: seven. Magic, simultaneously rough and refined, is afoot. Here is a work that draws on a deep well of the popular collective unconscious, and at the same time exemplifies an utterance of that difficult-élitist-decadent (*etc*) fellow Stéphane Mallarmé: 'Le *suggérer*, voilà le rêve/ To *suggest*, there's the dream').[19] Could not the public actually *prefer* a certain tantalising obscurity?

Conclusion

So let us call time on po-faced polarities which make little or no sense in European contexts—at which point it is perhaps apt to end on a note of some irony. Endre Ady may have enjoyed the role of transplanted *flâneur* on the Boul' Saint-Mich' but there was nothing greenery-yallery about him (come to think of it, there is not anything particularly greenery-yallery about such a milieu, apart from the colour of absinthe).

While I was in Budapest, I took up an Ady ballad which struck me as workable into a Scots ballad. It is based on the story of a Hungarian Princess Margaret—not the one who became Queen Margaret of Scotland—and her immurement for life in a convent on an island in the Danube. This was her punishment, imposed by her father, for rejecting all the suitors who had turned up at the palace. I first read my version at a bohemian dive in Buda; more recently (November 2009) I presented it at the Carrying Stream Festival in Edinburgh. The text has appeared in the online Hungarian jounal *Epona* and in the Dublin-based poetry magazine *Cyphers*, but it has not been published in Scotland. I suspect Hamish Henderson would agree that such order of appearance, performance first, text later, is just as it should be.

'The Legend o the Leddy Margret'
(after Endre Ady: Szent Margit legendája)

The lang island in the river
    Yieldit ti me its saft-toned secret:
The king kest inti the cloister there
    His dochter, the virgin Margret.

A lassie o dreams and muffled screams:
A sweary-word wad gar her faint.
Thir lords that rampaged through the coort
Were nae fit company fir a saint.

She socht her lover frae oot West,
    No the rough type wi hairy erse;
He'd be a peelie-wallie lad,
    And greet while singin his ain verse.

She waitit sair: it grupped her hairt.
    There came brave horsemen, coorse in jest,
Gallopin richt inti the haa,
    But no her lang-expectit guest.
He wadna wander bi thon shore:
    His rhymes and kisses she'd ken never.
She deed, a sacrifice ti Christ,
    On the lang island in the river.

References:

1   Sorley MacLean, *Pervigilium Scotiae (Scotland's Vigil): Tom Scott, Somhairle MacGill-Eain, Hamish Henderson* (Buckfastleigh: Etruscan, 1997).

2   Hamish Henderson, *Collected Poems and Songs*, edited by Raymond Ross (Edinburgh: Curly Snake Publishing, 2000).

3   See Mario Relich's chapter in the present volume.

4   See Tessa Ransford's chapter in the present volume.

5   Pablo Neruda, *Five Decades: a Selection (Poems 1925-1970)*, edited and translated by Ben Belitt (New York: Grove Press, 1974), pp. 72-73.

6   Leo Tolstoy, *What is Art? And Essays on Art*, translated by Aylmer Maude (London: Oxford University Press, 1969); George Orwell, 'Lear, Tolstoy and the Fool', in his *Inside the Whale and Other Essays*, (Harmondsworth: Penguin Books, 1962), pp. 101-19, p. 109.

7   Thomas Crawford, sleeve notes for *Freedom Come-All-Ye*, an LP of Hamish's poems and songs (Dublin: Claddagh Records, 1977). See also: Bert Wright, 'Politics and the Folksong Revival—Commitment or Complacency?', *Radical Scotland*, no. 24 (December 1986/January 1987), pp. 36-39.

8   See T S Law, *At the Pynt o the Pick and Other Poems*, edited by Tom Hubbard and John Law (Blackford: Fingerpost Publicatiouns, 2008).

9   Hugh MacDiarmid, 'A Theory of Scots Letters' in *The Thistle Rises: an Anthology of Poetry and Prose*, edited by Alan Bold (London: Hamish Hamilton, 1984), first published 1923, p. 131.

10 Quoted by Bill Newman in his sleeve note to Karol Szymanowski, *Symphonie concertante op. 60 and Pieces for Solo Piano*, various performers,

Unicorn label LP [RHS 347], 1977.

11 Although that could also be said of the avant-gardist Martyn Bennett's *Grit* (Real World, 2003); see also Margaret Bennett's chapter in this volume.

12 Erik Chisholm, 'Béla Bartók', *Men and Music: lectures given at University of Cape Town Summer School, February 1964*, p. 22. Document kindly supplied by Dr Morag Chisholm, the composer's daughter and chair of the Erik Chisholm Trust. For the work of the School of Scottish Studies, see Jim Gilchrist, 'The School of Scottish Studies', *Cencrastus*, no. 12 (Spring, 1983), pp. 15-17.

13 Quoted in Erik Chisholm, *Ibid*, p. 21.

14 See Tom Hubbard, 'Scottish-Hungarian Literary Connections: Past, Present and Possible Future', *HUSSE Papers 2005: Proceedings of the Seventh Biennial Conference* (Veszprém: Department of English and American Studies, University of Veszprém, 2006), vol. 1, pp 13-26. Also see László Marx, 'Robert Burns in Hungary', *Studies in Scottish Literature*, Vol. 15 (1980), pp. 3-27; Sárosi, Bálint (ed.), *Hungarian Folk Music Collected by Béla Bartók [on] Phonograph Cylinders* (Hungaroton LP [LPX 18069]), Budapest: Hungaroton, 1981); and Sándor Weöres, *If All the World Were a Blackbird*, poems translated from the Hungarian by Alexander Fenton (Aberdeen: Aberdeen University Press, 1985).

15 I would like to reiterate here my warm thanks for the information and advice which I received from them. John Purser's biography has since been published, with his own discussion and documentation of the Chisholm-Bartók encounters. See John Purser, *Erik Chisholm: Scottish Modernist 1904-1965: Chasing a Restless Muse* (Woodbridge: Boydell & Brewer, 2009).

16 Quoted in *Béla Bartók Memorial House*, edited by Máté Hollós (Budapest: Bartók Béla Emlékház, 2006), p. 10.

17 See Margaret A Mackay, 'Folk Religion in a Calvinist Context: Hungarian Models and Scottish Examples', *Folklore*, 113 (2002), pp. 139-49.

18 The Berlin cabaret and theatre/opera of Brecht/Weill of the Weimar period are another good example.

19 Quoted in Jules Huret, *Enquête sur l'évolution littéraire: conversations avec […] Stéphane Mallarmé [et al]* (Paris: Bibliothèque Charpentier, 1891), pp. 55-65, p. 60.

APOLLYON'S CHASM: THE POETRY OF HAMISH HENDERSON

Mario Relich

Responding to the publication of *Elegies for the Dead of Cyrenaica*, the Marxist historian E P Thompson wrote as follows in a letter of February 1949 to Hamish Henderson:

> I think this is your greatest danger and you must *never* let yourself, by the possible insensitivity or hostility of those who should be your greatest allies, be driven into the arms of the 'culture boys' who 'appreciate' pretentiousness and posturing. They would kill your writing, because you, more than any other poet I know, are an instrument through which thousands of others can become articulate... And you must not forget that your songs and ballads are not trivialities – they are quite as important as the *Elegies*.[1]

While cultural commissars of any stripe never conquered Henderson, quite the contrary, Thompson's letter of 10 February 1949 turned out to be prophetic about the trajectory of Henderson's career as a poet and, arguably, as Timothy Neat puts it in volume one of his biography of Henderson, 'the last champion of a genuinely druidic bardic tradition'.[2]

Thompson's letter reveals that while by implication he valued the complex word-play and imagery of the *Elegies*, he also wanted the poet to continue writing his more immediately accessible ballads. There is, indeed, something of a chasm in Henderson's achievement, that between his dourly heroic *Elegies for the Dead in Cyrenaica* (1948) and his poems and ballads in the folk idiom, even if a bridgeable one.

With the major exception of the *Elegies*, his poems appeared mainly in literary and political periodicals, and the occasional anthology. The publication of his *Collected Poems and Songs*, edited by Raymond Ross, which appeared soon after Henderson's eightieth birthday, was therefore very welcome and long overdue, although it is by no means complete. This appears to be particularly true with regard to his war poetry. As Neat points out, he is a poet ripe for re-evaluation as the author, adapter, translator and collector of something like one thousand songs and poems written during the six years of World War Two.'[3] Nevertheless, any assessment of Henderson's poetic output has to begin with *Elegies for the Dead in Cyrenaica*, which is generally considered to be one of the finest poetry sequences to emerge out of World War Two. Among early admirers Neat quotes Hugh MacDiarmid and Seán O'Casey, as well as the Surrealist poet David Gascoyne, who wrote to Henderson as follows: 'The *Elegies* made a real impact on me, and I regard them as the most significant martial poems to have come out of the war: something about them only to compare with Wilfred Owen, David Jones (maybe also Isaac Rosenberg?)',[4] thereby firmly relating him to the greatest British poets of World War One. And the sequence has certainly stood up well to the test of time; although, as will be seen, it has had its critics.

Henderson began writing these poems, forged in the heat of desert warfare, when serving as an intelligence officer with the Eighth Army, and while accompanying the 51st Highland Division through Libya, Tunisia and Sicily. Looking back on the desert campaign in a 1989 letter to Naomi Mitchison, the novelist and left-wing activist, he quoted Montgomery's words before eventual victory at El Alamein: 'If we cannot stay here alive, then let us stay here dead.'[5] It is those who died that the *Elegies* commemorate. But not only the British and Commonwealth dead at El Alamein. As his biographer points out, 'pity for the German dead was one of his starting points.'[6] The Battle of El Alamein itself has its place in the 'Interlude', which is subtitled 'Opening of an Offensive', between the fifth and sixth elegies, and here the 'pity of war' is most firmly replaced by its 'mak siccar!' These lines are from the conclusion:

> against the contemptuous triumphs of the big battalions
> mak siccar against the monkish adepts
> of total war against the oppressed oppressors...

against the executioner
against the tyrannous myth and the real terror
mak siccar

Henderson's notes draw attention to 'mak siccar' (make sure) as 'one of the famous phrases of mediaeval Scottish history,' referring to one of the Bruce's lieutenants wanting to make sure, 'after Bruce had stabbed the Red Comyn in Dumfries Kirk that the assassination wasn't botched.'[7]

Yet the opening stanza of the 'First Elegy', subtitled 'End of a Campaign', closes as follows: 'And sleep now. Sleep the sleep of the dust.' It is a line which subliminally suggests 'the sleep of the just', and makes for muted, yet powerful irony about the waste of war, even when the cause is just. Another line, 'There were no gods and precious few heroes,' has often been quoted in Scotland, not least by those unaware of its origin, as a jibe against pusillanimous politicians. Within the poem's context, however, it is very much a compassionate salute to those who died in the North African campaign, an attempt to bridge the gap between the living and the dead. One of the dead was Corporal Heinrich Mattens, killed in action, and in the conclusion to the First Elegy Henderson echoes lines about carefree birds above the battlefield from a poem which he had retrieved and translated from the German soldier's diary.[8]

It is the 'Ninth Elegy', subtitled 'Fort Capuzzo', which most directly encapsulates the liminal aspects of life and death experienced in desert warfare, and indeed it has been widely anthologised. Reputed to have been chosen by Edith Sitwell for her wartime poetry reading recitals, it is the most straightforward of the *Elegies*. To adapt E P Thompson in his letter quoted at the beginning of this chapter, the poem certainly 'makes articulate' one common, and deeply poignant, kind of soldierly feeling. The voice of the poem is that of the poet observing a soldier 'looking at the grave of a fallen enemy' and reminding himself of 'the meaning of the hard word 'pietas''. The poem is particularly appealing in how it reproduces the brutally colloquial language register of the ordinary soldier, yet without sacrificing dignity. Consequently, it convincingly conveys the observed soldier's thoughts:

—Here's another 'Good Jerry'!
Poor mucker. Just eighteen. Must be hard up for manpower.
Or else, he volunteered, silly bastard. That's the fatal.
the – fatal – mistake. Never volunteer for nothing.

While this elegy focuses on a specific moment of soldierly piety, indeed a lull in the fighting, the 'Eighth Elegy (Karnak)', looks back over millennia. The poem surveys life and death from the perspective of ancient Egyptian religion, and a vivid re-imagining of the ancient world: 'will the smooth priests/in bell-bottomed robes process between the sphinxes?' Taken as a whole, therefore, the *Elegies* display an epic grandeur, true to both personal experience and historical implications.

According to Angus Calder, Sorley MacLean, who had himself taken part in and written about the desert campaign, was the greatest influence on the *Elegies*. As Calder wrote:

> Henderson's magnificent *Elegies for the Dead in Cyrenaica* are in English, but the idiom seems heavily affected, like some of MacDiarmid's work, by consciousness of Gaelic. No English soldier of Henderson's generation wrote anything like them, yet they do relate to the Gaelic poems by Sorley Maclean, also from the desert war.[9]

He also points out that 'Henderson showed that one could be intensely 'Scottish' with the lexicon of standard English.' However, at the time that they were published, the nationalist poet Douglas Young expressed a very different view. He wrote to Henderson that 'many of your telling phrases are journalistic rather than poetic, eg, the 'sleep of the dust', the 'malevolent bomb-thumped desert', etc.,' that 'this is, of course, entirely in a certain fashion of decadent English bourgeois writing pretending to be poetry,'[10] and much more in similar abrasive fashion. A more recent critic, Robert Crawford, grudgingly accepts that 'the poems are often rescued by precise observation', but not before claiming that its 'free verse accounts' of the desert terrain are too derivative in their 'Eliotic and New Apocalyptic tremors',[11] a critique alluding not only to T S Eliot's *The Waste Land*, but also to the supposed excesses of Dylan Thomas, J F Hendry, Henry Treece and other poets of the 1940s. While there is certainly some rhetorical flamboyance in the *Elegies*, often associated with the New Apocalyptics,

Henderson forged something much more steely, hard-edged, and intense. As for Eliot's influence, Henderson's biographer justly reminds us that Eliot's influence on the sequence 'Over the years... has been over-emphasised.'[12] Perhaps the most balanced verdict is that of Raymond Ross, on the *Elegies* and Henderson's poetic *oeuvre* as a whole: 'these are poems of lyrical intensity and gentle humour, of subtle irony and satirical intent, of profound humanity and, on occasion, cold steel.'[13] The fact that the poet was born and brought up in Blairgowrie, Perthshire, historically an area of conflict between Highlanders and Lowlanders also undoubtedly contributed to his sensitivity with regard to landscape and history.

But as in MacLean's Gaelic poems, the *Elegies* also have a strong European dimension through the many allusions to Rilke and Hölderlin (the latter having been translated by Henderson), rather than W H Auden and Dylan Thomas who greatly influenced other British war poets. As for Owen's pervasive influence on the *Elegies*, conceded by Henderson himself, most British soldier-poets during World War Two wrote in his shadow. Yet for Henderson in both the *Elegies* and his ballads, the poetry was not 'in the pity,' but in going beyond it.

Sorley MacLean himself contributed a valuable introduction to the 1977 reprint of the *Elegies*, published by Polygon. He pointed out that desert warfare provided 'a good battle-ground in that there was little of human achievement in it that could be destroyed except soldiers themselves and human means of destruction.' As for the combatants, they were 'as if abstracted from a real world to fight on a remote moon-like terrain, and in general the only bitterness against the 'enemy' was when a soldier got news of the deaths of his near and dear by civilian bombing at home.' Henderson's poems assimilate this almost 'chivalrous' aspect of the desert war, which has been confirmed by other survivors and historians of the campaign. Often the real enemy turns out to be the bureaucrats and the propagandists, such as the newsreel commentator in the 'Ninth Elegy, (Fort Capuzzo)' likened 'to the pimp, the informer and the traitor'. MacLean's verdict about Henderson's achievement cannot be bettered:

> To me its dominant quality is the fusion of its very particular desert sensuousness with the particular and universal truth of its statement about the dead, reactions and actions of men under the stress of fast-moving war in such places as the North African desert;

and notably of the feelings of the survivor about the dead who have expiated their share of responsibility for the war.[14]

It is, indeed, the mesmerising aspects of desert warfare which the *Elegies* capture particularly well, or what Henderson called, in the foreword to the original edition, 'a curious 'doppelganger' effect.' His haunting memories of the desert campaign, moreover, led him to certain political conclusions. Here is how he put it:

> After the African campaign had ended, the memory of this odd effect of mirage and looking-glass illusion persisted, and gradually became for me a symbol of our human civil war, in which the roles seem constantly to change and the objectives to shift and vary. It suggested too a complete reversal of the alignments and alliances which we had come to accept as inevitable.[15]

His comments above are particularly applicable to the 'Third Elegy, (Leaving the City)', and the final 'Tenth Elegy, (The Frontier)'. The 'Third Elegy, (Leaving the City)', is also partly a response to, and appreciation of, C P Cavafy's poems about Alexandria, especially 'The God Leaves Antony'. Antony in Henderson's poem is transformed into those soldiers fated to die. Alexandria itself, or 'Alex' in soldierly parlance, was very much the place for rest and recreation before and after battle:

> ... So long then,
> holy filth of the living. We are going to the familiar
> filth of your negation, to rejoin the proletariat
> of levelling death. Stripes are shed and ranks levelled
> in death's proletariat...

The 'Tenth Elegy, (The Frontier)', with its echoes of Dante's 'Purgatorio', ends with a reconciliation between the living and the dead, 'spanning this history's apollyon chasm.' Apollyon, whose Greek name means 'the Destroyer', is the 'foul fiend' who could be defeated only by Christian standing up to him in Bunyan's *The Pilgrim's Progress*, an inspiring allegory familiar to many soldiers in the desert war, not least Montgomery. The dead become Dantesque in the following lines:

Here gulled, or stuck through the throat like Buonconte,
or haired to grey ash, they are caught in one corral.

Henderson's notes tell us that 'The episode of Buonconte was quoted
to me by a Tuscan partisan in the hills north of Florence.'[16]
It is evident that he came to think, as MacLean confirmed, of the
Elegies as expiation for what we would now call 'survivor's guilt'. His
view of the war as one between two main antagonists, but each riven
by internal class divisions—even if the Nazis were more culpable
than the Allies—was not so very different from Norman Mailer's in
The Naked and the Dead, itself, coincidentally, published in 1948. The
impetus which produced the *Elegies* was quite simple, yet profound
in its implications: 'It was the remark of a captured German officer
which first suggested to me the theme of these poems. He had said,
'Africa changes everything. In reality we are allies, and the desert is
our common enemy".[17]
Relatively neglected are Henderson's pre-war poems, in which
his voice and concerns were similar to those of other poets of the
1930s. Many of these stand up well beyond that intensely political
and ideological 'low, dishonest decade', as Auden called it. Like other
left-leaning poets, such as Auden himself, Spender and Day-Lewis,
he was a university graduate, though not of Oxford, but Cambridge,
where he read modern languages. One short poem, *4 September, 1939*,
is a good example in this vein:

Bonjour, misere

We had twenty years – twenty years for building and learning.
Those twenty years come back no more.
An incendiary dawn is prelude to this soft morning
First morning of the new war.

The notes to the poem are both evocative and informative concerning
Henderson's life at the time:

This quatrain was written about 6am in Kensington Gardens. I had
spent the night under a tree there, having almost no money, and no
place to stay in London. The previous day I had hitch-hiked from

Ledbury in Herefordshire, the HQ of a Quaker organisation for which I worked for several weeks in Nazi Germany that summer. I heard of the declaration of war en route to London.[18]

'Pictures in St Sebald's Church, Nuremberg' describes a mostly indifferent crowd who witness Christ crowned with thorns in a tone suffused with almost Audenesque irony:

> they were ahead of time
> most half disillusioned already
> maybe trying to summon up a little blood-lust
> (here and there some genuine sadists)

Another early poem, 'Ballad of the Twelve Stages of My Youth', is also strongly autobiographical and pictorial, but its striking woodcut sharpness is reminiscent of Brecht. The concluding stanzas read as a kind of farewell to the thirties style:

> From Spain return the Clyde-red brave Brigadiers.
> I clench my fist to greet the red flag furled.
> Our hold has slipped – now Hitler's voice is rasping
> From small square boxes over all the world.
>
> There's fog. I climb the cobbled streets of Oldham
> With other conscripts, and report to one
> Who writes with labour, and no satisfaction
> That I've turned up. – From now, my boyhood's done.

Both in the *Elegies*, and in his post-war poetry, Henderson left what he called 'the unvirile political badinage of the thirties'[19] behind, yet without relinquishing the deeply political nature of nearly everything he wrote.

Henderson also composed lyrics to traditional ballads and folk tunes during the war. Two of the best known are the 'The 51st Highland Division's Farewell to Sicily' and 'Ballad of the D-Day Dodgers'. After the war, he continued to compose ballads and became heavily involved in the folk song revival, which flourished not only in Scotland, but also in Canada and the United States. Kindred spirits in this endeavour were the American folklorist Alan Lomax and the playwright and folksinger Ewan MacColl, both of whom were friends. Henderson's enthusiastic advocacy of the folk song revival led to a famous, and still often debated, clash or 'flyting' with his prickly old friend Hugh MacDiarmid in the pages of the *Scotsman*, and elsewhere.[20] MacDiarmid had a highly elitist attitude towards folksong, even though he admired the old Scottish ballads, while Henderson pointed out how much the folk tradition had contributed to political protest, praising its democratic and egalitarian qualities. The battle was a very fierce one, with no quarter given by either poet, or their respective allies, such as Norman MacCaig in MacDiarmid's camp, and Ian Hamilton Finlay in Henderson's. Their flyting scorched the letters pages of the *Scotsman* for weeks in the spring of 1964. Yet in a letter to the same paper in 1980, after MacDiarmid had died, Henderson insisted there had been no personal animosity between them. As he put it, though their opposing views 'had taken on the high mottled complexion of a medieval flyting,' this was 'in accord with the rules of a traditional native bloodsport which neither of us (I am sure) would have disavowed, and of which furthermore we were both – although in vastly differing degrees of talent and aptitude – by no means unwilling practitioners.'[21]

But a flyting poem which had no direct response from the eminent poet was Henderson's 'To Hugh MacDiarmid'. Subtitled 'On Reading *Lucky Poet*', which refers to MacDiarmid's autobiography, it is in satirical couplets which identify the senior poet's anti-English feelings with small-mindedness and other vices that Henderson thought were endemic in Scottish society at the time, as in these blunt, hectoring lines:

> You list 'Anglophobia' as your recreation,
> But it's Scotland that's driven you to ruination.
> Why not admit it? The meanness, the rancour,
> The philistine baseness, the divisive canker,
> The sly Susanna elder-ism, McGrundyish muck-raking
> Are maladies of Scottish, not English making.

MacDiarmid did not respond to this provocation, at least not in verse, but had he done so, the flyting between them would have been closer in spirit to those between Renaissance makars such as William Dunbar and Walter Kennedy, more than the prose letters in the

Scotsman. Henderson's poem, moreover, certainly resembles that of the flyting makars in its inventively abusive vocabulary and intricate rhyme-scheme. His notes tell us that it was written from a perspective very much outside Scotland: 'This was written at Merarro, in the south Tyrol (Italy) in the autumn of 1945. I was sitting thinking about MacDiarmid. The more I thought, the more I was puzzled.'[22] His puzzlement was all the greater in that his own poems owed much to the elder poet's reinvention of Scots in the modernist vein of twentieth-century poetry.

This is certainly the case with 'The Flyting o' Life and Daith', which displays Henderson at his finest as both poet and songsmith. It is made up of quatrains in vigorous Scots, alternating the personified voices of Life and Death. He described its musical qualities in a letter to his old friend Marian Sugden in April 1963: 'Not long back I completed a new song... to a tune of my own which somewhat resembles the 'urlar' (or 'ground') of a pibroch,'[23] the most solemn kind of bagpipe music. The poem concludes:

> Quo daith, the warld is mine.
> I hae dug a grave, I hae dug it deep,
> For war an' the pest will gar ye sleep.
> Quo daith, the warld is mine.
>
> Quo life, the warld is mine.
> An open grave is a furrow syne.
> Ye'll no keep my seed frae fa'in in.
> Quo life the warld is mine.

Life has the last word, and victory in six of the eleven quatrains, but Death is always around the corner. Another letter, to the folksinger Jimmy MacGregor, in 1967, contained specific instructions about how the poet wanted it to be performed:

'The Flyting' is a song for a single singer. Life and Daith are present in one man. If it were done by two singers as a dialogue, it would be an empty dualism, and I don't think it could ever effectively be made into a group song. The tune is exceptionally exacting, and has to be sustained with grace-noting (which is up to the singer) for eleven verses.[24]

Henderson's ballad is not only reminiscent of traditional folk artistry, but also modernises the trenchant resonances of medieval allegory. It gestated in his mind for quite a long time, as Alec Finlay's notes indicate: 'The Flyting o' Life and Daith' was partly derived from an anonymous medieval German poem which Henderson saw in manuscript in the Library of the University of Göttingen in 1939.'[25] His commitment to the Scottish ballad tradition was so high that his creative energies were dedicated just as much to collecting, like Burns and Scott before him, and tape-recording as many extant ones as possible, hence his field-work for the School of Scottish Studies at the University of Edinburgh. He was also always generous in making his own ballads available to performers and musicians, which is strikingly unlike the current obsession with 'intellectual property rights'. How far Henderson had an entirely different perspective on the matter can be seen in a further 1967 letter to Jimmy MacGregor:

As you know, I have taken an exceedingly liberal attitude towards performances of my own songs by the folk singers of the revival, especially the ones who are just about making a living jigging around the clubs. However, you and Robin are now in a totally different position. I don't think that you could altogether deny, furthermore, that it is partly due to my own work… that you are in a totally different position… As for the songs I collected and put into circulation, I did this in the context of a definite cultural strategy, and as in war one must always allow for losses of one sort or another. (I am not now referring to financial losses.) My hope – and it has been realised in quite a large number of cases – has been to encourage young folk to approach their cultural heritage with real creative élan.[26]

Two of his most famous ballads are 'Rivonia' and 'The Freedom Come-All-Ye'. The former's refrain 'Free Mandela, Free Mandela' was highly prophetic as not only a protest, but also a weapon, and one which historically turned out to be very effective, in the struggle against apartheid in South Africa. Henderson's familiarity with Spanish Civil War songs served him well in composing 'Rivonia'. His description (in lecture notes) of its genesis captures some of the inspired excitement with which it was composed:

'Rivonia' is the name of the farm in South Africa where the South African National Congress leaders had taken refuge and where they were captured. Their trial was often referred to as the Rivonia trial. I made the song just after Nelson Mandela made that magnificent speech from the dock in November 1963. I was in London at the time and singing various Spanish Civil War songs, including 'Viva la Quince Brigada' which has this refrain 'Rumbala, rumbala, rumba-la...' and it struck me that that was rather like the sound of African drums and almost immediately I extemporised 'They have sentenced the men of Rivonia'. It was one of my songs that came together very quickly.[27]

Auden declared that 'poetry makes nothing happen,' but who can really say this about 'Rivonia', however small a factor it may have been in the liberation of the great South African?

As for 'The Freedom Come-All-Ye', it has become a kind of alternative, or dissidents' national anthem in a devolved Scotland. Yet it is anything but narrowly nationalist, and this is confirmed in the following lines, so explicit about Scottish complicity in the British Empire:

Nae mair will the bonnie callants
    Mairch tae war when oor braggarts crousely craw,
Nor wee weans frae pit-heid and clachan
    Mourn the ships sailin' doon the Broomielaw.
Broken families in lands we've herriet,
    Will curse Scotland the Brave nae mair, nae mair;
Black and white, ane til ither mairriet,
    Mak the vile barracks o' their maisters bare.

This ballad is sung so frequently in ceilidhs and protest rallies that many are totally unaware of its authorship. As in the case of Pablo Neruda, few poets have achieved greater immortality.

In his time, Henderson challenged the aesthetics of 'confessional' poetry, which was very much dominant in the late twentieth century, and still remains a challenge to the self-absorbed verse which is very much in vogue at present. What bridged the 'Apollyon's chasm' between the *Elegies for the Dead in Cyrenaica* and his later poems and songs in a more populist balladic form is his undeviating focus on common humanity in all his work.

He is also more European-minded than most late twentieth-century British poets, as is evident not only in his own poems, but also his translations. They are mainly of Italian and German poets, many of them unfamiliar to British and American readers. These include his powerfully felt translations of the Sudeten German war poet Louis Fürnberg (1909-57), with titles like 'Requiem for the Men the Nazis Murdered', which Henderson admired for its unflinching look at violence, and 'From the Serbian Spring 1941', Fürnberg's response to Hitler's invasion of Yugoslavia.

His translations of two poems by Corrado Govoni, 'Lament for the Son' and 'Dialogue of the Angel and the Dead Boy', are almost unbearably moving. Neither poem can be quoted in excerpt without completely distorting the tragedy depicted. They demand to be read in their entirety. Henderson's notes explain the circumstances in which Govoni originally wrote them: 'This is part of a long prose poem, here recast in verse, written by Govoni after the death of his son, Aladino, a partisan of Italy, who was one of 335 hostages shot by the SS under Kappler in the Ardeatine Caves, 24 March 1944.'[28] In a 1946 letter to the poet Maurice Lindsay, Henderson described how Colonel Kappler, at the time in Allied custody, actually requested a Gaelic primer, he was so interested in Scottish culture.[29] Kappler evaded the maximum penalty for war crimes, which only goes to show that the struggle with Apollyon is endless, and true poetry always an arduous pilgrim's progress. Hamish Henderson never shirked from the implications of this insight.

References:

1   Hamish Henderson, *The Armstrong Nose: Selected Letters of Hamish Henderson*, edited by Alec Finlay, (Edinburgh: Polygon, 1996), p. 29.

2   Timothy Neat, *Hamish Henderson: A Biography, Volume 1: The Making of the Poet* (Edinburgh: Polygon, 2007), p. 363.

3   *Ibid.*, p. 363.

4   *Ibid.*, p. 361.

5   Hamish Henderson, *The Armstrong Nose: Selected Letters of Hamish Henderson*, edited by Alec Finlay, (Edinburgh: Polygon, 1996), p. 287.

6   Neat (2007), p. 69.

7   Hamish Henderson, *Elegies for the Dead in Cyrenaica* (Edinburgh: EUSPB, 1977), first published 1948, p. 54.

8   Neat (2007), p. 71.

9   Angus Calder, 'Scots Language in Transition', *Chapman*, 82, 1995, pp. 63-7.

10   Neat (2007), p. 358.

11   Robert Crawford, *Scotland's Books* (London: Penguin Books, 2007), p. 603.

12   Neat (2007), p. 79.

13   Hamish Henderson, *Collected Poems and Songs*, edited by Raymond Ross (Edinburgh: Curly Snake Publishing, 2000), p. 8.

14   *Elegies*, p. 12.

15   *Ibid..*, p. 59.

16   *Ibid..*, p. 55.

17   *Ibid..*, p. 59.

18   *Collected Poems and Songs*, p. 156.

19   *Ibid.*, p. 162.

20   A selection of these letters can be found in *The Armstrong Nose*, edited by Alec Finlay, and Timothy Neat devotes an entire chapter to the context of their acrimonious exchanges in the second volume of his biography.

21   *The Armstrong Nose*, p. 236.

22   *Collected Poems and Songs*, p. 162.

23   *The Armstrong Nose*, p. 113.

24   *Ibid.*

25   *Ibid.*, p. 115.

26   *Ibid.*, pp. 158-59.

27   Timothy Neat, *Hamish Henderson: A Biography, Volume 2: Poetry Becomes People*, (Edinburgh: Polygon, 2009), p. 188.

28   *Collected Poems and Songs*, p. 162.

29   *The Armstrong Nose*, p. 8.

ENCOMPASS THE CROSS-SWORD BLADES: HAMISH HENDERSON'S POETRY

Tessa Ransford

In *Pilgrim's Progress,* John Bunyan describes the valley faced by Christian after his life and death struggle with Apollyon during which he had found strength by crying 'When I fall, I shall arise' as '…a wilderness, a land of deserts and of pits, a land of drought, and of the shadow of death'. When the battle was over 'there came to him a hand, with some of the leaves of the Tree of Life'.

Dino Campana's 'In Un Momento', translated by Hamish Henderson, contains the line 'They were her roses, they were my roses/ This journey we call love/ With our blood and tears we made the roses/ That shone for a moment in the morning sun…'[1]

Carla Sassi, an Italian academic who specialises in Scottish literature, claims that Henderson helped her to see 'the individual elements' of her own culture 'assembled' in a way she had not known before, a way that allowed 'high and folk literature to interact' and where language itself is 'a torrent of music'.[2]

Adrian Mitchell, in a short introductory piece for the 2008 Birlinn edition of Henderson's *Elegies for the Dead in Cyrenaica* writes: 'The poems work best in company. Listen to the music of their long and often melancholy lines – sometimes like the pipes heard from a distance'.[3]

Here we have an outline of four strands to guide us in the poetry of Hamish Henderson: firstly his Christian Humanism/Socialism on the pilgrimage journey of his own life, and its demands for commitment;[4] secondly, the journey as one energised by love (*Eros* and *Thanatos* in an eternal flyting) where beauty overcomes fear even if demanding 'blood and tears'; thirdly Henderson's integrative vision, seeking consumation in the understanding that the whole is more than the sum of the parts, but that each part is essential to the whole and is related to all other parts, however seemingly fragmented; lastly, Henderson's love of company, his sense of the bonds of brotherhood, and his delight in the auditory companionship also of both word and music.

Let us call them pilgrimage, love-energy, integration, companionship. The four are themselves integrated and indivisible, forming a core and impetus to the work and works Henderson produced in poetry, song and service to 'the cause of the people.'[5] Raymond Ross and Alec Finlay have written comprehensively and illuminatingly about Hamish Henderson's poetry in articles and introductory essays.[6] My proposal is to 'touch down' on these four prominent themes or aspects of the *oeuvre*, in each case taking poems as illustrative examples and allowing imaginative and connecting ripples to emanate from them.

Pilgrimage

The vision of life as a pilgrimage does not need to be linear. Life happens in curves, cycles and circles. It begins, waxes, wanes and ends on larger and smaller scales, even within an individual lifetime, and is transformed onto a new plane where it spirals again, but the gyre is itself onward. Yeats and Rilke often celebrate this kind of movement and pattern in their poetry (see Rilke's 'I live my life in widening rings').[7] In the 'First Elegy' Henderson describes 'the brutish desert' and asserts 'the dead land is insatiate/ and necrophilious.' As the Bible tells us, 'we are sojourners on the earth'. Henderson picks this up in the 'Fourth Elegy': 'We're uneasy, knowing ourselves to be nomads,/ impermanent guests on this bleak moon-surface/ of dents and ridges, craters and depressions.' This could be applied to the world in general, the whole of life on earth and of human life to which we belong, not possessively to a specific acre, race, genus or nation on it. We are here to both stay and not to stay, to be home and away, to give and to give up, to love and to leave, each of us completing a fragment of the pattern which is the whole. Nevertheless, it is significant that Henderson chose to settle and make his home in his motherland, Scotland, having left at the age of nine, after his education in England

and his service in Africa and Italy during the war. He made a decision and commitment to Scotland's culture, to Scottish poetry and to accepting the role as such of 'Scottish poet', but more than that as, in some respects, a leader, seer or bard.

Henderson's poem 'Jokers Abounding, for Peter Duval Smith' is headed 'Freedom Becomes People: Prologue' in the issue of *Chapman* celebrating Henderson's eightieth birthday.[8] This follows an introductory note quoting Heinrich Heine: 'Freedom, which has hitherto only become man here and there, must pass into the mass itself, into the lowest strata of society, and become people.'[9] Apart from the obvious direct link to Henderson's signature tune, the poem-song 'The Freedom Come-All-Ye', this shows how Henderson used Heine's theory about freedom, transferring it to or identifying it with poetry, so much so that Timothy Neat called the second volume of his biography of Henderson *Poetry Becomes People.*[10]

In his introductory note to *Chapman*, Henderson sets out his guiding ideas very clearly. He claims that 'poetry needs to become, to *be* everyone'; to achieve this 'we must not be ashamed to go to school with the folksingers—the traditional singers...' and 'we must abjure self-gratificatory elitism' and look for 'a people's culture' reflective of Heine's 'revolutionary humanism.' No doubt this clear outlining of his guiding principles was something Henderson could do at the end of his life, whereas in the thick of it he was inevitably following the thread of his destiny without certainty as to where it was leading. Peter Duval Smith, first encountered in Cambridge, produced the first BBC broadcast of the *Elegies*. In dedicating 'Jokers Abounding' to him, Henderson was rallying a comrade in arms who will need luck to emerge from 'history's ambuscades'. The metaphor is one of pilgrimage, in which the individual has to avoid ambush, the apollyon abysses, the uncouth dalliance of death, must walk 'through glowering ravine and too-silent valley', and 'encompass the crossed sword-blades'.

These metaphors spring from archetypal sources such as *Pilgrim's Progress* and the *Book of Revelation*, where 'the angel of the bottomless pit,' or King of the Locusts, is Abaddon, meaning 'destroyer' in Hebrew but Apollyon in Greek. The medieval *Totentanz* is also shadowed here and clearly evoked in other poems such as 'We show you that Death as a Dancer', and the ancient ritual of crossed swords in duel or dance feels almost Rosicrucian. The 'Tenth Elegy' echoes this theme at the end, with the hope of reconciliation between life and death 'spanning this history's Apollyon chasm'. Christian's bitter fight in *Pilgrim's Progress* with the fiend Apollyon in the Vale of Humiliation follows a long allegorical dialogue or flyting between them as to where allegiance lies. This was clearly significant to Henderson, who had to make his own choice of allegiance when the war against fascism developed and to fight it meant joining the forces led by 'the bosses' whose motivation for profits and privilege he despised.

'The Jokers Abounding' is lightly rhymed but strongly rhythmical, indeed a dance itself, almost mouth music in that its meanings are so deep as to seem almost nonsensical to the conscious mind. Indeed the jokers or tricksters in the title are those who defy categorisation, who slip between the demarcation lines and upset the paradigms. Charles Williams's novel *The Greater Trumps* (1932), which Henderson probably knew, celebrates 'The Fool' as the unobserved, unnoticed secret mover and shaker in the world.[11] Henderson declares that he carried a copy of Yeats's later poems with him during the war campaigns[12] and that he particularly responded to the poems 'Under Ben Bulben' and 'The Circus Animals' Desertion' (published in January 1939). The latter poem features The Fool and The Blind Man, characters from tarot cards, but the following lines may have been significant: 'Players and painted stage took all my love/ And not those things that they were emblems of'. That could surely be seen as a warning to any literary poet in time of war. No showing off with clever tricks ('circus animals'). No need self-indulgently to 'seek a theme' when confronted with the detritus of war and 'the foul rag and bone shop of the heart'. 'Under Ben Bulben' also enjoins the poet that his task is to 'Bring the soul of man to God'.[13]

Willa Muir had received a great deal of advice from Henderson while researching and writing her book *Living with Ballads*.[14] She discusses the origin of ballads and claims that they belong to 'the archetypal world of feeling' and that they 'bypass the conscious mind', a skill that belongs to the school of traditional singers. Henderson himself possessed this skill as is demonstrated in poems such as this, which are at the same time contemporary, engaged politically, yet historical, archetypal and riddling. He himself explains references to *The Thrie Estaitis* and to William Wallace before the battle of Stirling Bridge. Henderson has no problem in writing in English, yet adding Scots when allusion and sound demand. Words are dancers and swords. They must move and cut, delight and fight. They are not to be constrained within one language or idiom. The crossed sword blades might also bring to mind the Saltire or Leonardo da Vinci's Pythagorean man, for 'man the measure of all things.' Henderson's translations of Hölderlin are of significance. Hölderlin's 'Patmos' is an elegiac poem where earth is understood as bereft of the gods who are no longer accessible, yet even in their absence and anonymity 'the immortals must have a sacrifice'. The stark lines 'where danger is, grows/ that which can save' ('Wo aber Gefahr ist wächst/ das Rettende auch') is a beautiful example of the riddling that spars with life and death. Hölderlin liked to write in Greek metres, and Henderson translates some of Hölderlin's alcaics, as in 'The Applause of Men', (Menschenbeifall) where we find: 'Och, the mob is content with what counts in the market place,/ And the god of the slave is the man who kicks him around'.[15] Here is an admission that we have lost 'the archaic world of feeling', with its tribal, communal rather than individual, more self-conscious ethos. Yet that old world with its power structures and demand for sacrifice is never far away. Rescue is found only in confronting the danger, in demanding the freedom of the individual, not as apart from but as a member of 'the mob', the people, who have 'become freedom'. The struggle is against being unquestioningly obedient, as so many of the German prisoners were, whom Henderson interrogated in his duty as an intelligence officer in the North African and Italian campaigns, giving this phenomenon the grim German description of *Kadavergehorsam* (see 'Fourth Elegy': 'who shoulders his shovel with corpse-obedience'). The pilgrimage, then, can also be seen as that of individuation, for despite the corporate and shared nature of much experience, each is born, makes choices and dies alone.

Life-energy: Eros and Thanatos

Hamish Henderson, while studying at Moray House in the late 1940s, wrote in his personal notebook that, ' ...literature, to be literature, must desire to be life not an idea of life'. It is hard to be impartial if you have been 'in the midst of things', was a comment made by an editor in Rome on Henderson's *Elegies for the Dead in Cyrenaica*. Henderson's response, as he records in his foreword to the first edition of the *Elegies* in 1948, was to reflect: 'It certainly *is* terribly difficult, if one has been (to use his phrase) in the midst of things... I begin to feel that it is next to impossible if one has not.'

There is no doubt that in Henderson's poems, generally speaking, whether written before, during or after the war, there is distinctly an unflinching grappling with cruelty and horror, yet there is the core determination to both embrace and transcend it by acknowledging that the real war is one of life against death, humans against the desert, as a captured German officer told Henderson was the reality of the situation, and that 'the dead, the innocent' ('First Elegy'), deserve a Remembrancer ('Tenth Elegy') and a song ('First Elegy'). This is in the sense that without the singer there can be no heroes, even as Homer brought into being the forgotten heroes of the Trojan War. *Elegies for the Dead in Cyrenaica*, published first by John Lehmann in 1948, and winning the first Somerset Maugham Award, is a unity of stunning poems. I use that rather colloquial word advisedly: The whole being is stunned in order to be quickened. The *Elegies* achieve the aim of being literature that constitutes life, rather than an idea of it.

Begun during the North African desert campaigns as early as 1942, they ring true to the witness of another poet who fought in the desert and wrote about it: Sorley Maclean. In his introduction to the 1977 edition of the *Elegies*, MacLean (verses from whose poem 'Death Valley', about the young German soldier 'who showed no pleasure in his death', are quoted in Gaelic at the beginning of Part Two) vouches for the authenticity of 'the physical and psychological 'feel'' of the desert warfare scenario, and the tormenting guilt of survivors who may not have changed the world for the better even if they have helped to 'prevent its change for the worse'. The choice of Cyrenaica in the title resonates with the gospel record that Simon of Cyrene was forcibly volunteered by the Roman soldiers to help Jesus carry the heavy wooden cross through the via dolorosa on the way to Calvary. He was thus a reluctant hero, as were most of those fighting in the desert on both the Allied and the German side. Simon of Cyrene was doubtless one of 'precious few heroes' in that Gospel story, even as he came to the aid of the 'human and animal' Jesus (see 'First Elegy (End of a Campaign)': 'there were no gods and precious few heroes'). The title of the poem: 'The Heroic Song for the Runners of Cyrene', which concludes the *Elegies*, is another tribute to this emblematic figure, for Henderson explains: 'Cyrene... is for me a symbol of civilised humanity, or our 'human house'.' The human house—earth, as it

were, as home for the human race—is a phrase Henderson perhaps
borrowed from the writings and ideas of William Morris. Henderson acknowledges the influence of Eliot in the *Elegies*, of Whitman too, and even Kipling, but he also acknowledges German poets whom he had read before the war, such as Rilke, Heine and Hölderlin. He states: 'If any poems have directly influenced my *Elegies*, I think it is the poems of Hölderlin and especially the later poems, the poems of his madness. In a time of tremendous suffering and war, small wonder that poems of a poet's personal suffering, horror, ecstasy and extreme agony should influence another poet.'[16] It is possible that the unattributed quotation heading the 'Tenth Elegy':

> One must die because one knows them, die
> of their smile's ineffable blossom, die
> of their light hands

is from Rilke.[17] (Rilke's 'Sixth Elegy' ends with: 'For whenever the Hero stormed through the halts of love/ … / turning away, he'd stand at the end of smiles, another').[18] The structure with 'one' is German 'man'. However, the positioning of the word 'die' in emphasis at the end of each line, yet beginning a semantic unit, is similar to that used by Henderson in the poem 'Brosnachadh' ('martial music for the bagpipe classed under *ceol mor*,' according to *Dwelly's Gaelic Dictionary*), dedicated to 'the partisans of peace'. Here end-rhyming words begin sentences all through six verses, giving a heavy, rousing rhythm or summons, as is a feature of pipe music. 'Leben ist Tod und Tod ist auch ein Leben' ('Life is death and death is also a life') is the last line of Hölderlin's 'In Lieblicher Bläue…', a poem considering the sufferings of the Greek heroes, and 'Hyperion's Schicksalslied' must have seemed appropriate to the dice with death in battle:

> *To us has been granted*
> *No place on earth to abide;*
> *Tormented we creatures*
> *Totter and tumble*
> *Head over heels from*
> *Hour to hour*
> *Like water from rock-face*
> *To precipice hurtling*
> *On and on down into unknown depths.*[19]

Henderson also acknowledges the influence of MacDiarmid's 'Hymns to Lenin', dealing with social injustice. Henderson was only twenty-two, and had not yet met MacDiarmid, although he had read and championed his poetry, when he started working fragmentarily on the *Elegies*, 'written between March 1943 and December 1947 in North Africa, Italy and Scotland', as he tells us in the foreword to the first edition. Though no doubt aspiring to find a place among the accepted literary modernists of his era, as any such gifted young man would, Henderson very soon found what can with certainty be called his own voice and made his elegies unique and extraordinary poems, classifiable as war poems but far transcending any label. They became both Henderson's garland and his albatross, since more such literary 'art-poetry' of high quality was expected of him after the war, when he began to find his interest in what is fundamental and elemental leading him backwards through the folk tradition and, possibly even earlier, to 'King Orfeo' itself (a medieval ballad recorded by Child where the musician king tries to redeem his wife stolen by the king of faery), as a way of going forward in the right direction for bringing the people back from 'the underworld' or as a way of tuning in to 'the other world'? The Stewarts of Blairgowrie, who felt 'the Sidhe have never left Glenshee and they've never left Scotland', recognised something 'other' and unique in Henderson as they worked with him on song recordings.[20] In the poem 'My Way Home' we glimpse the lonely Orphic singer or seer, recognised only by the creatures of nature. It is almost as if Henderson alone could not accept the dichotomy (which he likened to an apartheid) which others, especially MacCaig and MacDiarmid, imposed on the diversity in types of poetic expression, particularly between oral and written forms, and the creative processes.[21]

The ten elegies plus the 'Interlude' and the 'Heroic Song for the Runners of the Cyrene', each unique and able to stand alone, often with a quotation as lead-in, are nevertheless woven into a unity. Although the Eros-Thanatos theme runs through them all, the 'Tenth Elegy (The Frontier)', has a particular over-view. Imagining tourists flying over the former scenes of battle and death and seeing nothing: 'they'll be certain/ they've seen it, they've seen all …' They are more interested in 'Trojan defence-works' than more recent history, equally heroic, bloody and tragic in that 'benighted deadland'. There is little to 'arrest them' beyond accidental survival of 'dried blood in the sangars'. The poem revives memories of the dead, 'not sleeping but dead'. Jesus on his way to raise Lazarus from the dead says 'Our friend Lazarus sleepeth but I go that I may awake him out of sleep.' Henderson's Christian Humanism is here denying any belief in supernatural resurrection.

The conflict between life and death is here and now on earth in life's time. The scene is a coastline, evocative of Scottish coastlines and perhaps also of the desertification of the Clearances, alluded to in the 'Fifth Elegy,' and of Hölderlin's lines in 'Der Einzige', (referring to Christ standing alone in a desert background and perhaps of Rilke's 'one single thing once prayed or tended or knelt to' in his seventh of the *Duino Elegies*,[22] and Rilke is alluded to in Henderson's 'Eighth Elegy'. Even as Hölderlin feels himself closer to the imaginary coast of Greece than to his 'Vaterland,' so Henderson, throughout the *Elegies,* is constantly touching German literature, demonstrating that he is writing for the dead on either side. Henderson picks out 'that bend of Halfaya' (subject of the 'Second Elegy') where 'the convoys used to stick, raw meat for the Jabos.' (Jabos were *Jagdbomber*, dive-bombers, accentuating the gruesomeness of this image). Turning aside 'to perform a duty', 'restoring a fallen cross-piece', the poet takes on the public role or task of 'remembrancer,' gathering the fragments and weaving them into song, creating the heroes.

A detailed remembering then ensues about how some fled towards the sea and 'darkened their waves'; were 'caught in one corral' as, running and stumbling, they were gutted, stuck through the throat like Buaconte (a reference to Dante's 'Purgatorio V,' recounted to Henderson by a Tuscan partisan) or 'charred to grey ash.' But the remembering brings torment and guilt for the survivors: 'their sleep's our unrest, we lie bound in their inferno'. This is also suggested by the lines quoted as subtitle: 'one must die because one knows them...' The poem suggests that such after-torment helps to allay the guilt, since it makes for an 'alliance' with those who were killed. The impulse is for revenge, evoked in an image of 'seedlings of lament like swordsmen' and 'bitter keening of women'—a conflating of Celtic with Arabic culture here—as those images are followed by the choking cloaks of 'back-edged vendetta'. The way out is to go further in: 'inhabit that desert of canyon and dream', in order to reconcile survivors with the dead, life with death, by embracing them: 'Take iron in your arms!'

But this is not so much physically as mentally, for it is implied that 'the tyrannous myth' (which traps its adherents into 'corpse-like obedience') is even harder to combat than 'the real terror'; therefore, as in the 'Interlude', quoting from Scottish history and the murder of the Red Comyn in Dumfries Kirk, we have no choice but to: 'mac siccar'.

There is a sense here, however, that, rather than a dualistic, antagonistic approach to life and death, Henderson seeks a complementary more holistic, dialectic understanding. This may have come to him to some extent from his familiarity with Rilke's *Duino Elegies*, where death is embraced and held gently as preceding life: 'den ganzen Tod, noch vor dem Leben so/ sanft zu enthalten...' ('Fourth Elegy')—and essential to life. In the midst of life there will be a presence of death and in the midst of death there will be a presence of life, as in the yin-yang emblem and as in Poussin's 'et in arcadia ego'. Water and aridity, fire and ice are similar complementary opposites, challenging and enabling one another in Henderson's poems, as in 'The Salamander'.

Seen in this light, Henderson's later poem, 'The Flyting o' Life and Daith', can be understood less as an argument to win through or lose, (as is the case in the *Pilgrim's Progress* archetype) than as an analysis of the eternal rhythm in which we are nonetheless required unambiguously, heroically, to struggle on the side of life at all times. A flyting is more a test of wits and enjoyment of repartee, a discussion, reminiscent of the Devil and God bargaining in their proposed game with Job, and certainly a reckoning, as in Dunbar's 'Done is a battell on the dragon blak'. Tom Scott writes about Dunbar's poem: 'This is a heroic poem, the triumph of spring over winter, good over evil, health over disease, life over death, man over himself... at once personal and communal, original and traditional.'[23] It would be hard to find a better description of Henderson's 'Flyting'. In a letter to Jimmie MacGregor in January 1967 Henderson explains: "'The Flyting' is a song for a single singer. Life and Death are present in the one man. If it were done by two singers as a dialogue, it would be an empty dualism...'[24]

The quietly triumphant ending of the poem—when Life states: 'The warld is mine/ An open grave is a furrow syne./ Ye'll no keep my seed frae fa'in in'—may seem verbally a victory. But Henderson knew that words are not unattached from the physical. The contemporary Leipzig German philosophical thinker and writer, Elmar Schenkel, in an essay on 'the Body in Poetry and Imagination' makes a case for the physical origins of poetry in the human body, and in the earth's soil: 'any poetic activity is close to one or more of the primeval attitudes of cultivation,' and he claims that 'the soil must be turned before it produces life' and that furrows can be approximated to lines of verse, turnings.[25] The King of the Locusts is there too in the threat: 'Your silly sheaves crine in my fire/ My worm keeks in your barn and byre…'

Henderson's concept of the life that contends with death is one of the substantiality of life, its toil, sweat, tears and laughter. And it is that life to which he wants his works of 'literature' to approximate. His attitude has echoes of John Macmurray's philosophical view that the unit of the person is an I-Thou, relational one, and that fear is the chief enemy of faith, (an obstacle to life and the servant of death therefore).[26] Henderson is reported by his biographer Timothy Neat to have written movingly, in a long list of all that love is and does, worthy of Corinthians 1:13: 'Love operates faster and surer than time or space or both' and 'Love cannot operate on your behalf as long as your own sickly fear will not permit love to operate on your behalf.' Thus life is conflated with Love in the Eros-Thanatos sense.

An integrative vision

Timothy Neat accords to Duncan Glen 'the best critique yet published of Henderson's anthem, 'The Freedom Come-All-Ye'.[27] Here Glen, identifying the song with the CND movement and anti-Polaris campaign of the 1960s, affirms that it 'is firmly rooted in Scotland and Scots vocabulary and the native song tradition' yet embraces the Third World and 'the new socialist freedom' in its last two lines. Glen calls the poem-song 'a masterpiece without qualification' belonging 'to all time and all people'. David Stenhouse makes clear, in a piece written for the *Sunday Herald*, that the song is deliberately international and, in Henderson's own words, 'is an anti-nationalist song' because it aims to 'unite the human race' against tyranny and injustice anywhere.[27]

On New Year's Day 2010 in the Old Town of Edinburgh—an extremely cold day—I was walking up the Canongate when I encountered a piper playing 'The Freedom Come-All-Ye'. The City was full of tourists who had thronged to Edinburgh for the Hogmanay parties which have suddenly become big business, so that the familiar shut-down of a Scottish New Year has been transformed into a dark, cold scenario for almost enforced jollity. I attended prayers and poems for peace in St Giles Kirk, having wandered round Holyrood Palace and thought about the dire destruction of medieval glory in the old Abbey where a radiantly beautiful, cultured young queen had been married, before being systematically destroyed by a death-worshipping, beauty-hating, patriarchal religion. Somehow the strains of the 'Freedom' sounded a call for sanity and hope amidst it all.

Henderson was fully aware of the entertainment type of folksy 'come-all-ye' song of Irish origin, which overacts and coaxes its audience in an almost pantomime fashion with topicality and knowing jokes. He understood the Irish-rooted poet William MacGonagall as being in this tradition, and therefore not so much a poor poet as a valid, poetic version of popular entertainment. This is in contrast to the great ballads in their 'sensuous austerity',[29] where the audience is mentally and emotionally at one with the singer and does not need to be wooed. However, the inclusive aspect of the 'come all-ye' tradition was not something Henderson deplored; on the contrary. For poetry and song to 'become people,' in the sense of 'freedom becomes people,' it must connect at a deep level to human communities and movements, nationally and internationally, passed from singer to singer with varying versions and becoming part of an anonymous treasure in due course, attributable only to this or that singer's version, rather than to an individual 'author'.

While studying at Moray House for a teaching qualification in 1946-47, Henderson 'began a systematic study of the philosophy of A N Whitehead, whose unified vision complemented many aspects of Hamish's own thinking'.[30] While accepting that nature is not passive but in constant transformation, Henderson understood Whitehead as seeking a common principle—the principle of 'life'—in the hope of abolishing 'all the contradictions and dualism implicit in most philosophy...' Due to an increasing understanding of dialectics, thanks to Marx's theories, post-war thinking in Europe was struggling to find systems that unified, or synthesised opposites and dualisms. MacDiarmid himself famously cried that he wanted to be 'whaur extremes meet'. However he did not seem able to escape from the ever-persistent, underlying concept of the existence of extremes. Buddhist and Hindu philosophies, which understand the phenomenal world as a veil for an invisible unity, have vocabularies which make non-dualistic thinking possible, but western languages themselves are riddled with either-or vocabulary. If Whitehead, according to Henderson's reflective notes, has 'a vision of the Universe evolving dialectically under the imminent control of God', so also did the French Jesuit thinker, Teilhard de Chardin; and John Macmurray's applied philosophical views were also based on dialectical theory.

It is interesting that the concept of *autopoesis*, developed in the last decade or two of the twentieth century by scientifically-based writers such as Steven Rose, Fritjof Capra and Rupert Sheldrake, make a neat argument for the kind of integrative vision Henderson himself both had and sought to have. Rose states that 'Living systems need to be dynamic if they are to survive', and that 'self-organisation and self-repair are essential autopoetic properties'. He continues: 'All living forms are active players in their own futures.' And sums up, 'The organism is both the weaver and the pattern it weaves, the choreographer and the dance that is danced.' (This closely echoes Yeats' 'How can we tell the dancer from the dance?')[31] Capra defines the concept of autopoesis as a system that is 'self-bounded, self-generating and self-perpetuating', keeping itself constantly in a being-with-becoming state of 'poised equilibrium'. Built into the concept of autopoesis, however, is the understanding of self-limitation. When the conditions for life no longer pertain, there will be decline and ending.[32] Sheldrake propounds a theory of morphic resonance, which shapes and stabilises morphic fields, in nested levels of complexity. And he claims that at all levels of complexity organisms will display 'holistic properties'. He suggests that 'a collective memory underlies our mental activity', rather as Jung suggested we are enveloped in a collective unconscious,[33] even as our individual memory of our past self organises our present consciousness.

To return to 'The Freedom Come-All-Ye'. The MacDiarmid/Henderson controversy about the value of folk or high-art poetry is surely transcended here. The poem is a poem and not eminently memorable in terms of the words for singing. It is without repetition or chorus. As with many German *lieder*, hymns and ballads, each verse has two parts of four lines, rhyming ABAB and CDCD, the second part introducing a tune change in lines five and six and returning to base in the last two lines. Although each of the three verses repeats the tune, swaying towards and away antiphonally as in a dance, it is also 'through-composed', in that there is a progression of mental process culminating in a climax in the last line. Based on a bagpipe tune, 'The Bloody Fields of Flanders', the poem is flowing and sinuous, with grace notes and tripping sequences.

The words themselves are subtle, though seemingly simple, and the line-ending rhymes play the variations, with the first of each pair of lines having a two-syllable 'weak', open ending and the second a single-syllable closed ending. In a ballad, however, the second syllable is often given due stress, as is the case in 'The Freedom Come-All-Ye' Thus 'dawin' is the way to pronounce 'dawn', rather than a Scots pronunciation for dawn. This lets light and air into the poem, giving it the exuberance of sailing down the river. The Scots idiom prevails, often with words of particular significance and colour with no English equivalent such as 'rottans' and 'loanins', 'crousely craw', 'roch', 'heelster-gowdie', 'callants', 'gallus', but the poem does not shun a word in English here and there. In that sense it expresses what Gavin Greig called 'bilingualism in one language, which includes English and goes beyond it'.[34] It is in a Scots known as ballad Scots, used in the traditional ballads, which transcends particular dialect or dating, (Willa Muir describes time as 'a felt process' in the ballads), making the words carry the images and narrative regardless of their linguistic parentage. In this poem words are related by sound and assonance so that they make their own music, even if not being sung.

Throughout the series of flyting letters in the *Scotsman* between MacDiarmid and Henderson in 1964 as to the importance of the folk tradition in song and poetry, Henderson was never in doubt that it was a false dichotomy and that 'separation of poetry from music is a passing phenomenon'.[35] Even if afforded the scholarly term 'troubadour', Henderson insisted that troubadour/intellectual was a false antithesis: 'I don't think of myself as a troubadour'.[36] He felt that there should not be a barrier between poetry and song. 'I think that the two have to go together. I intend to go on writing in this way.' MacDiarmid clearly felt 'menaced', however, by the folk revival and its seeming herd-mentality. He writes, referring to his earlier sympathies, ' …the folksong movement had not then assumed its present menacing form'.[37] As David Craig observed, for his part, in the letters, MacDiarmid was at that time 'obdurately anti-folksong.'[38] Yet he wanted his poems 'spoken in the factories and fields', as articulated in his 'Second Hymn to Lenin'. The greatest composers and poets of whatever nation and whatever age have drawn creative inspiration from the folk tradition. However, as MacDiarmid contended, this is not the same as reviving the folk tradition for its own sake, rather than as a political or creative tool for modernism. It is somewhat ironic that Marxism, which produced the intellectual Sardinian thinker, Gramsci, whose letters from prison were translated by Henderson, and who championed community arts as a way of fostering an alternative to official bourgeois culture, should also have produced Stalinism and the need for a *Samisdat*.

Contentiously, probably neither Henderson nor MacDiarmid was interested in the folk tradition *intrinsically*. Henderson valued the popular endorsement it gave him, a literature of 'presentification', a theory taken from Gramsci, and a lively direct contact and platform for practising his skill in word and music in the service of the people; whereas MacDiarmid feared it would keep people submerged in some kind of cultural opiate for the masses, whence they would not be able to awaken to their own condition and stir themselves to improve it. Henderson's sense of his own pilgrimage, however, gave him impetus for a spirit of resistance to imposition from above and commitment to an integrated vision in all he undertook. The fact that two such great thinkers should have tussled with the place of culture nationally and internationally over those mid-century decades is perhaps a reproach to the arguments based solely on commercial outcomes, which prevail nowadays in this sphere. Indeed, Henderson was always fearful that commercialism would bully and sully the ballad-singing integrity of the travelling people and other tradition-bearers. As stated earlier, the nature of the folk songs and ballads was of their being passed from singer to singer, community to community, and for words and tunes to have many variants, often losing all trace of any original author. That was how Henderson was happy for it to be with his own folk-song-related poems and ballads.

Most of the themes in Henderson's life experience and interests can be found woven into 'The Freedom Come-All-Ye' which Adam McNaughtan describes as 'the perfect match of text and tune'.[39] We can feel Henderson's love of the Scottish landscape and identification with it whether in sky, mountain or city, in the most memorable phrase of the poem:' the great glen of the world', but also in 'roses and geans' as they 'turn tae bloom', and in outrage at the 'sport and play' that replaced people in the Highland glens as a result of the Clearances. We can sense the young Henderson's memory of the

Highland community he shared with his mother, listening to singers and storytellers in Scots and Gaelic when they lived at Spittal of Glenshee and in his early schooldays in Blairgowrie, in the evocation of 'the bairns o' Adam finding 'breid, barley bree and painted room' in freedom's 'hoose'. We are reminded of Henderson's gut hatred (see 'Hate Poem') of the oppression of the 'bonnie callants' ordered by their empire-building overlords (gallus rogues and 'rottans'), to 'mairch tae war when oor braggarts crousely craw'. The grief and sorrow of being forced by poverty to emigrate or enlist is evoked as 'wee weans' 'mourn the ships sailin' doon the Broomielaw' but the wreaking of equal oppression through 'vile barracks' in the lands that were settled or enslaved is not overlooked in the next lines: 'Broken families in lands we've herriet' and the ironic suggestion of 'Scotland the Brave', Scotland of the Declaration of Arbroath, being a curse to such nations. Thus Henderson is recalling the oppression of Scots by Scots and Anglo-Scots as it went hand in hand with the oppression by Scots in the service of Empire elsewhere in the world. The two are interlinked, as the oppressed all too often become expert oppressors in their turn. Intermarriage, which had been a vicious taboo in apartheid South Africa, is welcomed as something that will become the norm.

Throughout these first two verses in succinct and vivid imagery a deep, heartfelt, gut-felt love of the land and its people is conveyed, despite awareness of the failures and dangers inherent in the population having for so long been traumatised by oppression and loss, so that Scots were/are so deprived of their languages, culture and self-confidence that they were/are capable of speaking up for independence in any part of the world save that of their own country. For Scots it seems, freedom is alien. All too easily, heeding 'whit the hoodies croak for doom', any vision of freedom for Scotland seems unimaginable, of freedom as something that can be accepted as real within Scotland, to be 'at hame wi'. In the last four lines Henderson recalls John MacLean, imprisoned for his stand on behalf of international workers against World War One. His 'John MacLean March' finds a place in 'The Freedom Come-All-Ye'. The march was written for the memorial gathering for the twenty-fifth anniversary of his death in November 1948, (a time when communism was still very much espoused in its idealism by Henderson and others, such as MacDiarmid and Sorley MacLean), sung to Henderson's own arrangement of a traditional pipe tune, in its manner a calling to arms of the clans and the troops. Thus, Henderson is so in tune with the almost anonymity of folksongs and ballads that he can allude to his own such compositions without embarrassment! Indeed, Adam McNaughtan has shown how several traditional songs from 'the shared song stock' are alluded to in the vocabulary and imagery of the poem.[40] And finally, Henderson's ballad-chant on behalf of the South African struggle against apartheid, 'Rivonia', written to a Spanish Republican tune, identifying with the stand for the freedom of his people taken by Nelson Mandela, also imprisoned, is called to mind in the last two lines: 'a black boy frae yont Nyanga... ' Nyanga was a township in Cape Town in which a great deal of suffering was endured, which therefore stands as a symbol for such centres of oppression and resistance in the Third World.

Henderson's inclusive integrity of vision is something that cannot be split up into analytical segments. His work also settles itself into an integrated whole, one poem or song linking to the others and beyond. His aims in his work transcend convenient divisions of culture, such as oral and literary, heich and laich, national and international, protestant or catholic, town and country, past and present, heritage and innovation, intellectual and sensual, male and female, this or that language, popular or elite. Moreover, they also transcend the literary factions themselves, warring as to who should be included in which latest anthology. Political factions are also transcended in his desire for a peaceful, integrated world, free from tyrannies of class or commerce, fanatically-imposed political or religious structures or empire-building. As Henderson says himself in his introduction to *Chapman* 42: 'What Heine says of freedom applies also to poetry. Poetry becomes everyone, and should be everyone.'

Companionship

In the poem 'Journey to a Kingdom', the introductory phrase— 'Alone and alonie/ I climb Balmano Street' —is repeated twice more: the second time at the start of the second stanza and the third time running over the second last and last line of the third stanza. It is a stark poem, comparing the conditions of life in the slums of the city to 'early morning by Schiehallion', and the 'lovely tongues' wave-beating language' of the Gaeltachd, where there is still no comfort to be found, since 'Brigades of innocent sheep/ Have put a race to rout.'

The poem demonstrates the difficulty of identifying 'community' in Scotland and of reviving it, and the almost impossibility for the twentieth-century poet of speaking with and for the people. In this light an existential loneliness is detectable in Henderson, orphaned as he was at thirteen and with no support from extended family. In his 'Ballad of the Twelve Stations of My·Youth' the first verse opens with 'I climb with Neil the shiny braes of Lornty/ Or walk my lane by drumlie Ericht side.'

Henderson needed friends and companions and he sought and found them in Cambridge, in the army, among the travelling people, among fellow folk-song enthusiasts, among colleagues, but remained at a deep level vulnerable and 'alonie'. Even his years with the 51st Highland Brigade in North Africa and Italy, full of comradeship in hardship as they were, must have been at a practical level also lonely for an intelligence officer. His choice of the ceilidh, oral culture, companionship, as a priority over art-poetry with its modernist mask, was perhaps an instinctive one of need. 'Foregather in the Balavil for ceilidh/ And drink malt whisky, swapping song for song' is one of the vivid images in the 'Ballad of the Twelve Stations of My Youth'. As Alec Finlay points out, Henderson came increasingly to idealise the communal values of song... which was perhaps 'an avoidance of a kind...'[41] A dozen or more of Henderson's poems, shorter and longer are entitled 'ballad' and others are 'blues' or songs. Song is at the heart of his poetry, but singing is also something that we do together in groups and crowds as well as small gatherings. This social aspect of song is therefore implicit in Henderson's poetry, however cerebral it may appear to be, and is also something that quite simply was the essence of life for him personally.

Henderson had the ability to empower, not only the travelling people and rural ballad-singers by bringing them to public notice and validating their traditions, but also to empower sophisticated academics such as Carla Sassi who asserts: 'I have learnt to look at my own country with difference eyes' and identifies 'beauty, passion and humanity' as underlying Henderson's devotion to song which is the key to the 'house of freedom'.[42]

James Elroy Flecker's verse play, *Hassan*, was familiar to Henderson since his school days at Dulwich Academy, where he organised a public reading of it. Flecker died at the age of thirty of tuberculosis in 1915. He had studied classics at Oxford and served in the Levant

Consular Service. A virtuoso poet, his writings are a blend of the classic and romantic and on the cusp of modernism. He puts a clear commitment to the importance of poetry at the heart of culture in his famous dialogue between Hassan, the sweet–maker, and the Caliph of Baghdad: The caliph waxes philosophical saying:

> In poems and in tales alone shall live the eternal memory of this city when I am dust and thou art dust, when all Baghdad is broken to the ground. If there shall ever arise a nation whose people have forgotten poetry or whose poets have forgotten the people, though they send their ships round Taprobane and their armies across the hills of Hindustan, though their cities be greater than Babylon of old, though they mine a league into the earth or mount to the stars on wings – what of them?[45]

And Hassan replies, 'they will be a dark patch upon the world.' I quote this extensively because it seems to me that it is in the face of that 'dark patch upon the world', so fiercely confronted in the battle against Fascism and the desert landscape itself, but also felt in the emasculated populations of the Scottish glens and the crowded slums of Scottish cities, that Henderson felt compelled to commit himself with all his strength and ability, even as he had witnessed the deeds of brave resistance leaders in Italy, such as Corbora, 'yon wuddifu callant' for whom he wrote a ballad. And the form that resistance had to take for a poet was not to be guilty of forgetting the people, or allowing the conditions in which the people forget poetry. A line from Henderson's translation of Quasimodo, 'Colour of Rain and Iron'[46] touches on this sense of a burden of responsibility though couched in a question to the crucified Christ: 'how shall I answer those who ask? / Now, now: before another silence...' Hence the Edinburgh People's Festivals which, despite their success and support from such as Norman Buchan, were banned by the Labour-ruled Edinburgh City Council in 1952. Presumably this was from of fear of nationalism and communism. (A Labour Council in Edinburgh similarly closed down the 'Women Live' festivals in 1983 after two successful years.)

Folk includes women in a way that 'art-poetry' certainly did not, until the efforts of the woman's movement and innovative women's publishing houses gradually began to change the situation from the 1970s onwards. The woman's movement and the hippie culture's espousal of music all contributed to the feel of people power returning after subservient war and post-war years. Henderson will have been caught up in this as well as contributing to it and he understood its compelling strength, even seeming to threaten to sweep away high culture in its flow. He therefore sought a fusion, not a conquest, of folk with high culture, an integration and encompassing, whereby each was enhanced and could bring forth new and exciting work. Interarts activities, theatre groups, such as the 7.84 Company playing in community and church halls, and the increase of young traditional yet innovative musicians graduating from the School of Scottish Studies or the RSAMD, were products of this groundswell. As Donald Smith has noted, 'it was not the text, the music, the performer or the audience that counted but what happened between them.'[45]

The 'duende', celebrated by Lorca, was applied by Henderson to Jeannie Robertson and other great ballad singers from the Highlands and the north-east of Scotland. The 'duende' or indefinable artistic power, which Lorca perceived in Andalusian *cante jondo,* became equivalent to the 'conyach' acknowledged by the Scottish travellers as the ground of their ballad-singing art, without which even a superb voice was hollow. Smith connects Henderson's friendship and work with Calum MacLean in collecting songs from the Highlands and with other folk-song collectors as another shared work, shared love, 'a darg of love', as is implied in Timothy Neat's record of Henderson's entire life.

Some of Henderson's 'ballads' may be and may remain no more than versions of occasional songs that were circulating, but this is no reason why they cannot sometimes become great poems, when moulded by a poet of his skill. Charming as is the tune and sentiment of 'The 51st Highland Division's Farewell to Sicily', the 'Ballad of the D-Day Dodgers' is succinct and deeply satirical with its refrain of 'Italy', turning it to pathos in the last verse, entirely Henderson's composition, with the last line: 'Those are the D-Day Dodgers who'll stay in Italy'—because they 'slumber on' beneath 'the scattered crosses' on the mountains, some with no name. The poem, as poem, is memorable and irresistible in its magnetism. Dennis Healey, for instance, who fought in the Sicily campaign, referred to it when he was interviewed for *Desert Island Discs* in 2009. In September 1944, Henderson heard an organ playing 'Lili Marlene' in a ransacked church in Castaglia after the attack on Florence and he wrote this 'timeless ballad', as Timothy Neat rightly calls it, during five days of wind and rain 'horizontal in my wind-thumped tent' in the Appenines.[46]

Conclusion

The four themes I have identified: pilgrimage, eros/thanatos, integration and companionship, weave in and out of Henderson's work, however slight or weighty. The work, as also the life, should itself be taken as a whole, rather than picking this and that as more serious poetry or more folksy. Timothy Neat prefaces the second volume of his biography with a quotation from Keats: 'A man's life of any worth is a continual allegory'. All four themes are certainly interwoven into the lovely lyric 'Under the Earth I Go', in which the poet charges his successors to 'change elegy into hymn,' even as 'the twin dragons, Life and Death' joust under the maypole, for 'new voices [will] be borne on the carrying stream'. Then, with a traditional child's rhyme, we have Monday to Sunday and Aberlardian 'rest forever' (O quanta qualia/ sunt illa sabbata… Perhaps by 'rest' Henderson intended a pun with the meaning of continuation, because he hoped there would be no rest for his compositions. The amen, the so-be-it, is also an inclusive, international expression of loving acceptance—akin to Dante's 'in his will is our peace'.

Henderson's poem 'Brosnachadh,' sums up his legacy. Its strong commanding rhythms, and end rhymes which begin new commands, are singularly effective and unusual. For pilgrimage we have the apollyonian injunction 'Throw/ Your shadow across valleys'. For eros/ thanatos, minded that quick means alive, we find 'Above all be quick, Love/ Never outlasts its movement. Prove/ That with us is no 'villainy of hatred'/ and history will uphold us – justify and forgive'. For integration we find 'a new legend,/ our human house greatly to grace.' And for companionship we have the rousing second verse: 'Tell of the rebellious truth. Foretell/ At street corners an awakening. Swell/ The insurgent armies of knowledge./ Foregather on field and fell.' 'Fell' is a word meaning mountainside but also indicating foreboding or evil.

In a delightful early lyric, 'When we were Children, Time ran errands for us', Henderson binds it all together with the instruction: 'Face the imperative choice', and 'O child, child hurry./ For life our mortal blow quickly we'll strike'. He knew even then that the deathly blow, or the blow that only mortals can strike, must be on behalf of life. This is a poet we should treasure among our centuries of Scottish bards in many languages for, while embedding us in the past, he inspires us for the present, wherever that may find us, and also leads us into the future. Time is on his side and will continue to run 'errands' for this earthy son of man.

References:

1   Hamish Henderson, *The Obscure Voice: Translations from Italian Poetry* (Under the Moon Series 1/3), introduced by Carla Sassi, Edinburgh: (Morning Star Publications, August 1994).

2   *Ibid.*

3   Hamish Henderson, *Elegies for the Dead in Cyrenaica*, London: Lehmann, 1948; Edinburgh: Polygon, 2008).

4   Poems referred to or quoted are taken from Hamish Henderson, *Collected Poems and Songs*, edited by Raymond Ross (Edinburgh: Curly Snake Publishing, 2000) unless otherwise indicated.

5   See the inscription on the Thomas Muir monument, Old Calton Cemetery, Edinburgh.

6   See Hamish Henderson, *Elegies for the Dead in Cyrenaica* (Edinburgh: Polygon, 2008), first published 1948; Hamish Henderson, *Alias MacAlias: Collected Essays*, edited by Alec Finlay (Edinburgh: Polygon, 1992); Hamish Henderson, *The Armstrong Nose: Selected Letters of Hamish Henderson*, edited by Alec Finlay (Edinburgh: Polygon, 1996).

7   Rainer Maria Rilke: 'Ich lebe mein Leben in wachsenden Ringen', in Rilke, *Das Stundenbuch* (Frankfurt: Insel Verlag, 1905).

8   *Freedom Come-all-Ye, an 80th Birthday Souvenir for Hamish Henderson*, (Edinburgh: Chapman Publishing, 1999).

9   Heinrich Heine, 'Essays II: Über Frankreich, Lutetia, Zweiter Teil, LVII, (Paris, 6 Mai 1843)', in H Heine, *Vermischte Schriften* (Hamburg: Hoffmann und Campe, 1854).

10 Timothy Neat, *Hamish Henderson: A Biography, Volume 2 Poetry Becomes People (1952-2002)*, Edinburgh: Polygon, 2009.

11 Charles Williams, *The Greater Trumps* (London: Sphere Books, 1976), first published 1932, p. 168.

12 Interview by Peter Orr in *The Poet Speaks* (London: Routledge, 1966), Also in *Alias MacAlias*.

13 See William Butler Yeats, *A New Selection* (London: Macmillan, 1984), pp. 91, 284.

14 Willa Muir, *Living with Ballads* (London: The Hogarth Press, 1965).

15 Friedrich Hölderlin, *Gedichte* (Ditzingen: Reclam, 1979). Translated by Tessa Ransford.

16 Interview by Peter Orr.

17 Rainer Maria Rilke, *Uncollected Poems*, bilingual edition (San Francisco: North Point Press, 1997).

18 Rainer Maria Rilke, *Duino Elegies*, bilingual edition, translated by J B Leishman and Stephen Spender (London Chatto and Windus, 1981).

19 Friedrich Hölderlin, 'Hyperions Schicksalslied', in Friedrich Hölderlin, *Gedichte* (Stuttgart: Reclam, 1979), p. 46. Translated by Tessa Ransford.

20 Neat (2009), pp. 49-50.

21 See 'The Folksong Flyting', in *The Armstrong Nose*.

22 Rilke (1981).

23 Tom Scott, *Dunbar: a critical exposition of the poems* (Edinburgh: Oliver and Boyd, 1966).

24 *The Armstrong's Nose*, p. 156.

25 Elmar Schenkel, 'Breathing Space', *Lines Review*, 119 (1991).

26 John Macmurray: *The Self as Agent and Persons in Relation (Gifford Lectures)* (London: Faber and Faber, 1953).

27 Neat (2009), p. 186.

28 David Stenhouse, 'Scotland's Internationale', *Sunday Herald* (7 November 1999); reprinted in the sixth Carrying Stream Festival programme (Edinburgh: Edinburgh Folk Club, 2007).

29 Prologue (for John Speirs) to *Elegies for the Dead in Cyrenaica*.

30 Timothy Neat. *Hamish Henderson: A Biography: Volume 1, The Making of a Poet, (1919-1953)* (Edinburgh: Polygon, 2007), p. 189.

31 Steven Rose, *Lifelines* (London: The Penguin Press, 1997).

32 Fritjof Capra, *The Web of Life* (London: HarperCollins, 1996), p. 202.

33 Rupert Sheldrake, *The Presence of the Past* (London: Fontana/Collins, 1988).

34 *Alias MacAlias*, p. 51.

35 *The Armstrong's Nose*, p. 134.

36 Interview by Peter Orr.

37 *The Armstrong Nose*, p. 121.

38 *Ibid.*

39 Adam McNaughtan, 'Hamish Henderson – Folk Hero', *Chapman*, 42 (1985).

40 *Ibid.*

41 *Alias MacAlias*, p. x.

41 *Ibid.*

42 Henderson, *The Obscure Voice*.

43 James Elroy Flecker, *Hassan: A Play in Five Acts* (London: William Heinemann, 1923).

44 Henderson, *The Obscure Voice*.

45 Donald Smith, 'Libraries of Love and Passion', in Geddes and Grosset (ed.), *A Sense of Place* (New Lanark: Waverley Books, 2005), reprinted in this volume.

46 Neat (2007), p. 153.

HAMISH HENDERSON:
AS THE POETS SAW HIM (1940-2004)

Timothy Neat

As a boy and youth I knew that I was different; my clairvoyant experiences had begun even then. Sometimes part of me appeared to move outside time and communicate with the departed.[1]

Educated people in contemporary society find the clairvoyant and mystical difficult, but many great artists, across millennia, have been inspired by the supernatural and mysterious and, in this essay, I am concerned about Hamish Henderson—as the poets saw him. For, unlike many educated people, the poets enjoyed Hamish's mystical side. Most recognised him, from the start, as a visionary prone to exert an almost uncanny impact on those around him. Their responses will, I think, play a key role in the continuing evolution of the Hamish story.

I first met Hamish on Mayday 1967. We became friends and later worked together on numerous projects—films, books, cultural and political campaigns. I was with him on the day he died, in March 2002. At that first meeting I recognised what I can only describe as 'a greatness' in Hamish. There was something special about him—as a man, as a poet, as a force for good in Scotland and in the world. In our academically, institutionalised society I have been highly conscious that this kind of 'partisan enthusiasm' would be seen as undermining my credentials as Hamish's biographer. Consequently, as my research progressed, I was pleased to find humerous equally partisan enthusiasts amongst his literary contemporaries: my word may be of no account—but the word of Hugh MacDiarmid and two of the greatest of Nobel Laureates deserve attention. Like Hamish himself, I make no apologies for writing from within 'the thick of it'. The closeness of a Boswell inspires me more than the scholasticism of an R F Foster. Future writers will be free to look back from the mountain top, I speak from the rock-face—as did those poets on whose writings I shall base this chapter.

Poetry is unusual source material for a biographer. The lives of poets rarely stimulate poetry in others. Most modern poets live rather private lives. Hamish lived a life of adventure, in the public realm. In 1941 he wrote, 'I am tired of reading poems which have an atmosphere of 'Here is Art'. I want poems with the atmosphere 'Here is Life', and here is Hamish Henderson living it.' In the prologue to *Elegies for the Dead in Cyrenaica,* Hamish gives expression to a wish to write 'a true and valid testament' that will hold 'against the armour of the storm':

Let my words knit what now we lack
The demon and the heritage,
And fancy strapped to logic's rock.
A chastened wantonness, a bit
That sets on song a discipline,
A sensuous austerity.

There was always something of the teacher in Hamish. His address was always to his fellows. That he saw his *Elegies* as a testament tells us much. From boyhood he was determined to use poetry as a cultural base camp—from which he would go out to change the world and renew a Scotland, broken by war, poverty, exploitation and disease. Hamish was always a political animal and his impact on politics is clearly hinted at in this poem written by George Gunn, in 1989, the year the Berlin Wall came down—'Liberty Ode for the Ghillie Mor, at Seventy':

As I write this empires crumble.
Can we blame it all on you
Hamish Henderson?
Russia, America, cracking open
in there different ways
like an old damp Gorbals tenement
Russia, where the wild wind of freedom
blows loud at last
America, a desert of rabid dogs
and the poor sleeping beneath their feet.
'All those tired old men" you said to me once...[2]

Some critics will dismiss this suggestion as grandiose nonsense—the mindless conceit of a 'nationalist lefty'—but others will look for the reasons why Gunn was moved to conjure this conceit and, perhaps call 'chaos theory' up—in his defence. Stuff happens. John the Baptist, William Wallace, Vincent van Gogh were all once dismissed as callow louts—with scorn! If George Gunn's suggestion existed in a vacuum, it could be dismissed, but my purpose here is to show how many other poets, across many years, found themselves witness to similar phenomena—a poet who, in addressing the public zone of experience, raised strange hopes and realised things till then deemed impossible.

Hamish's Henderson's preoccupation with human being—joy, song, peace, plenty—was established early. All his teachers found themselves embraced by 'renaissances' he effected: in Blairgowrie, at his prep school in Devon and at Dulwich College in London. Going up to Cambridge University in October 1938, he got himself appointed as a stage-manager at the Arts Theatre for a production of the Auden/Isherwood play, *On the Frontier*. that November. Benjamin Britten was musical director, and there are sound reasons to believe that the crusading, ballad-singing, young Scot influenced the choice of at least one song sung in the production. Consequently, the idea that Hamish's demonic championship of the ballad form influenced the conception of Britten's wartime, ground-breaking opera, *Billy Budd*, is less preposterous than music historians might have us believe.

In the spring of 1939 Hamish got engaged in a public spat with Nicholas Moore, leader of the younger English poets at Cambridge— writing to the editor of the anti-war literary magazine *Cambridge Front,* denouncing 'the mindless moral stance' taken by Moore in a previous issue. Hamish himself was anti-war but believed war to be an aspect of human behaviour that had to be addressed head-on, in all its savagery, not shied away from.

> If you publish this letter sir, I hope it will work in a salutary way in the minds of those young poets who may have been tempted by Mr Moore to forego creative freedom and start writing with an eye to the spread of the New Morality... It seems from your editorial and its reference to the subconscious that you disapprove of the surrealist method. The subconscious is and always has been, an infinitely more valuable source of poetry than the mind; and if it be urged that a philosophy of Meaninglessness is sometimes the result of it, one can answer that it is to be found in Sophocles... One who has courage to see life whole and pin no easy faith in 'goodness' has, in my opinion, a truer sense of values and a better claim to be called civilised in the Clive Bell sense of the word than the exponent of a naive ichthyosaurus-ego philosophy of moral good... Any attempt to provide the poet with even the base ground-work of a philosophy, and the first blow has been struck at his spiritual

freedom. Mr Nicholas Moore inclines towards a *simple* optimistic conception of life; many others towards the tragic conception of life which - I am convinced is not only the more profound philosophy but also the better attuned to the demonic spirit in man which is the source of the greatest poetry—springs not from a recognition of the good things of life but from the splendid certainty of religious ecstasy... *(Henderson archive)*

The letter goes on to recognise 'war as the supreme expression of the violence in man's nature', and Hamish quotes from one of his own songs, 'A Triumphant Song for Rorie Mor', to blood-curdling effect. This onslaught seems to have stimulated Moore to write a series of energised counter-poems. One published in *Cambridge Front*, was entitled *Caravan* (the title of an 'alternative magazine' Hamish had created at Dulwich College).

> You look like history. All the bright caravans
> That ended in no more than a mad man's whisper,
> The cavalcade of honour that led to death,
> Is history you have loved and suffered beneath...
>
> You look like fable, myth and the fairy tale,
> But you are real as the boy was in the stable.
> What agony is to suffer will still be true,
> Though the future open out like a flower in you.

Hamish is presented as a force-of-nature, a throw-back from another age, a political zealot, a victim of his nation's history, a man of Christ-like innocence and power. Moore was clearly impressed by Hamish and, four years later, in the summer of 1944, wrote to ask him (then fighting on the Anzio Beachhead) to contribute to his magazine, *New Poetry*. By return Hamish sent his Sicilian war-song 'Battle of the Simeto' which duly appeared in *New Poetry, No II*.

Cambridge Front also brought Hamish into contact with the poet Paul Potts, an Irish Canadian Londoner. Potts was gay and, almost immediately, found himself overwhelmed by Hamish's Celtic persona, political passion and spiritual idealism. In pubs, Potts liked to introduce Hamish as 'one of the wandering kings of Scotland', whilst Hamish would introduce Potts as 'the People's Poet/ the poet who heard his poems in the streets/ and only wrote them down...' They shared folklore enthusiasms, a Shakespearean hunger for London low-life and the friendship of Dylan Thomas. In the summer of 1940 *Cambridge Front* published a poem by Potts about Hamish. It was entitled 'The Poet and the Harvester': Hamish is the poet, Potts the harvester.

...Then a man like you has come along
Who has no wealth to give away
But a can opener for the mind.
You make me want to cease, to be a brother to an ox.
You make me want to read,
To see the beauties of the field,
To walk the earth.
Poet you, not my father, made me become a man.

Hamish, however, ever conscious of his duty to Scotland, shied away from any kind of close commitment to Potts, or to London. This caused Potts long-term pain but, twenty years later, the closeness of their relation provided Potts with the creative fulcrum of a splendid autobiographical exploration: *Dante Called You Beatrice*.[3] Hamish's name does not appear in the book but his presence is everywhere apparent. For Potts, Hamish embodied the ideals Dante had found and bestowed on his love, Beatrice.

Love is my poetry, I have no other... She looked as beautiful as I thought she would before I met her. Men seldom thought so, women always. Her hands were as marvellous as St Francis of Assisi's must have been that day he held the host above his head during the consecration of his first mass in the city of Jerusalem. This metaphor is even more worthy of her, when I remember that St Francis never did say Mass, as he was too humble to allow himself to be ordained. She had the simplicity of a Highland Chief's daughter mixed up with the arrogance of a Borgia cardinal. She had a face a bit like Shelley's and the body of a Chinese empress. Determined to a fault, she was a gentle as a prayer in Gaelic. She always thought of Canada as a colony of Scotland. She had an urge to self-destruction and a taste in pretty boys. She tried to cure all the ills of the thirties on her own... because of both her parent's early death... She was a victim of that kind of communism which killed by guilt young sensitive cultured rich people... She imagined her privilege and her leisure were being paid for by other people's work, pain and restrictions... The last time I saw her she was a destitute lunatic of over forty, in a public institution. The first time I saw her she looked like Our lady's younger sister in a painting by Botticelli... My feeling towards her have not changed...

The friendship of the two men was interrupted in January 1942 by Hamish's decampment to Egypt where he quickly found himself a new literary companion, G S Fraser (poet and academic). He, too, seems to have been overwhelmed by the dynamism of the Henderson personality. Fraser was a young Aberdonian working for the British Army's Information Service in Cairo and his autobiography, *A Stranger and Afraid*, written thirty years later, paints a vivid portrait of Hamish as soldier and revolutionary.

It was refreshing from time to time to meet a man of action... I looked up from my desk in *Parades* offices one day to find a very tall, gawky, bony young lieutenant in battledress looking down at me. I could place him at once as a Highlander, by something fierce and gentle in his whole bearing. His voice confirmed my guess, soft and lilting, with long vowels and snaky sibilants. 'Would you by any chance be Mis-s-ter George Fras-s-er?' I looked up at a strange face, with a short nose, a broad forehead and high cheekbones, fierce dark short-sighted eyes enlarged by strong glasses, and a wide, loose, sensitive adolescent mouth under an absurd small moustache. The wrists and the huge hands thrust out of a battledress jacket a little too tight and too short. The tall figure held itself with a military vigour but swayed a little on its feet, in a way that seemed to match the voices lilting of its formal syllables. One large hand dived into a haversack to produce a little pamphlet, which it thrust onto the desk before me. 'These are some verses of yours and I'm very pleased to meet you.' ...The young man was Hamish Henderson... With Keith Douglas, whom I was also to meet later in Cairo, Hamish proved to be one of the two best battle poets of the war... But in early 1942 Hamish was still fresh out from home and still on the edge of battle. Though I thought of him, from the first, as a fighter, I was merely recognising a type. He had not yet seen any action. He took me out for a drink and began to tell me all about himself... He was obviously a born soldier; and ideally fitted for Intelligence in that he had a spontaneous sympathy for the Germans and their romantic attitude to history—just as obviously, he was out of sympathy with the English, with their tepid self-control, mild dislikes, liberal hesitations, and their passion for compromise. When Hamish loved or hated, he liked to be thorough... When we sat down over our drinks, Hamish at once began to discuss philosophy... Hegelian—as developed by Marx... with the rather Germanic mind that overlaid his Celtic temperament—(he wanted) some inclusive philosophy of change... It meant a fight and his Celtic temperament was spoiling for a fight. The war had exalted and transformed him... Yet I sensed a contradiction in his attitude. He was not only a Marxist but a Scottish Nationalist, and in Scottish history his sympathy was not with the winning faction, the Lowland

Whigs, but with the Highlanders, who rode into battle, but they were defeated. Hamish's instincts were with the last stand and the lost cause; his mind trained in the schools of Germany, sought to hallow any victory. For the moment, Marxism was helping him to solve his emotional problem. It must, he thought, win in the end; but it was not winning at that time in Western Europe, and by standing by it he was standing by a threatened minority. He saw Marxian Socialism as the means by which the Highlands of Scotland and the Celtic enclaves of Europe generally, from Scotland and Wales to Brittany and Spanish Galicia, could regain their old cultural autonomy... Scotland was going through a cultural revival —but that was not enough. The politically central power always imposed its own culture on the outlying provinces. Look, Hamish said at the case of Provence... So it was, he said, with the Highlands of Scotland; when the Lowland Whigs became supreme in Scotland, their policy towards the Highlanders was to destroy their clan system and 'root out their Irish language'. The '15 and the '45 were the last desperate rallies of a proud, ancient people in defence of old ways, and Hamish, a Marxist in the Modern World became, when he considered Scottish history, a Jacobite and a Tory. He was so eager about the old feuds, which he felt stirring again beneath the surface of our time, that it was hard not to catch his enthusiasm. An age of battles! What a splendid prospect... If one had a temperament like his... 'A thrawn little dominie' he called me... (but) sometimes I tried to enter into Hamish's enthusiasms. When he was dictator of Scotland, I said, I would write his propaganda for him. 'Ah, man Geordie, but it had better be I who carry the pistols!' So he rallied me and, in the middle of our most obstinate arguments, suddenly broke into a lilting Gaelic song...

Fraser's portrait verges on hero-worship but is also highly informative. Hamish's response to Fraser was more brutal: 'Fraser asked me what I thought of his poetry. I told him I considered his tight-rope act under the parasol most admirable—every conscious tremor of the muscles gauged to a nicety—but I was still listening for the sound of Niagara below. 'Is there a Niagara below?'...There is about as much lyricism in George Fraser's songs as in a *Times* leading article. Poetry must free itself from this degrading case of being a kind of supplement to a treatise on psycho-analysis.' The two men maintained a correspondence throughout the war, and Fraser wrote a series of poems in which Hamish features: one is 'Three Characters in a Bar':

Charming gentle bohemian
Last, last of the Jacobites
Lighting my countless cigarettes.

Pleasant to meet indeed, old man!
No one to talk to all these nights
About the prompters behind the sets.

This image of Hamish as being a prompter 'behind the sets' is another
important insight: life-long, Hamish, as poet, song-writer, folklorist
and political activist, consciously pursued a theatrical role in public
life—as prompter, puppet master, clown, tragedian and director.
Fraser develops the idea in another poem, 'Monologue for a Cairo
Evening'. It is dedicated to their mutual friend John Waller (poet) but
the man it describes is Hamish:

                              ...who
Among the projectors on this floating island
Is such an honest Gulliver as you?

Old friend, who being simple and merciless
And kind and subtle, can enjoy a show
Where every part's pat in your repertory:
Crude Caliban to priggish Prospero!

To you I dedicate this inconclusive
Conclusion to an unmethodical
Method of being the mass and the observer:
To you, the critical, this curtain call...

Fraser's recognition of Hamish as somehow being both 'the mass and
the observer' throws light on Hamish's future career as a folklorist,
and in a poem completed in the fifties, after Hamish had discovered
the great ballad singer Jeannie Robertson, Fraser documents the
visionary determination with which Hamish presumed he would
change Scotland, by celebrating the poetry dormant in 'the folk':

Goddess or ghost you say by shuddering,
    And ominous of evil to our land,
Twisting to ugliness the mouths that sing,
    Parching the lover's moist and balmy hand.
Goddess or ghost, you say, by silence known,
    The silence ticking in the rotten wood

Like our numb pain, that can no longer groan;
A grief so old it gives the mind no food.

...Then I have thought my country might arise
Like these half-sleeping girls with tawny necks
And summer's sensual softness in their eyes.

These skies bled warmth: and while my blood stays young,
That starving peace, or this protracted war,
Vows broken, or friends lost, or songs unsung
Shall leave no permanent or vexing scar...

On New Year's Day 1945, Fraser wrote to Hamish, then in the Apennines: 'Dear Hamish—I've often enough thought of that phrase in your last letter—Jerry has had it, but an army of one-eyed half-wits could hold you up in these hills of sorrow..., and thought of us in our comfort here in Cairo, our intrigues, petty quarrels, paper wars, and you out there in the night, in the cold, in the rain and mud, and yet as always (as Haig Gudenian wrote to me when he met you once and drank wine with you in some mountain village) "like the laird of the surrounding hills." God (or Time, or History) keep you safe this year... I thought your last fragment of an Elegy strong and moving like the others; like Whitman, the whole thing will be even more impressive when you have it in bulk. It's like a broad river carrying a lot of gravel along with it...' Fraser's recognition of the *Elegies* as, essentially, one poem, was to the point and when the collection was published, in 1948, it was the poets—not the critics or academics—who offered praise and succinct criticism. First was Hamish's Cambridge friend, E P Thompson, the Marxist historian and poet:

I also proffer you some heavy advice which I hope you will take as carefully considered and deeply felt – and not dismiss as Marxist phrase-mongering... I greet you with humility, *compagno*, for you are that rare man, a poet. You have achieved poems out of our dead century. I hope you have had bad reviews from the culture boys, because their approval today is cause only for shame. But you must remain a poet. Remember always who you are writing for— the people of Glasgow, of Halifax, of Dublin—not of Edinburgh and Hampstead. I don't mean always, today, or for all of them— but for the vanguard of the people, the thoughtful ones. You will know Mayakovsky's reflections on the difficulties of writing 'Big Poetry—poetry genuinely created', which can be understood by the people. I think this is your greatest danger—you must *never* let yourself, by the possible insensitivity or even hostility of those who should be your greatest allies—into the arms of the culture boys who 'appreciate' pretentiousness and posturing. They would kill your writing—because you, more than any other poet I know, are an instrument through which thousands of others can become articulate. And you must not forget that your songs and ballads are not trivialities—they are quite as important as the 'Elegies'.

This letter helped affirm Hamish's perception of himself as a teacher committed to the folk tradition and the concept of art as largely communal creation. The idea that Hamish was a teacher with responsibilities best described as religious seems implicit in this letter from the surrealist English/French poet, David Gascoigne:

Dear Hamish... Since I read your Elegies last Spring, your name has been in my mind as one of the small group of contemporary poets whose work especially interests me. The Elegies made a real impact on me, and I regard them as the most significant martial poems to have come out of the war: something about them only to compare with Wilfred Owen, David Jones (maybe also Isaac Rosenberg?). The form and manipulation are enterprising and efficient enough to attract unusual attention, no doubt; but the spirit is what makes them rare and unforgettable. Not much warm-blooded, aristocratic authenticity and humanity about like yours... It occurs to me that you may not care for the epithet 'aristocratic' as applied to the spirit of your poetry: but of course I don't mean anything 'ruling class' by the word, only the sense in which the Carpenter's Son was aristocratic...'

The Irish playwright Sean O'Casey—exiled to Devon—was equally impressed by the universality and ambition of Hamish's poem: 'Good man—a grand book, thank you for sending it to me. I get in it the brown snarly rocks, the suffocating sand, the sigh of all the *laochrais*, German & English, Scots and Irish, falling forever into the sniffling sand, falling forever from the hills, the dales, the streets they knew, and the warm kiss from a favoured lass when the times were quiet... *Na laochrai Eirean agus na Laochrai Alban.* I am so glad you got the Somerset Maugham award for the work; it deserves it. And I hear in it that the desert that has buried so many dead, should now itself be buried by the living, that we might see the blossoming of the rose.' O'Casey's letter suggests that there is Rosicrucian symbolism in the *Elegies* and this is true. For example the poem's movement from imagery of arid sterility to sparkling life is typically Rosicrucian. The poem opens with the line 'There are many dead in the brutish desert' but ends with the words 'locking like lovers/ down the thunderous cataract of day.'

Three years earlier, in the spring of 1946, Hamish had translated Primo Levi's then unpublished, now famous, poem 'Se Questo e' un Uomo'. Its subject is barbarian Europe and 'the communal crucifixion' of the Jewish people. Levi's poem is not about Hamish, but the fact that he was sent it and translated it into English—before anyone else —suggests that Levi, or mutual friends in Italy, believed that Hamish must see this landmark poem of Europe's post-war trauma. Strangely, the poem also anticipates aspects of Hamish's own struggle to make a living in post-war Britain.

In March 1948 Hamish was employed as guide to the Italian writers Eugenio Montale, Alberto Moravia and Elsa Morante on cultural visits to Britain (organised by the British Council). Hamish and Montale got on well, and at least two poems written by Montale during his visit are about Hamish who, immediately, translated and adapted them. The first is entitled, 'Wind on the Crescent, Edinburgh 1948':

> The great bridge did not lead to you.
> I would have reached you even at the cost of sailing
> along the sewers, if at your command.
> But already my energy, like the sun on the glass
> of the verandas, was weakening.
>
> The man preaching on the Crescent
> asked me 'Do you know where God is?
> I knew where, and told him. He shook his head.
> Then he vanished in the whirlwind that caught up
>   men and house
> and lifted them on high on a colour of pitch.

The two men then travelled south to Cambridge where, after a visit to Ely Cathedral, Montale wrote, 'Letting Go of a Dove—Ely Cathedral, 1948'. Montale knew that Hamish believed himself destined to give his literary and political energies to Scotland; that, having enjoyed his moment in the sun (of youth and Italy), he must now—in MacDiarmid's words—take up 'the burden of his people's doom' and suffer in the dark and cold of home. Montale's Ely poem can thus be read as a message of farewell to youth and happiness, but a farewell also resonant with inspirational solidarity:

A white dove has flown from me
among stelae, under vaults where the sky nests.
Dawns and lights suspended; I have loved the sun,
The colour of honey—now I crave the dark.
I desire the broody fire, and this immobile tomb.
And I want to see your gaze downfacing it.

Montale recognised Hamish as a Celtic poet—with tribal
responsibilities; a man destined to challenge the death-longing of
Scotch Calvinism (presented in the Edinburgh poem) by the sacrifice
of his life and art at the altar of his nation's need and, in the Ely poem,
Montale suggested that Hamish's life's work is to do for the Scots
people (through song?) what the magnificent Gothic Lantern at Ely
has done over the centuries for East Anglia: lift the spirit.

When Hamish arrived in Italy in March 1951 to complete his
translations of the prison letters of Antonio Gramsci, Montale
presented him with a new poem, 'Il rosso e il negro'. It was dedicated
'to Hamish Henderson, in friendship, Eugenio Montale, 24th March
1950'. Its subject was the atrocities committed in the Ardeatine caves
in 1944, and Montale sought to honour Hamish as a Partisan war-
hero, a catalyst of the Italian post-war Resorgimento and as a leader
of the International Peace Movement. He was also saluting Hamish
as the translator of Corrado Govoni's poem for his son, Aladino—one
of the 335 men massacred in the caves. Today, many Italians believe
Hamish's translation to be a finer poem than the original:

'Lament for the Son' (after Corrodo Govoni)

He was the most beautiful son on earth,
braver than a hero of antiquity,
gentler than an angel of God:
tall and dark, his hair like a forest,
or that intoxicating canopy
which spreads over the Po valley;
and you, without pity for me, killed him
—there in a cave of dull, red sandstone.

He was the whole treasure
of war, of sanctuary and of crown,
of my accepted human poverty,
of my discounted poetry –
you, once his hiding place was discovered
(after which no angel could sleep)—

you, with your thieving hands
that were strangers to no sacrilege,
you carried him away at the run
into the darkness
to destroy him without being seen—
before I had time to cry out:
'Stop!
Put him down!
That is my son!'

He was my new son, he was the triumph
of my betrayed boyhood;
and you changed him in front of my praying hands
into a heap of worms and ashes.
     Mutilated, hurt, blinded,
only I know the tragic weight I am carrying.
I am the living cross of my dead son...

In Italy, Hamish championed Gramsci and the programme of the Italian Communist Party but also took every opportunity to advance the reputations of MacDiarmid and Sorley MacLean as European poets. He met Einaudi (Gramsci's Italian publisher) and Mario Motta (editor of 'Cultura e Realta'), made contact with Sereni, Aldovrandi, Rossi, Italo Calvino and Cesare Pavese. And Pier Paolo Pasalini (at that time an aspiring poet, now recognised as one of the world's great film-makers) seems to have been swept forward by Hendersonian values, as his great poems 'The Ashes of Gramsci', 'The Appenines' (owing much to Sorley MacLean?) and 'The Religion of My Time' demonstrate.

When Hamish was expelled from Italy in October 1950, he established a brief friendship with the Greek poet Odysseus Elytis—in London and Cambridge. It was at this time that Elytis was writing 'Axion Esti', one of his finest poems. It carries clear echoes of Sorley MacLean's Marxist epic, 'The Cuillin', and, just as MacLean had cried out for Highland Scotland, so Elytis cries out for a socialist transformation of post-war Greece. 'My foundations on mountains/ and the people carry the mountains on their shoulders/ and on these mountains memory burns.' Before leaving London, in May 1951, Elytis gave Hamish two poems for issue No 4 of the *Cambridge Poetry Broadsheets* he edited. Both seem to have been selected (or written?) as tributes to Hamish and his vision of a revived Scotland in a new Europe:

Yet one day the vision awakes flesh
And where but naked solitude glittered before
Now smiles a city, beautiful as you wish her;
You almost see her, she awaits you.

Give me your hand, let us go down before the dawn
Pours down on her with cries of triumph,
Give me your hand, before birds gather
On the shoulders of men and sing this;
That she appeared at last coming from afar,
Across the sea, the virgin of Hope.

Let us together, though they lynch us
Though they may call us head-in-air,
My friend, those who have never guessed
With what metal, what stones, what blood, what fire,
We build, we dream, we sing.[4]

During the post-war period Hamish made an impression on most modernist poets in Scotland: I have selected six for brief analysis: James Burns Singer, Norman MacCaig, Thurso Berwick, Alan Riddell, Hugh MacDiarmid, and Stuart MacGregor. James Burns Singer was a half Jewish marine biologist from Glasgow. As a young man he sought mentors; he admired MacDiarmid, he was close to W S Graham, and very close to Hamish. It was Hamish's war experience, political vision and personal gentleness that appealed to Burns Singer. They met in 1946 and Hamish encouraged him to sign his poetry 'Burns Singer'. The first poem so signed was 'The Transparent Prisoner' and deals with action in the Western Desert—something that Singer was much to young to have experienced himself but which Hamish had been in the thick of. Another very early Burns Singer poem, 'Epilogue to another man's book', was sent in manuscript to Hamish and inscribed 'for Hamish'. The importance of their relationship is made movingly clear in this poem entitled 'The best of it':

...Your words make hay of me, but I'm released
By them from standing shivering and distant.
The best of it is that I am at least.

Knees soaked rheumatic by the promised harvest
You razed with scythe and sickle what I meant:
Reached by these words now, measure what's increased.

But you, like a horizon or a priest,
Past every boundary of the round land, went:
The best of it is that I am at least
Reached by these words now measuring what's increased.

Hamish and Norman MacCaig famously 'never got on', but at least one of MacCaig's poems was directly inspired by a Henderson incident. Geoff Dutton, the Dundee poet and mathematician, has informed me about an evening in MacCaig's flat during an Edinburgh Festival (c. 1950). Sam Wanamaker, the American actor was there. This is Dutton's account:

> When MacCaig spoke of 'the philistine, uncouthness of the Scottish working class; they see nothing in life beyond football…', Hamish demanded: 'Norman, what do you know about the Scottish Working Class? What it is. What it might be.' MacCaig stood his ground, handsome and arrogant. When he added a smile, suddenly, Hamish let fly with a hay-maker that knocked MacCaig to the ground. He got to his feet and said, 'Am I meant to be insulted!' Wanamaker said, 'I like to see a man felled with a blow – delivered in anger!' After that everything then settled down.

Within a short time MacCaig wrote a poem that seems clearly based on the incident; entitled 'Hero', it places Hamish (and Scotland) in a time-warp in which barbarism and civilisation battle in a very Celtic melting pot.

Cuchulain
Or any other great legend's man
Salted white with the blue Aegean
Or ruddy on an Irish strand,
What was the simplicity that made
Time tender with you and your uncrooked shade.

No need to look
For plume, carved chessmen, golden torque.
We, more than they, are your relic.
Passion remains; and south and north
Happens to us, as to you. We seek
No other than gay Celt and subtle Greek.

Cuchulain
Fighting suffered a transformation
To still Cuchulain but more than man.
—Only once Time's repetition
Showed us in him, when staring mad,
He died fighting the waves on a friendly strand.[5]

Hamish's relationship with Morris Blythman (the poet Thurso Berwick) was founded on political allegiance, Lallans and a love of song. Blythman and his wife Marian were Communists. One of Berwick's best Lallans poems was written to be recited at celebrations marking the twenty-fifth anniversary of the death of John MacLean. The main event took place in St Andrews Hall, Glasgow, on St Andrews Day 1948. Berwick knew Hamish would be in the chair— before two thousand people— and he seems to have deliberately sought to honour Hamish as 'the new John MacLean': Glasgow being, in 1948, in many ways a revolutionary city. After sixty years, Berwick's poem, 'Til the City o John Maclean', retains a thrilling power:

They rieved the live rose frae the leaf
An bluidit aa hir snawy bosom;
Bit rose-buds wheesh the rose-tree's grief
An fresh hir rue til reasoun.

They've rowpt oor hames an gien us slums,
Black-reekit, chokit wi thri factries;
Bit rivets, reid-hot in thir wames,
Wull eftir-birth thir victries.

They've taen oor bluid ti mak thir gowd
An stuid us idle, lean an lankit;
Bit nou black's birlan rou ti reid
—They're drunk at Yankee's banquet.

Then get the lethers on the waa,
An gie thir gates Auld Scotland's shouther;
An suid thir heids til fredom faa,
Twull red them oot the smother
The doors are doun – the stairs are doun –
Lat nane come near athout bean thankit!
Fur Auld Lang Syne, then – aa breenge in!
—A MacLean is at yuir Banquet!

As Berwick spoke that last line the whole audience erupted in spontaneous applause. Years later Hamish noted it as 'a moment that made my hair stand on end!'

An thank ye braw. An thank ye rife.
We thank ye, John, we reid o roses,
Thit, lowan wi life abuin yuir grave,
Wull mind us aye where lies—No!—ryses
The giant wha toured up in the dock
Wi eagle een o Scotland's wrackers,
An rowed aside that muckle rock,
Thit stappt the mou o hir makers.

They've reived the live rose frae the leaf
An bluidit aa hir snawy bosom
Bit rose-buds laved wi reivers' bluid,
Wull lowe wi loe, come simmer seasoun,
Whin, City, prood o John MacLean,
Ye ryse again!
An, braw wi reid rutes in the Clyde,
Ye guide the warld
To flourish

Thurso Berwick is also important in the Hamish story because in an article he wrote for the magazine *Chapbook* Vol. 4, no.6, in 1966, he makes it clear that it was Hamish Henderson who blew up the EIIR letterbox, at the Inch in Edinburgh in February 1953.

Another friend tempted, but not seduced, by Hamish's revolutionary ardour was Alan Riddell, poet and magazine editor. The two men met first at International House, during the third Edinburgh Festival, in 1949. Riddell was a twenty-two year old Australian/Scot who, after service in the Royal Navy, was hungry for contact with the Scots literary scene. In January 1951, Hamish published two poems by Riddell in the last issue of his *Cambridge Poetry Broadsheets*, No.11. Both are about Hamish. The first is entitled 'Free One':

All joys are his
   Wind-free to hover
Still over mountain
   And snarling sea.

Hump-backed clouds
   Under him are beautiful

As he rises, only
   Perfect one, eagle.

Day and night
   He spans the world;
Wings wonderful
   Lift him swimming,

Fill falling from him,
   Falling, the earth
Grows small as he
   Shoulders the sun.

Riddell's second poem describes a scene in an Edinburgh Street. It counter-points Montale's 'Wind on the Crescent' and is entitled 'The Shower':

Sudden the shower burst on the street,
   an agony of falling stars
till we ran for shelter.
The awning cried gold tears
   as you shook the rain from your hair.

The rain was rainbow
   falling, a golden halo
circling your hair
   the sunlight was.

And as suddenly passed
   the shower,
and we were walking the street
   again walking the street
so lately filled with stars.

Riddell admired Hamish as a man and as a poet but quickly became disillusioned by his revolutionary politics. Anyone associated with the Scottish Republican Army (SRA) at a time when any EIIR letterbox in Scotland was liable to be blown-up was likely to find their career blighted, or incarcerated in a prison or asylum. One of Riddell's poems can be interpreted as documenting his need to free himself from Hamish's all-pervasive literary and political influence. It is called 'Interloper':

It seems so strange to me
That the sun sitting outside my window munching an orange
Really is the sun, will go on really *being* the sun
As long as I live, and that's more than a million years
The way I feel now...

It seems so strange to me I could almost cry out -
Hey there, ragamuffin,
Stop throwing orange rinds into my window,
Take your pumpkin face out of my seed-beds,
And SCRAM!'

That last word—in capitals—is the only word in capitals in the whole book in which the poem was published.[6] Another poem in the book, 'The Burden', addresses Riddell's need to free himself of life – a life focused, then made weary, by Hamish.

The relationship between Hamish and Hugh MacDiarmid has been a subject of speculation and debate for sixty years. The accepted wisdom is that their intellectual feud *re* the merits of the folk and literary traditions in Scots culture was sterile and their personal antagonism mutually destructive. However, one of the most surprising discoveries I have made whilst writing Hamish's biography has been how close and stimulating the MacDairmid/Henderson relationship was. They had dialectical disagreements: certainly MacDiarmid guarded 'his' Scottish Renaissance with a wilful jealousy but, beyond that, the two men admired and influenced each other to the great advantage of creative and intellectual life in Scotland. Indeed, it is now clear that Hamish, and the ideas he carried, makes repeated appearances in MacDiarmid's post-war poetry. The first example is a poem written in June 1947, which followed hard on the heels of their first, very intense, weekend together. MacDiarmid had been hugely impressed by the appearance of this revolutionary, all-singing, all-knowing, motor-cycling soldier poet—as his poem 'Glasgow' (*Voice of Scotland*, July 1947) makes clear.[7] The poem addresses urban destitution and civic corruption in Glasgow but, recognising that his own powers are now waning, MacDiarmid cries out for support—for a new man (someone like Hamish), who, might build the New Scotland he had so long envisioned—a new Glasgow of the kind Charles Rennie Mackintosh had sought to nurture into being fifty years previously.

... Glasgow
Thinks nothing, and is content to be
Just what it is, not caring or knowing what...
Everything is dead except stupidity here...

...Ah no! I am too old,
Too old, too old, too old, and as for Scott
The only other 'whole' and 'seldom man' I know here,
The cabal of his foes gives all this insensate welter
Of a city an expression of idiot fury...

...Wherever the faintest promise, the slightest integrity,
Dares to show in any of the arts or thought or politics,
At once the jealous senile jabber breaks out
Striking with sure instinct at everything
with courage and sincerity...
'Confound it all!' If once we let these young folk in
What is to become of us?
...Who knows – in this infernal brothlike fog
There maybe greater artists yet by far than we
Unheard of, even by us, condemned to be invisible
In this tarnhelm of unconscionable ignorance
Where 'everyone is entitled to their own opinion.'?

'Unconscionable' was one of Hamish's favourite words, and there can
be little doubt that Hamish was source and subject of this poem. Over
the next decade Hamish and MacDiarmid remained, recurrently,
close, and numerous poems bear the Hamish imprint: 'The Universal
Man' (To Lady Astor), 'Old Woman in High Spirits', and 'Faugh-a-
Ballagh' (to the SRA) are examples. It is, however, three long poems,
written in the early fifties that provide us with substantial information
about MacDiarmid's response to, and admiration for, the Henderson
phenomenon. And, despite the combative jealousy endemic in Chris
Grieve's 'borderland' personality, Hugh MacDiarmid cannot but
speak well of Hamish—as a multi-talented and very Scottish genius.
In 1952 he wrote a poem entitled 'A New Scots Poet' which reads like
the 'extended review' he had failed to write when Hamish's *Elegies for
the Dead in Cyrenaica* were first published in 1948:

It was difficult for his work at first
To secure the reception it required
Among such sentimentalists as the Scots.

They did not realise he had
Already put such emotion and feeling
Into it that all *they* had to do
Was to accept it straight forwardly,

Directly and simply, and that the emotion
Would liberate itself like a volatile vapour
Of its own accord,
Without any efforts on their part...

...The Scots were always devils
For adding rouge to a rose
And guilt to a lily,
And prone to the pet vices of Liedersänger
—Scooping and unnecessarily marked dynamics.

Though simple in the sense of single,
Of unified in aspiration,
His work of course is not imply in any way.

Bringing Scotland alive in people's blood again
Rather than in their minds at first,
Through their instinctive actions and sense perceptions,
Through their sight, touch, smell and hearing,
Making them vividly aware
Of every element in the Scottish scene.

He was like the Piob Mhor, or the Great Highland Bagpipe,
The only instrument extant whose manual is derived
In enharmonic concord with a fixed fundamental bass.
Piobaireachd is derived from the upper responses of
    the human heart
To the fundamental sequence of the elements.

In 1953 MacDiarmid wrote another highly ambitious poem—'The Poet as Prophet'—addressing a future Scots poet of genius. This man is, evidentially, not MacDiarmid; nor is it Sorley MacLean, the pre-eminent Gaelic poet. Perhaps MacDiarmid seeks to conjure an apocryphal, composite genius-poet, but the skills, experience and qualities he gives his 'prophet' are exactly those MacDiarmid had been so amazed and thrilled to find in Hamish. Indeed, he welcomes the new poet with pride because he has acknowledged himself as MacDiarmid's apprentice, as his *filidh*. Since his school days Hamish had honoured MacDiarmid and believed himself destined to develop, humanise and make substantial the Scottish renaissance MacDiarmid had initiated; revolutions need their Robespierres and their Dantons. MacDiarmid describes 'The Poet as Prophet—*The Man for whom Gaeldom is waiting*' as being a man

Au fait with the whole range of European arts and letters
As few have ever been, he proudly proclaimed himself
A barbarian, in the sense that that the art
Of the Celtic lands and Scandinavia
Were both on the edge of the world...

His sympathies were wholly with [the Communism
    vision of the world]...
Which alone, he knew, had anything of value
To say to Gaeldom, and under which alone
Gaelic independence and the Gaelic languages
Would be respected and encouraged,
A view in which alone the disastrous split
Between Highlander and Lowlander might be healed
And a united Scotland arise in the world...

The reason was that he rose
Out of the category of men
And entered the category of the elements.
He was the wind, the sea, the tempest, the hurricane.
He was the marvellous embodiment
Of the complete identification
Of the Celtic mind with all nature and all life...

For the real Gael has something that the old Greeks had ...
He has an ideal, a plan of life,
Transcending the mere means and apparatus of living,
Feverish immersion in secondary and ancillary matters
Leaves him unsatisfied.
He has a craving for essentials.
The miracle of literature,
Of culture, in racial history
Is that it is at once the bow and the mark,
The inspiration and the aim...

Suddenly, splitting the sky
Was heard a great voice
Which echoes round the firmament.
'Stand fast for Scotland!'

Finally, in 1955, MacDiarmid wrote, 'King Over Himself', a eulogy
written shortly after Hamish had returned from Sutherland with

his historic recordings of the Ossianic tinker patriarch *Ailidh Dall* (Blind Alec Stewart of Lairg). It was a folklore discovery of European importance and MacDiarmid wrote a pangyric in praise of Hamish— and auld Caledonia—as a twentieth-century bard who personifies his nation. MacDiarmid paints a picture of a hero, a confrontational intellectual who loves to sing, who makes the poorest citizens feel like kings: he exults a hero—in thrall to both human frailties and Leninite discipline, a man who lives free as a bird, yet at one with the common man.

How he loved to survey the lands of Scotland
From some nest of eagles in a cloud of stone
—to let his soul pasture in valleys
And frolic on her mountains,
Roam from her Northmost to her Southmost point,
Watch her skies, drink her waters,
And breath her forests and fields!
And all the flowers of Scotland grew in his soul,
And he felt the savour of his own soul rise to his head.
All the people of Scotland once more
Were timeless, aflame and virile.
Their speech rang like steel.
They talked in poems and their words
Held echoes of miracle.
Miracle followed the man like a domestic animal.

Ere the great day on which he declared himself
Had he not looked at Anglo-Scotland and
   understood and judged,
Here there was no justice, or love of justice, he thought,
No reality or love of reality.
Here there was only expediency and love of expediency.
Here all was venal, and to feign worth
Was better than to possess it.
There was too much outward showing,
Too little inward meaning,
Too much appearance,
Too little reality.
And instantly, summing up in himself
The whole range of Gaelic wisdom…

...to every man in Scotland he cried:
'Remember that thou art a man',
And there is nothing like him
Who is king over himself.

As the years passed, however, Hamish did not fulfil MacDiarmid's visionary hopes, and the older man determined to bring the younger low.

Two other writers who recognised the crisis Hamish was facing in the sixties were Tom Scott and Stuart MacGregor. Both believed Hamish could and should do something astounding for literature, and for Scotland. Hamish, by the mid-sixties, knew that fulfilling such expectations was an impossibility, in his time, at least alone. And Scott articulated the great problem facing any original thinker in Scotland by raising the spectre of the brutalism ever ready to destroy creative goodness in Scotland—in a letter concerning an article about Hamish in the folk magazine *Chapbook* (1967):

Dear Hamish, Chapbook certainly does you proud...You have deserved well of your country... and if your country, as is its wont, repays you with impalement on the thistle, its highest award for its benefactors, at least the folksong elements are in no doubt at all about your importance, and rightly hail you, as the father of the folksong revival in Scotland... the mother of art poetry is the folk, out of whom the rocket soars – even Grieve – and back to whom it sinks.

Stuart MacGregor, doctor, folk enthusiast, poet and novelist, remained close to Hamish over many years but, like MacDiarmid, seems to have felt bound to 'betray' him and the ideals he represented. 'Hamish' characters dominate MacGregor's two major novels, *The Myrtle and the Ivy* and *The Sinner*. Both are formally experimental, strongly biographical, and set in mid-twentieth-century Edinburgh. MacGregor was fascinated by Hamish as a shamanic, messianic revolutionary, and his ideas provide the philosophical subtext of both books. In *The Myrtle and the Ivy* (MacDonald, 1967), Hamish provides a template for the character named Hector Gunn, a radical Scots nationalist, university lecturer and folk-entrepreneur. In *The Sinner* (Calder and Boyars, 1973), Hamish is Nicol Ross, a folk-prophet betrayed by his friend Denis Sellers (MacGregor himself). The names of all MacGregor's characters were chosen with care. Hector was the Trojan hero killed by Achilles but whose descendents went forth to found the Roman republic. Gunn is the Norse clan name of the

Henderson family. Nichol is the Old Norse name for a warrior, Ross another name for Red; Sellers was one of the villains in the history of the Sutherland Clearances… *The Sinner* is an important Scots novel and merits analysis *re* the Henderson story. When the novel opens, its chief protagonist, Nichol Ross, is already dead—killed, we are informed, by Scotch Calvinism and repressive bourgeoisie Edinburgh. Dennis Sellers states: 'We both crucified him, and rightly so'. Ross is an enigma and remains one throughout the novel:

> The rumours, particularly in Connor's [Sandy Bell's]: a ruined aristocrat, the bottle. A fisherman's son, left home because of a woman, said Joe the Rat. Really an Englishman, said Starkey Shearer, there are Oxford undertones in thet eccent. An unfrocked priest, from Ollie the Bull, the Harlem schizophrenic. Deals in black magic, queer noises from his house at night. Best novelist we had fifteen years ago, hasn't written much since.
>
> We talk about you, Nichol, how could we help it? Were you a fragment of God? But it's too late now. The Powers of Darkness, the two mad Johns, still rule this City…Together we raised a new rebel standard, then like all the others we went the way of history, turned on each other and…

The two mad Johns referred to are John Calvin and John Knox. Nichol Ross, as a modern man, a saintly poet and metaphysical philosopher stands against these personifications of reductive intellectualism. He is, also, a man of action, a modern Montrose. One scene describes Ross taking two young lovers from Connor's Bar to Edinburgh High Street, to the spot where Montrose was executed. There Nichol Ross, raising his arms like a druid, sees them given Gaelic oaths of allegiance—to each other and to Scotland: and he marries them.

> We stopped by a plaque. Montrose. Nichol scanned the street for the Crows [the police], but not a speck of black to be seen. His arms upthrust to the tall sharp roofs. 'In place of the conventional hypocritic oath that binds most lovers, let us be more reverent. Here he died, one of the noblest of our poets, and all the Black Ministers drooling with bloodlust and the whole city black with shame. Stand on his blood, children, stand on his death!' The night wind stilled; strangely powerless we obeyed. 'Murdo,' he commanded, 'bless them in Gaelic!'…
>
> Murdo intoning, his voice an elegy, but so slightly mechanical, brother you also are hypnotised. The round diphthonged vowels faded through the night; Nicol's flat icy palms on our heads:

'And I order all that I hold sacred to bless and guard this union that is right beyond all calculated knowledge,' he muttered in a voice charged with affection. 'As I know that your feet now point towards the light, so I beseech you to love each other out of lust and away from darkness.'

Lawnmarket, cobbled square, Cathedral moaning Amen... Hope lies somewhere inside that uncanny skull. And here we stand on martyrdom, knowing nothing, but I feel your hand in mine, lassie, and above the last note of a rebel benediction the tolerant stars wink and watch like wedding women.

> Dear Man of Men so strange thy words and strong
> Below the spires that John had screamed among
> Yet under madness in my heart a song.

Ross's suicide (in *The Sinner*) seems to be symbolic of what MacGregor saw as Hamish's inability to go on writing great poetry and of his failure to lead Scotland back to political independence. Having made himself into a Judas figure, MacGregor ends the novel with the 'discovery' of a clutch of posthumous letters—left by Ross—that read as testaments to the dead man's values. The Christ comparison seems clear. And the questions relating to Hamish's 'failure' and MacGregor's own, possible suicide are left very open. Certainly MacGregor's books demand serious study, not least because of the 'first-hand' light they throw on Hamish in the fifties and sixties.

MacGregor and Hamish were both members of a radical cultural group called the Heretics, a forum for writers and artists wishing to ginger-up the cultural scene in Edinburgh. Another member was the trilingual poet William Neill. His poem, 'Edinburgh Don, 1971', adds something profound to our knowledge of how Hamish was perceived by his literary friends at this time. It was, probably, written after a lunchtime session in Sandy Bell's had been followed by a visit to Hamish's Socratic attic in the School of Scottish Studies:

> In this high centre
> of all that's known and ever can be known
> I gaze across the cities of the plain
> to clearer skies beyond.
>
> Soon they will come,
> secure in their new prophecies,
> sure their causes have the best effects.

Soon they will come, eager disciples;
seeking yearned truths, at last they will come to wisdom,
seeing the years bring no knowledge,
syllogisms no surety.

For my disciples I resurrect no gods,
only the whispering phantoms of old words,
the gibbering ghosts of long dead certainties.

I am the living link of the old chain,
my cell a little warmer than Lindisfarne,
a little less remote than Icolmkill.

Our faltering guidance still remains unhonoured,
the well-born lackey of the worldly-wise.

I pull my gown around me, close my window
lest in the traitor moment I should hurl
my body concretewards from this high temple.[8]

This monastic side to Hamish's character is also finely caught in
Hayden Murphy's poem, 'Your Welcome'. Having met Hamish in
Dublin in 1966, Murphy began working as a journalist in Edinburgh.
After deciding to settle permanently in Scotland, in 1979, Murphy
wrote this poem—to his mentor:

It always begins with your smile:
Then the hand-clasp,
Each finger an embrace
Of knowledge delivered
With affection. Then
The embrace of comrade
Generosity with Brother Pleasure
At our meeting.

It is the warmth
Of knowledge heated
By the sure fire of intellect.
And, I hope,
Lit by friendship.

The Franciscan references in Murphy's poem are strangely echoed in
a letter Hamish received in February 1991 from Jim Henderson of One
Tree Farm, Auckland. A former ANZAC soldier, wounded in Italy, Jim

Henderson had long felt personally addressed by Hamish's 'Banks o' Sicily' and, in old age, he wrote to honour a man whose words had meant much across a life marked by tragedy and resilience:

Dear Swaddie Effendi Hamish, I salute a namesake and a fellow desert rat—war amputee [left leg off, gangrene at Bari]—and was deeply moved, ancestral echoes maybe, when years ago I heard 'puir bloody swaddies are weary'—the wonderful bone-tired weariness of it... Oh, the ever referred sound (to a Kiwi)—'Close 51st Highland Division...' – Aye. Close and personal now... I named our third son Hamish—and before and after—I visualised him as dark, powerful, semi-grumbling, yet with sudden arm-flung leaps of love—but alas Hamish was stillborn, Hutt Hospital—ending the family of three, thirty years ago. I'm 72, classified 160% disabled! But don't you believe that—I got to, and stood on the exact South Pole twenty minutes, courtesy of a Hercules—the first monopod to stand there, marvelling—the sky a gentle—soft—hedge-sparrow-egg blue and no wind (the killer). Afterwards I did a book 'One Foot on the Pole'.

Hamish stimulated highly personal responses. One night in October 1997, I had a dream about him:

'Hamish Henderson's Last Good Night'

A body broke the clouds below me,
Rising Tintoretto-like an arm and man
Came up at me through space,
His left hand reaching for my right –
Half the world was spread beneath us,
His grasp not worth the name.

I am become the Morning Star, he whispered,
My hour in the night-sky of life falls away,
The light of the morning of daybreak has found me –
This glisten of sweat is death having its way.

Life-long imprints the palm slipping from me,
In slow-motion a life is unlocking for ever:
The voice coming up is now thought more than whisper –
I loved you like a father and a son,
The secret is both one and all
As Cornishmen would say.

Hark Away! The Raven rolls his glossy wing—Hark Away!
A lady birds alighted on my breeches by the bed—Hark Away!
Ben Vorlich's there, and Dublin Toon
And Auld Reekie like a lang dried rose.

Look on me now not as I am
But as I was—in song—
When I was young
And in the Appenines
—in Italy, in sun.

The darkest hour is moments now and long,
My strength light-years away—
Back into the melting pot I go—I joke!
These rolling captions mark the end:

As when I sang John Berger out onto the Barra Strand.
Addio! Addio! It was in music those words came—
Like beastings atop a milking pail;
'The first and last of life is herding'
And that song older than all stories told.

Ah look—the sun is up—
Easing its shadow down Glas Maol,
Lighting the brig o'er the Glenshee Water.
Look - there on the road the rain lights to the hill—
A piper leaning on his son:

The Siege of Delhi fills my ears.
The Siege of Delhi
Sounding across the sands
As it did when he went down, at Anzio.

Silenzio.

The sound of oars, rested and dripping.
Fluorescent the boys who dive the Blue Grotto,
Amber the nectar in Keith and Kinross—
The Green Man and the Jew's harp!

Euphoric—I see Schiehallion illumined—
Ask Margaret sing, *The Cave of Gold.*

Ask Janet come. It was for Life and Love I sang.
I see Him shining in her eyes—my Champion.

In the same year, the year of the successful Scottish Referendum, Angus Calder wrote a rather similar poem, 'Anent that Referendum—for Hamish Henderson': it looks back before looking forward to affirm Hamish's abiding influence on modern Scotland.

It was as if the forests where kings hunted
Still stood on the Boroughmuir, by the Water of Leith
And after dark a silent army had massed
Befriending the gypsies, succouring those people plague
And leprosy had driven furth of the walls,
Then, in the small hours, moved
To reoccupy the Old Town by vanishing
Into its stones, giving each a radiance
As dawn leapt from the grey North Sea
Over a city where ghosts had reclaimed their own,
Flowed in and out of each other and made peace...

In 1999, the Gaelic Rock Band Runrig wrote a song called 'The Summer Walkers'. This was the title of a film I made with Hamish in 1977. Later I wrote a book with the same title. This in turn inspired Calum and Rory MacDonald to write a thumping Ceilidh-dance song—for their band Runrig. The song honours Ailidh Dall, the Traveller way of life, Hamish, and the book:

Sometimes when you journey
Through the pages of a book
You're taken places beyond words
You let them speak their truth
Today I've opened treasures
That my eyes could scarce believe
They're words of confirmation
Everything that makes me sing...

Now your words are not of sentiment
Shallow or untrue
But wells of living water
And from their clear deep sides we drew
The songs, the tin, the horse,
This countries great and ancient wilds
Your faith in God and man and nature

And the keenness of your guile...
For you were the Summer walkers
And the fishers of the pearl.[9]

In the wake of Hamish's death, in 2002, a stream of songs were created in his honour. Paraig MacNeill wrote, 'Tae Hamish'; Iain and Neil MacDonald, 'The Songs That He Left'; Geordie McIntyre, 'Beinn Gulabeinn'; Elizabeth Stewart, 'Lament for Hamish Henderson'... My concern here, however, is with the poets, and the most remarkable posthumous poem for Hamish is Donald Smith's visionary work, 'A Long Stride Shortens the Road'. Donald Smith's life had been significantly shaped by Hamish long before he became the first director of the Scottish Storytelling Centre in Edinburgh and, once in post, Smith began to use his Centre to advance many of the cultural forces to which Hamish had dedicated his life. Smith's poem is ambitious, wide-ranging and long. I quote from a section that describes Hamish on a coach—going westwards—at election time:

> ...Suddenly he was up into the aisle
> No longer dozing by my shoulder,
> But towering to the rooflights
> Leaflets flourished in his hand from nowhere.
> 'Have you voted yet today?
> Ladies, it's your parliament at stake.
> Scotland's right belongs to you as well.
> Aye, look around ye lads,
> Nationless, the workers' cause unwon.
> For King and Country, Mam?
> I fought to beat the fascists,
> Now I want to win the peace,
> For us and for the nations of the world.'
> He had the bus alight and laughing.
> Then he set them singing,
> Clydeside red, the weavers' ballads,
> Polaris and the CND, with bawdy numbers in between
> Then unexpectedly the bus arrived.
> 'Jesus Christ,' the driver spat contentedly,
> 'Will you be on my shift the morn?'
> Men shook his hand, women hugged.
> 'God' he said, 'But I could use a drink.'

Donald Smith's portrait echoes those painted by earlier poets. His Hamish is a man of demotic energy and boyish, Christ-like enthusiasm;

he is also a born leader who accepts public responsibilities not as irksome but a sublime reality. This is a man, at once other-worldly and down-to-earth; a man of vision but committed to the here and now; a man 'of values as old fashioned as the Walls of Jerusalem.'

It is easy to say of Hamish—as it is of Coleridge—that here was a man who fulfilled little of his promise. Yet Coleridge wrote 'The Ancient Mariner' and influenced many of the finest minds of his generation, Hazlitt writing that if 'he had not been the finest talker of his age he would have been its finest writer'. Likewise, Hamish wrote his *Elegies* and engaged in talk that made him one of the wonders of Edinburgh. These two men shared much in character and what they shared affirms something real about vitality in life and literature. What Coleridge found in his 'ancient mariner', Hamish found amongst the Highland Travellers, the Red Clydesiders and the bothy folk of Auld Pictland. And what Hamish did—'slumming it amongst the beggarmen' was only what most of the world's great literary figures have done: trawl the banks of oral tradition to the glory of mankind. He followed in the footsteps of Homer and Ossian; Matthew, Mark, Luke, and John; Dante and Shakespeare; Burns and Wordsworth; Yeats and Synge; Joyce, Eliot and MacDiarmid...Hamish, like Coleridge, enjoyed the Rabelaisian life but, retaining a Highland edge, saw the future, 'if there is a future', as an ascetic future.

In conclusion, I quote from *The History of Alyth Parish Church*, written by the Rev. James Meickle in 1933. Alyth lies next door to Blairgowrie, where Hamish was born, and just a few miles from the Spittal of Glenshee where he spent his early boyhood. Alyth was a Christian settlement founded by St Moluag, an Irish contemporary of St Columba. Having founded his community on the Isle of Lismore (an ancient centre of druidism and deer-hunting), Moluag set out to civilise barbaric, poetical Caledonia:

> St Moluag's monks, working amongst the Picts, were very different to the monks of the Roman Church—the Celtic monks did it all, and they alone; and their monasteries were never palatial buildings but groups of round huts with a common kitchen, a separate dining hut, a writing hut, a hut or huts for teaching student missionaries and a church... all of these were surrounded according to tradition by a dyke, which caused them sometimes to be known as forts... These Celtic monks were not all preachers. Some were readers, some singers, some artisans and agriculturalists—all under the authority of an Ab or Abbot ('Abba', father).

Like the Reverend Meickle, Hamish admired these Celtic/Pictish monks and the values they cultivated. They were not celibate and, under their Ab, enjoyed remarkable freedoms—personal, social, intellectual and religious. They enjoyed lives of 'sensuous austerity'. The kind of life Hamish advocates in the prologue to his *Elegies*, the kind of art to which Charles Rennie Mackintosh gave form. In retrospect, Hamish can be seen to have lived the bardic life of a modern 'Ab'—nurturing poetry, learning the common good and the social discipline necessary for the pursuit of happiness. Like the good Ab, Hamish was a man at ease with singers, scholars, soldiers, craftsmen, farm workers, the young and very old. He enjoyed life as 'a contemporary ancestor'. He was at once boyish and, apparently, irresponsible; but fatherly, and utterly responsibly. It was a combination that exulted life, and many of the poets who knew him loved and honoured him—as their words prove.

References:

1   This quotation is from Stuart MacGregor's novel, *The Sinner* (London: Calder and Boyars, 1973). It comes from a letter written by Nichol Ross, a major character in the novel, widely accepted as being based on MacGregor's friend and mentor, Hamish Henderson.

2   *Cencrastus*, no. 36 (Spring, 1990).

3   Paul Potts, *Dante called you Beatrice* (London: Writers Union, 1961).

4   'Sun the First', *Cambridge Poetry Broadsheet*, no. 4.

5   Norman MacCaig, *Collected Poems* (London: Chatto & Windus, 1985).

6   Alan Riddell, *The Stopped Landscape, and other poems* (London: Hutchinson, 1968), p. 7.

7   Hamish's dramatic meeting he with MacDiarmid is described in *Cencrastus*, no. 48 (Summer, 1994).

8   *Aquarius*, no. 6, Scottish Issue, (1973).

9   Calum MacDonald and Rory MacDonald, *Flower of the West: the Runrig Songbook* (Aberdeen: Ridge Press, 2000).

THE SCOTTISH ACCENT OF THE MIND: INTRODUCTION TO THE SYMPATHETIC IMAGINATION: SCOTTISH POETS OF THE SECOND WORLD WAR

Joy Hendry

Born of a post-war marriage of an ex-commando turned policeman to a hospital nurse, I suppose war has always been with me (like most of my generation). My paternal grandfather had fought in the trenches and survived. My father had been caught only two years into the war and served three years as a prisoner of war. He told me that he need not have been caught, having seen trouble and taken evasive action, but his other three colleagues had not noticed and were apprehended. So, in a gesture of solidarity, he gave himself up too. He was, by all accounts, pretty lucky. His last two years of internment were with an Austrian small-farmer family who could not have been kinder to him: he became known in the locality as 'Der Willie' [*pace* Mrs Thatcher!]. Six foot three and a half, he was handsome and so brimful of ingenuity at acquiring 'perquisites' that some of his fellow prisoners thought he must be a 'fifth columnist'. But in front of me and my mother, at least, only the funny stories (and they were *very* funny) came out.

I definitely remember meeting Hamish in the early 1970s, predictably, in Sandy Bell's while selling *Chapman* and other literary magazines, and he backed me to the hilt from Day One. (Actually, I think we *had* met before that when I was only 17 and still trying to be a folk singer, and Hamish, an *avant-garde* folk-blues band and I did probably not very good improvisations to Hamish's *Elegies* in what was then the men's union of Edinburgh University. This must have been 1970.) 'Sie macht eine wunderschöne Arbeit,' I remember him telling two German students in Sandy Bells—about my work with *Chapman*. He also greatly approved of my selling hand to hand. We soon got to know each other pretty well. I talked to him often about the need to publish his poetry, offering *Chapman* (indeed *any* medium)—more or less at his disposal.

'No,' he said, time and again. For Hamish, in the 1970s and early 1980s, his commitment to the oral tradition was so firm that he would not allow his poetry to be published. His faith that his work would survive was implacable and total. But I often pointed out, poetry is not like song. People do not or cannot commit it to memory and pass it on… (I often pricked him about the *Elegies*: why had he allowed these to be published?) And of course I told him about my father, at some point, though right now I cannot remember when, and Hamish positively glowed with fellow-feeling. I spent far too much of my undergraduate years on *Chapman*, working on it, selling it, meeting poets like Hamish, Norman MacCaig, Tom Scott, Sorley MacLean, even Hugh MacDiarmid, the philosopher George Davie (almost scorned by some in the philosophy department I studied in) and many others. This opened up a world I had hardly known existed and one almost totally unrecognised at the time by education at any level. It was a real revolution of the soul and I became avid and utterly committed to 'the cause' of Scottish literature, language and culture.

After university, I taught English in Haddington, and quickly adopted the policy of trying to open the doors to Scottish literature for the young people I encountered. Whenever possible, I would substitute Scottish poems where English poems were advocated, and I grew increasingly infuriated at the mindless torture of innocent minds with 'Dulce et Decorum Est' and other stuff from World War One. I managed to keep *Chapman* going on top of teaching, and my contacts with Scottish poets grew ever wider and stronger. I had had the privilege of getting to know the *Elegies* and the war poetry from other writers such as Sorley MacLean, Tom Scott, Robert Garioch or George Campbell Hay.

Almost *all* the poets of that generation—Hamish, Tom, Sorley, Norman, Edwin Morgan, Iain Crichton Smith, William Neill, T S Law, Sydney Goodsir Smith—were absolutely perfervid in their support for the 'little' magazines. Hamish's attitude to publication in printed form changed when he learned my father was dying: he suddenly agreed to let me have some of the poems he had been writing since the *Elegies* for *Chapman*, and I suspect that what he knew about my father was the clincher. So the poems began to arrive, mainly handwritten. I commissioned articles from Raymond Ross and Adam McNaughtan and before I knew it I had an extensive feature on Hamish for *Chapman* 42.[1] Thereafter, hardly a day passed without the post delivering yet another poem or idea or something from Hamish. It was an exciting collaboration. Almost all aspects of Hamish's work are at least referred to, and the poems (almost 20 pages worth) range from his magnificent long post-*Elegies* war poem 'Freedom Becomes People', which takes its cue from Heinrich Heine's 'Freedom Becomes People', his early Cambridge poems, translations of Friedrich Hölderlin, C P Cavafy and Dino Campana, his MacDiarmid salvo, written on reading the latter's *Lucky Poet*, and some much lighter material from 'Auld Reekie's Roses', celebrating events in 'ordinary' life. The tenor of his war poetry had changed from the *Elegies*. For Hamish, what Heine said about the necessity of freedom becoming people, was also true of poetry—it too must 'become people': accessible to all. And the mood had changed from one of the need for the passive endurance of suffering to one of 'resolve, of transformation, of insurrection' which would 'leave the desert behind'. Miraculously, the issue appeared only two or three months later, in early December 1985, and Hamish was tireless then too in his efforts to help me promote it. We toured the radio stations together!

I had left teaching the previous year to devote more time to the magazine and literary life and, increasingly, more work for radio, including extended interviews with poets and writers. Working with Raymond Ross, I co-edited two books of *Critical Essays*, one on Sorley MacLean, published in 1986, and one on Norman MacCaig,[2] which brought me into very close contact with both of them, especially Sorley, since my contribution to the volume was a biographical essay.[3] Raymond and I had also collaborated on major events: working sometimes with him, sometimes with others—Morris Blythman, Alan Taylor, Brian McCabe. We marked and celebrated birthdays for Norman, Sorley and Hamish, all this intensifying my relationship with them. I also met George Campbell Hay in his favourite howff, The Canny Man's, and, after he died in 1984, produced a couple of special features on his work.[4] For all of these writers, war played a huge part in their lives and in their poetry, and the seeds of this programme were steadily developing.

I felt a strong mission to get these voices heard on radio before it was too late. Thus, *The Sympathetic Imagination: Scottish Poets of the Second World War* evolved out of my work with *Chapman*, teaching experience, and the need to draw the attention of the world to the unique 'take' we in Scotland have on things from this *extremis* of the planet, and in particular *our* experience of and response to war. Norman MacCaig often quoted Douglas Young's expression, 'the Scottish accent of the mind', as something virtually worth dying for. I had also fought with Norman about his stance on politics and war, trying to convince him that it was in fact aggressive, not passive, as he insisted it was, and spent several evenings enjoyably damaging my liver, pointing out to him poems of his which could readily be all about war, or if not intentionally so, had something profound and important to say about it, however obliquely.

So I put a proposal up to Radio Scotland for this programme. 'What is the hook?' they said, repeatedly. 'Armistice Day?' I just wilted under the chronic cultural myopia. Radio Scotland had first right of access to this gold-mine but were not interested in picking up the shovel. They seemed not very comfortable with poetry anyway. But I did have the good fortune to meet Julian May, himself a poet, who came with Joyce McMillan to interview me about Scots language. When next in London I phoned him and petitioned him in the canteen over pie and beans (which I would *never* otherwise eat) and after five minutes we had a programme—no hooks, no nothing. So it was a resounding 'yes' from Radio 3—but sadly not Radio Scotland where it really might have stuck and been listened to by more 'ordinary' Scots fowk? Ah well. Attempts were made to 'sell' it to them afterwards, but they did not want that either. As Norman points out in the programme, 'You have to go to London…'

Listening to this again has been a life-changing experience for me. I am reminded of the grandeur of spirit so evident in Hamish, and indeed all of them—and of course the sheer quality of all the poetry. I think it can be safely said that at the time (1990) most of the poets interviewed were not speaking to at least one or two of the others. But look at the mutual respect (*not* admiration). Look at the common ground. Look at the quality of attention to the key aspects of each other's work paid in spite of whatever feuds might have been going on, in some cases, for decades. The Scottish accent of the mind again. The import of the subject, their humility in the face of it, the *absolute* values underlying their commitment to literature and life, allowed them to ignore all other *trivia* with ease. 'Allowed' is the wrong word. It was the right thing to do, and they did it, putting any personal animosities to one side. The Scottish accent of the mind at work, methinks.

'Fate' sometimes makes itself almost visible through 'serendipity' and what landed in our laps was Dennis Healey launching his autobiography and being overtaken by emotion when singing Hamish's 'D-Day Dodgers' (beautifully out of tune). When I revealed this to Hamish, he had two reactions: one, rather dismissive and almost aristocratic, that that is what happens when you do the right thing; and the other was to be delightfully and childlikely *pleased*. But, yet again, he passed the buck back to the oral tradition: the song belonged not to him, but to the soldiers who added bits to it, or lustfully sang it. Healey was happy to allow us to use this extract from his launch speech—and, indeed, to learn (I gather) a bit more about its origins.

Each of the poets' 'war experience' was very different.. Hamish was probably the most 'clued in' of all of them, being, I suspect, politically aware from the moment he 'squirmed out of his mother's womb,' to borrow yet another phrase from Norman's contribution. I think this is borne out in Hamish's interest in—and commitment to—so many things furth of poetry—song, religion, you name it. His view of what was going on in the 1930s was unsullied by any personal emotional concerns. He was initially turned down because of his eyesight, but later conscripted anyway. He had a personal ruthlessness which could make him a fearsome opponent if he chose. Sorley's path to war was more difficult. He had suffered an intense emotional dilemma during the Spanish Civil War: he wanted to go and fight but could not, essentially for family reasons—his teacher's wage was crucial to the family survival. But he tormented himself endlessly, a torment documented in 'The Cry of Europe', 'The Choice' and other poems, in which he puts himself through what was really a hypothetical mangle—given the choice between fighting on the right side, and the love of an Irish woman—which would he choose? He feared he would choose the woman—and hated himself for it. When World War Two came, he enthusiastically acquiesced in his own conscription, and eventually was sent to the desert hoping not to come back—in anguish again over a different, this time a Scottish, woman.[5] J K Annand was never one for disclosing much about his personal life, but I could not detect any reluctance about fighting in that war scenario. Tom Scott was fundamentally against war, but once he understood what Hitler was doing, put to himself this question: 'If Hitler was in this room, would I shoot him?' His answer was an unequivocal 'yes' —and so he happily offered his services.

Robert Garioch was also a conscript, and spent most of the war as a prisoner in Italy, where he learned Italian and in particular the 'Romanesco' dialect and began a huge project to translate Giuseppe Belli into Scots, but his memoir *Two Men and a Blanket* documents his POW experience.[6] Indeed, his death in 1981 was one of the things which added to my sense of urgency to get this kind of work done before it was too late. George Campbell Hay was initially a conscientious objector, appearing twice at an appellate tribunal. When his plea was refused, he ignored the summons to a medical and instead took to the Argyll hills for eight months before being apprehended, hiding in various places, including Wendy Wood's highland retreat in Moidart. Given George's febrile sensitivity, and the history of madness in his family, he should never have been near *any* war front, but he was duly put there, and cruelly punished by the army for fraternising with the enemy. He simply could not help it: they were human beings, after all, and he wanted to learn their language. He became especially friendly with Arabs in North Africa, fascinated by the parallels he saw between their situation and ours, and Greeks in Macedonia after the war. His ability to fraternise with the 'natives' (given his incredible facility with languages) and instinctive sympathy with them led right-wing Greeks to suspect him of being a communist. There was even an assassination attempt—a tremendous fracas involving knives and guns in 1946 which left him physically unscathed (he was apparently capable of tholing an extraordinary degree of physical discomfort) but severely mentally scarred. He spent the rest of his life in and out of the Royal Edinburgh Hospital as a psychiatric patient. What a waste!

Two other poets in the programme were more robust souls: Douglas Young and Norman MacCaig. Young was a fervent Scottish Nationalist and questioned the right of the British Government, in terms of the Act of Union, to require a Scot to fight outside the British Isles without the explicit consent of the Scottish people. He refused to be conscripted and was duly incarcerated for three years in Saughton prison. From there, he conducted an enormously revealing correspondence with Sorley MacLean in which, amongst many other things, Sorley discussed his anguish over 'the Scottish woman'. Sorley despised the attitude of the likes of W H Auden, who had scarpered to America to avoid conscription. He hated his 'saving his art' in this manner, and wrote to Douglas Young: 'Still, with one of us in gaol and the other in the front line, I think we are in the only really honourable places a man can be in a war!'[7]

Norman always insisted that he was a pacifist, and he too refused conscription and spent about three months in jail before being allowed to join the Non-Combatant Corps. He simply refused to be put in a position in which he was expected to kill people. Anyone who knew Norman will know that he was no coward—he would take on any fecht that was going—verbally. Indeed, he suffered for his conscientious objection for the rest of his teaching life—turned down repeatedly for that reason for the promotion he more than deserved.

Hector MacMillan once said to me that one of the 'keys' to a good play is to have someone who never appears, but who is somehow 'there' all the time. In the case of this programme, that 'ghost' is William Soutar—in my mind, at least. (We're both 'Perth', born and bred—and he lived less than a mile from where my parents stayed.) He died in 1943, having been bedridden for the previous thirteen years due to ankylosing spondylitis. He would have been too old to fight by then, and he became increasingly pacifist as the 1920s and '30s marched on—he had served the navy in World War One and thoroughly enjoyed it. Soutar has a great deal to say about war, in general, and, in particular, the two world wars, in his poems, but also his diaries and journals. As well as many individual poems, he wrote a long, book length sequence, *But the Earth Abideth*,[8] in ballad form, which tackles war head on—and there is that heartbreaking *tour de force*, 'The Children', about the bombing of Guernica.[9]

The recording of the interviews was crammed into four days of intense activity: an evening at Norman's flat in Leamington Terrace, another with Tom at his house near Portobello, an afternoon at the School of Scottish Studies, visiting Jim Annand in sheltered accommodation in Stockbridge—and Sorley came down from Skye. It was exhausting but hugely memorable—each interview brought out something quite unforgettable and Julian and I were moved, nearly or actually, to tears several times. Hand on heart, the wind *did* turn up precisely on cue for Hamish and Sorley's description of his young German hero in 'Death Valley'—which was so emotive I find it difficult even now to allow my mind to dwell on it. It was absolutely necessary to drink rather a lot of whisky or wine, depending on who was being interviewed, and both Julian and I were quite ill by the end of the week. I had to go down to London to make the actual programme and remember vividly, after the cuts had been made and the programme loosely stitched together, being given *two* hours to do the script on a rather old and battered BBC typewriter.

The resulting programme presents the cream of the Scottish literary renaissance having 'their say' about war, each expressing in his individual way 'the Scottish accent of the mind'. My producer, Julian, (who's Cornish), readily agreed that here was a rather special body of work, a 'bunch' of poets who were, somehow, different. In spite of estrangements, feuds, reclusiveness, whatever, all were singing from a unique and very special hymn sheet. What a lucky country we are to have had all of them at the same time—and there are others not so far mentioned at all—Derick Thomson, George Mackay Brown, George Bruce, Iain Crichton Smith (too young to serve)—and, going back, Edwin Muir.

So, what was, or is, on the hymn sheet? Can I dare to try to put my finger on it? It would be something like this: an unshakable faith and belief in the work and lives of ordinary people whose voices *must* be heard; that there are communities who must be allowed to define themselves in their own way. All of them, to different extents were nationalists, believing that 'Scotland' matters because it still thinks itself a nation (and even if it does not *think* itself a nation still *acts* as if it is one). All were hyper-aware of the importance of 'minority' languages like Scots and Gaelic, including those like Norman, writing only in English. They saw a profound 'common cause' between the individual, the town/city, the country, the continent—indeed right across the planet, which extended into an acute consciousness of basic humanity, even between enemies. None of them felt that money mattered much —and decades ago had reached the conclusion that it is those who control it who need to be controlled. Each felt under a compulsion to give to the world their version of *our* response to the cruel North Sea, the Atlantic Ocean, the rigours of Scottish topography, our troubled history—our 'all sorts of things'—and nothing, nobody, would ever stop them singing their 'songs'. And finally, for all of them, an unusually powerful sense that it is not about 'me', but about History, Memory, Now, the Future—and what they could *contribute* to it.

Hamish, in his bringing together of so many different worlds, perhaps did it all, lived it all, more intensely and universally, than anybody else. He, above all others, was the creator of possibility, and possibilities, for so many people. That is why Hamish matters. That is why all these poets matter. And, so, in the words of Robert Garioch, let us get on with putting our 'chuckies on the cairn'.[10]

References:

1 *Chapman* 42 (1985).

2 Raymond J Ross & Joy Hendry (ed.), *Norman MacCaig: Critical Essays*, ed. (Edinburgh: Edinburgh University Press, 1991).

3 Joy Hendry, 'Sorley MacLean: The Man and His Work' in *Sorley MacLean: Critical Essays*, edited by Raymond J Ross and Joy Hendry, (Edinburgh: Scottish Academic Press, 1986).

4 *Chapman* 39 (1984) and *Chapman* 40 (1985).

5 Ross & Hendry (1986), p. 27.

6 Robert Garioch, *Two Men and a Blanket* (Edinburgh: Southside, 1975).

7 The correspondence is in the National Library of Scotland

8 William Soutar, *But the Earth Abideth* (London: Andrew Dakers, 1943).

9 William Soutar, *In the Time of Tyrants* (Perth: privately printed, Perth, 1939), reprinted in *Poems of William Soutar, a New Selection*, edited by W R Aitken (Edinburgh: Scottish Academic Press, 1988), p. 26.

10 Robert Garioch, *Chuckies on the Cairn* (Hayes: The Chalmers Press, 1949).

THE SYMPATHETIC IMAGINATION: SCOTTISH POETS OF WORLD WAR TWO

A BBC Radio 3 Programme compiled and presented by Joy Hendry

Tom Scott (TS):

> Where are the war poets?
> cried the whores of the press.
> Can a dirty business have its poetry?
> The poetry of war is in the pity, said Owen,
> whose fierce compassion burns in his every line.
>
> Like Rosenberg and other poet martyrs
> he bore his personal witness and passed on.
> But the challenge is to understand.
> The poetry is in the understanding.[1]

Joy Hendry (JH): That was Tom Scott, reading from the beginning of *The Dirty Business*, one of the few epic poems to be written about the Second World War, despite the global nature of the conflict and the epic proportions of the horrors which attended it. The First World War, with its lessons learned from the ghastly experience of the trenches, spawned many poets, Owen, Sassoon, Rosenberg—and so many others. And their poetry has eclipsed that of the Second World War. Perhaps we need to discover these poets of the Second World War, to see if they can take us further than the First World War poets did, or could. The staggering scale of World War Two surely issues this challenge. And there are indeed many fine poets of the Second War. Apart from the well-known Keith Douglas, here are a few of them: Hamish Henderson, Sorley MacLean, Tom Scott, whom you have just heard, George Campbell Hay, Robert Garioch. If you don't know these names, it may be because they're Scots, not English, and, in many cases, writing in a language other than English. Both Tom Scott and the Scottish poet Norman MacCaig, jailed for his pacifism in the Second World War, believe that the gulf between England and Scotland goes far beyond mere geography.

Norman MacCaig (NM): There is a psychological barrier, in the arts, between Scotland and England—and these poets—I've never seen them referred to, in all the literary magazines I read, as being poets of extraordinary quality. I don't know the reason, except the familiar one for centuries that London of course is the most parochial place outside Achiltibuie in Europe! And it's a shame!

TS: We Scots were always part of Europe—became isolated from Europe by the Union of the Parliaments particularly, and ever since then England has stood between us and our natural heritage of Europe. To this day, you get this insularity, which is unnatural to the Scots.

NM: If a Scottish painter has to make a name, he has to go to London, meaning 'making a name' to the boys in the south—in Douglas Young's 'The adjacent kingdom of England'—(doh)—beautiful phrase!

JH: That the Scots should see the metropolis as parochial parish pump, or England as an irritating obstacle between them and Europe, may strike you with a dunt of surprise, but that European influence is at the heart of the work of many Scottish poets and writers. Tom Scott's major influences have been the French poets, François Villon and Charles Baudelaire. T S Eliot greatly admired Tom Scott's translations of Villon, not into English, but into Scots. Hamish Henderson is certainly the best known of the Scottish war poets for his *Elegies for the Dead in Cyrenaica*, which won him the Somerset Maugham Prize when the book first appeared, in 1948. In the summer of 1939, Hamish was reading Hölderlin and Heine in Germany and smuggling letters into the country for English Quakers—he smuggled a young Jewish boy out, too! The poets of the Second World War, unlike those of the previous world war, went into conflict with their eyes entirely open.

TS: You know, in the European War, there was a tremendous shift of sensibility, from Rupert Brooke at the beginning, of the war as being played by gentlemen—it was honour and all that—'If I should die, think only this of me...'—kind of thing—through the experience of the trenches and this thing becoming 'the dirty business', through Rosenberg, Graves and particularly Owen, you see this change taking place. War has ceased to be 'the grand illusion' —it has become a terrible reality. Now, we didn't have to suffer that change of sensibility —we knew, from the start, what is was going to be like. We had no illusions to lose. We had grown up to it, we'd been bred up for it, nothing took us by surprise.

JH: And as their perception of war had matured and developed, so had the poetry they wrote about it. No longer was it enough to describe the horrors of war and to evoke feelings about the pity and tragedy of it, the challenge now, as stated in Tom Scott's *The Dirty Business*, was to strive towards an understanding of it, and to articulate that understanding coherently. Perhaps Scottish poets, with their European outlook, their cultural minorities and their long experience of being the underdog in relation to England, were peculiarly well-equipped to face that challenge—their political commitment to nationalism and, on the other hand, to socialism, with small or capital 'n's' and 's's'—according to taste—is nonetheless almost universal. And their centuries-old literary tradition of not keeping politics out of poetry also sharpened their poetic wits. Hamish Henderson was no exception:

Hamish Henderson (HH): Well, I should maybe explain at the start, Joy, that I at one time was a member of the YCL—the Young Communist League—and so consequently the Spanish Civil War seemed to me to be very much a conflict between right and wrong. At any rate, it seemed to me that the new young republic of Spain was fighting our battle, and I still think that. I was only a kid at the time —18 when the war finished—and I know that other younger people did go, but, anyway, I did not.

JH: Nor did Sorley MacLean, the great Gaelic poet from Oscaig on Raasay, a small island between Skye and the mainland. MacLean's hatred of fascism, and commitment to socialism, impelled him to join the International Brigade, but family responsibilities made this impossible. In 'The Cry of Europe' ('Gaoir na h-Eòrpa')—and many other poems, MacLean presents himself with an ideological dilemma: given a free choice between the woman he loved, and the fight against Franco – which would he choose? The poem reflects the intensity of MacLean's conflicting passions.

Sorley MacLean (SM):

'The Cry of Europe'

Girl of the yellow, heavy-yellow, gold-yellow hair,
the song of your mouth and Europe's shivering cry,
fair, heavy-haired, spirited, beautiful girl,
the disgrace of our day would not be bitter in your kiss.

Would your song and splendid beauty
take from me the dead loathsomeness of these ways,
the brute and the brigand at the head of Europe
and your mouth red and proud with the old song?

The Gaelic is — 'Gaoir na h'Eòrpa' — and 'Gaior' is a wonderful word
because it covers the cry of lament, a cry of agony, or, something like a
very unpleasant electric shock put through someone — I can't think of
an English word for it...

A nighean a' chùil bhuidhe, throm-bhuidh, òr-bhuidh,
fonn do bheòil-sa 's gaoir na h-Eòrpa,
a nighean gheal chasurlach aighearach bhòidheach,
cha bhiodh masladh ar latha-ne searbh 'nad phòig-sa.

An tugadh t' fhonn no t' àilleachd ghlòrmhor
bhuam-sa gràinealachd mharbh nan dòigh seo,
a' bhrùid 's am meàirleach air ceann na h-Eòrpa
's do bhial-sa uaill-dhearg 'san t-seann òran?[2]

JH: The power of that poem, given here in extract, is beyond question.
'Letter from Italy', a poem by Robert Garioch who died in 1981, is
singled out by Hamish Henderson for its remarkable quality. And,
unusually for Garioch, it's in English.
HH: It's a love poem to his wife, but it has such reverberations,
that poem. He was a prisoner of war at that time, and this fantastic
Mediterranean sky united him with people outside 'the wire':

From large red bugs, a refugee,
I make my bed beneath the sky,
safe from the crawling enemy
though not secure from nimbler flea.

Late summer darkness comes, and now
I see again the homely Plough
and wonder: do you also see
the seven stars as well as I?
And it is good to find a tie
of seven stars from you to me.
Lying on deck, on friendly seas,
I used to watch, with no delight,
new unsuggestive stars that light
the tedious Antipodes.
Now in a hostile land I lie,
but share with you these ancient high
familiar named divinities.
Perimeters have bounded me,
sad rims of desert and of sea,
the famous one around Tobruck
and now barbed wire, which way I look,
except above—the Pléiades.[3]

It is such a beautifully turned poem, that – it's the craftsmanship of,
well, as never shown with such skill as in that poem, in my opinion,
in the way it leads up to Pléiades—it always brings a tear to my eye.
JH: That poem establishes an exquisite link between Garioch and his
wife, Peg. But, apart from maintaining a consistently European point
of view, and a socialist outlook, the Scottish poets, irrespective of class
background, shared an egalitarian feeling which made distinctions
of rank and class disappear. Unlike English poets of the First World
War, they were not 'officer types'—even if they were officers—and
shared an instinctive community of interest with the humblest of their
comrades, and an ability to appreciate the importance of the most
ordinary events of military life.
TS:

'Canteen'

This boy, dressed in dungarees, draws my attention.
He stands alone in this smoke and haze,
the air of a tropical AFN and army canteen
among snappy, white, khaki-clad soldiers
and over the counter, the white-dressed, white actresses.

He stands alone, his dungarees dirty,
his old blue shirt stained with grease from some ship.
And I wonder why, browsing in the latest books,
seeking the pimpernel unity, unbuttoned bright tunic.
Suddenly this tousie-haired boy disturbs me,
not that I want to be again in dungarees—
true to my time, I'm too proud, too afraid, for that.
Nor is it some fashionable flame.
But still, coldly, distantly,
I watch him alone among the bright uniforms.
I find his presence, like forgotten words, a bit puzzling.

HH: I think there is a community feeling between the Scottish other ranks and officers. Certainly I saw some English regiments of whom you could not say that, you know. I was on the Anzio Beachhead, and I was attached by that time to the First British Infantry Division and, I mean, some of the officers in that were like parodies of World War One, so to speak. You know, they… It was almost laughable. My own attitudes and ideas were, naturally, not very much to their liking. I made no secret about egalitarian feelings, you know…

JH: Hamish Henderson—a sergeant, later rising to captain in the Intelligence Corps—composed a bawdy song—'The Ballad of Section 3'—with a verse for each member of that section. Tom Scott, in the Pay Corps in Nigeria, made friends with his clerks, not only as underlings, but also black.

TS: Before I left the Coast, I was known as 'The White Wog' (laughs) for being friendly with the Africans. We were definitely given the line, you know, that we were to keep them in their place. I just befriended Africans. I felt an understanding; I knew what it was to be an underdog, I knew what it was to be ill-treated—I was on their side.

JH: This recognition of common humanity, of unity, one-ness with others, extended even further among the Scottish war poets.

NM: Thinking of Scottish poets, for example, three come into my head: George Campbell Hay's poems, some of them, some of Sorley MacLean's poems and some of Hamish Henderson's poems—who are all completely different—but they share the recognition that the enemy over there that they were trying to kill, and who were trying to kill them—are just like themselves. They were there because they were forced to it, by the machinations of governments and ideologies—

they only want to go home. And these three poets have expressed that beautifully, in a number of poems.

SM: On the 22 of July 1942, there was a big counter-offensive, what became the Alamein line later. Everything went wrong; there were very big casualties on all sides. I was in an armoured brigade, we were in the centre of the line – and the place was littered with corpses—of all kinds. There was one young German—oh he looked so young—he was sitting, quite upright, with his feet in a slit trench—not a mark on him—must have been killed by shell blast, or bomb blast—or something like that. I've never... he haunts me...

'Death Valley'

Some Nazi or other has said that the Fuehrer had restored to German manhood the 'right and joy of dying in battle'.

Sitting dead in "Death Valley"
below the Ruweisat Ridge,
a boy with his forelock down about his cheek
and his face slate-grey;

I thought of the right and the joy
that he got from his Fuehrer,
of falling in the field of slaughter
to rise no more;

of the pomp and the fame
that he had, not alone,
though he was the most piteous to see
in a valley gone to seed

with flies about grey corpses
on a dun sand
dirty yellow and full of the rubbish
and fragments of battle.

Was the boy of the band
who abused the Jews
and Communists, or of the greater

band of those

led, from the beginning of generations,
unwilling to the trial
and mad delirium of every war
for the sake of rulers?

Whatever his desire or mishap,
his innocence or malignity,
he showed no pleasure in his death
below the Ruweisat Ridge.

The Gaelic is 'Glac a' Bhàis'

'Na shuidhe marbh an "Glaic a' Bhàis"
fo Dhruim Ruidhiseit,
gill' òg 's a logan sìos m' a ghruaidh
's a thuar grìsionn.

Smaoinich mi air a' chòir 's an àgh
a fhuair e bho Fhurair,
bhith tuiteam ann an raon an àir
gun éirigh tuilleadh;

air a' ghreadhnachas 's air a' chliù
nach d' fhuair e 'na aonar,
ged b' esan bu bhrònaiche snuadh
ann an glaic air laomadh

le cuileagan mu chuirp ghlas'
air gainmhich lachduinn
's i salach-bhuidhe 's làn de raip
's de sprùidhlich catha.

An robh an gillie air an dream
a mhàb na h-Iùdhaich
's na Comunnaich, no air an dream
Bu mhotha, dhiùbh-san

a threòraicheadh bho thoiseach àl,
gun deòin gu buaireadh
agus bruaillean cuthaich gach blàir
air sgàth uachdaran?

Ge b'e a dheòin-san no a chàs,
a neoichiontas no mhìorun,
cha do nochd e toileachadh 'na bhàs
fo Dhruim Ruidhìseit.[4]

HH: Each of my elegies has got an aim, and this one is called 'El Adem'. And El Adem, though you could hardly distinguish it from miles and miles of sweet FA in the desert—you know, the Germans who were in the desert, the ordinary Wehrmacht soldiers, were just doing their job, much as we were doing. That didn't alter the fact that I was trying to kill as many of them as possible. But I had a certain fellow feeling with them, naturally. I mean, there they were, they were in the same ghastly plight that we were in and they were as guilty or as innocent as we were—so … this is 'El Adem'—this is the 'Fourth Elegy'—the plight of soldiers on both sides, and because I'm thinking of the Germans as well as our own troops, I interweave, in this poem, echoes of German soldiers' slang as well as British soldiers' slang. The beginning 'Sow cold wind of the desert' is a literal translation of 'Saukalt' which is – 'bloody cold' in German:

Sow cold wind of the desert. Embittered
reflections on discomfort and protracted absence.
Cold, and resentment stirred at this seeming
winter, most cruel reversal of seasons.
The weather clogs thought: we give way to griping
and malicious ill turns, or instinctive actions
appearing without rhyme or reason. The landsknechte
read mail, play scat, lie mute under greatcoats.
We know that our minds are as slack and rootless
as the tent-pegs driven into cracks of limestone,
and we feel the harm of inactions's erosion.
We're uneasy, knowing ourselves to be nomads,
impermanent guests on this bleak moon-surface
of dents and ridges, craters and depressions.

Yet they make us theirs: we know it, and abhor them,
vile three in one of the heretic desert...
sand rock and sky... And the sow wind, whipping
the face of a working (or a dying) unit
who shoulders his shovel with corpse obedience.

The sons of man
grow and go down in pain: they kneel for the load
and bow likes brutes, in patience accepting the burden,
the pain fort and dour... Out of shuttered Europe
not even a shriek or a howl for its doomed children
is heard through the nihilist windvoice. Tomorrow's victors
survey with grief too profound for mere lamentation
their own approaching defeat: while even the defeated
await dry-eyed their ineluctable triumph.
Cages are crammed: on guard crouch the fearful oppressors
and wait for their judgement day.
Therefore recollecting
the ice-bound paths, and now this gap in the minefields
through which (from one side or the other) all must pass
shall I not speak and condemn?

Or must it always
seem premature: the moment always at hand,
and never arriving, to use
our rebellious anger for breaking
the vicious fetters that bind us?

Endure, endure. There is as yet no solution
and no short cut, no escape and no remedy
but our human iron.
            And this Egypt teaches us
that mankind, put to the torment, can bear
on their breast the stone tomb of immolation
for millennia. The wind. We can build our cairn.[5]

HH: There it is!
JH: George Campbell Hay went to considerable lengths to avoid
conscription, partly because of his position as a nationalist

conscientious objector and partly, too, because of the strength of his empathy for other people. For eight months he was on the run in Argyll to avoid imprisonment but was eventually forced to join the Royal Army Ordinance Corps. Hay's father, the novelist John MacDougall Hay, was a Tarbert man, from Kintyre in mid Argyll, and George, though not himself a native Gaelic speaker, taught himself the language from listening to the fisherman of Loch Fyne. He became thoroughly tri-lingual, writing and translating freely in English, Gaelic and Scots, and various mixtures of all three. Sorley MacLean spoke to me of the loving delicacy that was so characteristic of his genius. Having learned what everyone knows is the language of heaven among these fishermen, he was extra-sensitive to the conditions they faced on their small boats. 'Cold is the wind over Islay that blows on them in Kintyre'.[6]

SM: It is the same sympathetic imagination that has produced the wonderful poem of bombed Bizerta, so haunting with its wistful, questioning rhythms.

> What is their name tonight,
> the poor streets where every window spews
> its flame and smoke,
> its sparks and the screaming of its inmates,
> while house upon house is rent
> and collapses in a gust of smoke?
> And who tonight are beseeching
> Death to come quickly in all their tongues,
> or are struggling among stones and beams,
> crying in frenzy for help, and are not heard?
> Who tonight is paying
> the old accustomed tax of common blood?[7]

JH: That was just a taste of Campbell Hay's extraordinary account of the bombing of Bizerta. All these poets exhibit a highly sensitised and febrile awareness of the human condition, such as Owen displayed in poems like 'Strange Meeting'. Yet the ease with which they empathised, not only with their fellow soldiers or the alien races they moved among, but with the very enemy themselves, is hardly likely to endear them to the xenophobic British state. Perhaps another reason for their neglect as war poets. Mrs Thatcher's ire at the Archbishop of Canterbury for including the Argentinean enemy in his prayers during the Falklands War Memorial Service, and the banning of the Peace Pledge Union with their white poppies from official attendance at the Cenotaph would seem to indicate that this moral myopia is still very much with us. The emotional and intellectual intricacy of this body of Scottish war poetry extends further still. Despite the exercise of that 'sympathetic imagination', their first-hand understanding of the suffering of war, their brotherhood with the enemy, they are nonetheless utterly dedicated to the grim necessity of killing them. Sorley MacLean's poem,

'Going Westwards':

There is no rancour in my heart
against the hardy soldiers of the Enemy,
but the kinship that there is among
men in prison on a tidal rock

waiting for the sea flowing
and making cold the warm stone;
and the coldness of life is
in the hot sun of the Desert.

But this is the struggle not to be avoided,
the sore extreme of human-kind,
and though I do not hate Rommel's army
the brain's eye is not squinting.

Chan eil gamhlas 'na mo chridhe
ri saighdearan calma 'n Nàmhaid
ach an càirdeas a tha eadar
fir am prìosan air sgeir-thràghad,

a' fuireach ris a' mhuir a' lìonadh
's a' fuarachadh na creige blàithe,
agus fuaralachd na beatha
ann an gréin theth na Fàsaich.

Ach 's e seo an spàirn nach seachnar
éiginn ghoirt a' chinne-daonna,
's ged nach fuath liom armailt Roimeil
tha sùil na h-eanchainn gun chlaonadh.[8]

HH: I didn't feel then, and I don't feel now, as if these people were devils incarnate, or anything like that. But I did feel that they were the almost sheep-like subservient servants of probably the most, what Sorley MacLean called the worst, threat to humanity that's ever come over the horizon. Consequently, it was absolutely necessary to defeat them on the field of battle.

JH: And it was that determination to win that really informs the 'Fifth Elegy (Opening of an Offensive)' — presumably you are talking about El Alamein.

HH: I am talking about El Alamein, yes, the great battle of El Alamein that started on 23 October 1942 and was, as Churchill said, the turning point of the war for us. There are three parts, 'The Waiting', 'The Barrage' and 'The Jocks'. And I just read 'The Jocks'.

Now again! The shrill war-song: it flaunts
aggression to the sullen desert. It mounts. Its scream
tops the valkyrie, tops the colossal
artillery.

Meaning that many
German Fascists will not be going home
meaning that many
will die, doomed in their false dream

We'll mak siccar!
Against the bashing cudgel
against the contemptuous triumphs of the big battalions
mak siccar against the monkish adepts
of total war against the oppressed oppressors
mak siccar against the leaching lies
against the worked out systems of sick perversion
mak siccar against the executioner
against the tyrannous myth and the real terror
mak siccar.[9]

JH: That evocative phrase 'mak siccar', 'make sure', brings up another facet of the neglect of this poetry—its being written in a language other than English. With Gaelic, the difficulty's obvious, but Scots faces the added complexity of not being recognised by many south of the border, and some to the north, as being a language at all. Some deny it even the status of a dialect. Yet this 'auld Scots leid' is the first language of Robert Garioch, Tom Scott, and J K Annand whose 'Arctic Convoy', in Scots, has a descriptive power, capturing the sound of a ship on the North Atlantic run to Murmansk, and a vitality which English would be hard put to beat.

> Intil the pitmirk nicht we northwart sail
> Facin the bleffarts and the gurly seas
> That ser' out muckle skaith to mortal men.
> Whummlin about like a waukrife feverit bairn
> The gude ship snowks the waters o a wave.
> Swithers, syne pokes her neb intil the air,
> Hings for a wee thing, dinnlin, on the crest,
> And clatters in the trouch wi sic a dunt
> As gey near rives the platin frae her ribs
> And flypes the tripes o unsuspecting man.[10]

JH: Douglas Young was anither o the Scots makars. Like George Campbell Hay, he was also a nationalist objector and a fierce and articulate propagandist for all things Scottish.

NM: He was a pacifist on political grounds, and he was a great scholar. He proved, conclusively, that the Act of Union had been broken over and over again and therefore it was broken and it doesn't exist. And he wouldn't fight for a, to us, a foreign country. Logically his case was unanswerable.

TS: Of course, he was jailed for it, but although he took that stance, he had a student who was killed in Libya and he wrote this very fine little poem about him—and it's simply called:

'For Alasdair'[11]

Written while fishing on the banks of the Calder at Lochwinnoch in 1941, in memory of a Highland student at Aberdeen, killed during the German advance into Libya.

Standan here on a fogg-yirdit stane
drappan the bricht flees on the broun spate,
I'm thinkin o ye, liggan thonder your lain
i the het Libyan sand, cauld and quate,
The spate rins drumlie an broun,
whummlan aathing doun.

The fouk about Inverness an auld Aiberdeen
aye likeit ye weel, for a wyce an a bonny man.
Ye were gleg at the Greekan o't, and unco keen
at gowf and the lave. Noo deid i the Libyan sand.
The spate rins drumlie an broun,
whummlan aathing doun.

Hauldan the Germans awa frae the Suez Canal,
ye dee'd. Suld this be Scotland's pride, or shame?
Siccar it is, your gallant, kindly saul
maun lea thon land and tak the laich road hame.
The spate rins drumlie an broun,
whummlan aathing doun.[12]

JH: It's perhaps ironic that the Scottish poet who has received most acclaim furth of Scotland, including, in 1986, the Queen's Gold Medal for Poetry, was also a pacifist—Norman MacCaig. Insisting that he writes only of those things he intimately knows, he's written no poetry directly about war, yet his poems are full of the consciousness of the dangers of weapons used by those who govern us—weapons which draw no blood, but words which dupe us into sheep-like subservience:
NM:

'Smuggler'

Watch him when he opens
his bulging words – justice,
fraternity, freedom, internationalism, peace,
peace, peace. Make it your custom
to pay no heed
to his frank look, his visas, his stamps

and signatures. Make it
your duty to spread out their contents
in a clear light.

Nobody with such luggage
has nothing to declare.[13]

JH: In poem after poem, MacCaig reminds us of the need for love:
NM:

'No Choice'

I think about you
in as many ways as rain comes.

(I am growing, as I get older,
to hate metaphors—their exactness
and their inadequacy.)

Sometimes these thoughts are
a moistness, hardly falling, than which
nothing is more gentle:
sometimes, a rattling shower, a
bustling Spring-cleaning of the mind:
sometimes, a drowning downpour.

I am growing, as I get older,
to hate metaphors
to love gentleness
to fear downpours.[14]

Well, that is about my love of a woman, of course, apart from the fact
that it hates metaphors and uses nothing but all the way through.
'Love' is a difficult word and it took me a lot of years to realise that
it meant more than a man and a woman in a bed, you know. A lot of
years. The only thing that'll rescue the world from the brutality and
the aggressive self-aggrandisement of governments is a recognition
that nobody wants wars: they want to like each other. And, they're

prevented. As, in a way, that poem tries to say, I'm prevented from speaking directly to you because I plunge myself and flee awa in metaphors.

JH: Do you remember at what point in your development did you actually make that intellectual decision that you were a pacifist?

NM: It was just as I squirmed out of my mother's womb. I remember saying to my father at the time... now... I won't get ridiculous... what I mean is that I was a pacifist all my life: it was my nature—nothing to do with religion, nothing to do with morals, nothing to do with ethics—or something to do with all three in some strange way—I knew that I would have nothing to do with killing people who—who were innocent.

JH: Did you come across much hostility?

NM: Oh, civilians shouted at us, you know... 'yellow bellies' and things of that sort. But not the members in the forces, because they'd had to think about what they're doing.

JH: Did they ever approach you and discuss the thing with you?

NM: Oh yes. I was once coming up to Edinburgh on leave with eight soldiers in the compartment, and they saw this badge 'NCC'. And one said: 'What does 'NCC' stand for? 'Norwegian Camel Corps'?' And I said, 'No, no, we're a bunch of conscies,' and not only did they not abuse me. Some of them said, 'Oh, I'm not clever enough... all these tribunals.' And the other one said: 'I just haven't got the courage to do it'. And it made it even clearer to me that the boys in the forces —they didn't want to go and drop thousands of bombs on Hamburg and Cologne and other places. No, no, no... Everybody hates war. It's governments, governments, governments—they love war. But the people don't.

JH: But, what do you do, Norman, with the position of people like, for example, Hamish Henderson and Sorley MacLean? Their position was not that they were being made to fight for the sake of rulers, to quote a line from one of Sorley's poems, but that they were actually actively wanting to fight on ideological grounds.

NM: Yes, but you don't fight ideologies: you fight people. They were fighting ideologies. I was refusing to kill people. There's that distinction.

TS: We must think people, not statistics.

Think that yae nicht bombs faa
(Scotland aye thirled to the English Treasury)
on unlikely Glesca, hooses turn rubble
and in the rubble Maisie deid,
wee Tosh in her airms,
Jean and Alan beside her deid.
But Bill, in his barracks at Perth
lives to come hame to bury his loves,
syne gaes back ti the war. Back? The war
is aa aroond us, follaes us like oor shadow.[15]

JH: In exactly the same spirit as Norman MacCaig, the main concern of Tom Scott's *The Dirty Business*, which began this programme, is people, as individuals, and their fate. Scott reminds us that each human life is utterly unique.

TS: I try to bring the reality of war through to people. Back to flesh and blood. Out of this abstract kind of thinking which doesn't involve your feelings by presenting one horror after another horror in terms of people. Giving them names, you know, so that I want the reader to be aware of this in terms of actual people and their sympathy, their sympathetic imaginations to be involved, and appreciate what this is really all about, not just in their heads, but on their nerve ends. And the hope is of course that they'll be so shocked that everybody will be anti-war for ever after:

Marilka, Daddy's pet, in Auschwitz
reduced to skin and bone, one day
stoops to pick up potato peelings.
Strapped to the flogging block in public
against regulations her backside bared
takes twenty-five measured strokes of the whip,
and each time she faints is soused with water
until she comes round, then the torture goes on.
Zwanzig. Einundzwanzig. Zweiundzwanzig.
Later, in London, in the room above me
where Tadek nightly caresses her scars,
her screams on the block whiles tear the night.[16]

You know, the last word tends to become just history, and what I wanted to do here is keep alive the sheer horror of it. The question in my own mind, all the time, was of course: is it possible to make poetry out of such horror? I take it up from Owen: Owen said the poetry was in the pity and I say, yes, but beyond pity there must be understanding. There must be both. And the poetry is in the understanding—I'm answering my own question—'is it possible to make poetry out of this horror?'

> Multiply that by a million, add
> atrocities and depths of dehumanization
> unimaginable but true
> in every area of the Earth
> and you get some notion
> beyond sensibility
> of the unprecendented, machine-wrought agony
> the dirty business perpetrated.
> Not Owen's compassion could encompass it,
> nor could Dante's, for Hell
> was only for sinners—so-called by Aquinas—
> while war is for innocent victims.[17]

JH: Tom, what you've got there, in fact, is a poem which is an epic rather than just an individual poem…

TS: An epic is essentially a heroic poetry about a nation, about its people, about its heroes, about its wars. The challenge of war is not to write lyrics about war or lyrical poems within the war. The challenge is to write an epic about the war itself which contains it, in the way that Homer tried to contain the Trojan siege in *The Illiad*. I think our time calls for epic poetry, if ever a time did. It calls for a public poetry—and epic is the one and only form that will fit.

> And in the desert
> Sorley proves himself again
> a Gael of the heroic age,
> while George, surviving the desert war
> is driven mad by fascists in Greece.
> Garioch taken prisoner, muses
> pent up at night behind the wire,

on how the self-same stars he sees
look down on his Peg in Edinburgh.[18]

JH: Tom Scott's task is to take war poetry on to that next stage, towards understanding, for if war poetry has a purpose or function, it is to enter the conscience of a nation, to trigger little explosions in people's heads that may yet make war an absurdity and an impossibility. I wondered if something like this happened to Denis Healey, sparked off by tactless remarks from an infamous aristocrat as he fought with 'the forgotten army' in 1944.

Denis Healey (DH): We were infuriated when Lady Astor, who was a conservative MP, called us 'D-Day Dodgers' and… a very good poem was invented which was quite rude about Lady Astor and people who thought like her. 'We are the D-Day Dodgers out in Italy'. [He starts to sing]

> We hope the boys in France will soon be getting leave
> After six months' service it's a shame they're not relieved
> But we can still carry on out here for another
>   two or three more years
> For we're the D-Day Dodgers, out in Italy.
>
> Old Lady Astor please listen dear to this
> Don't stand upon the platform and talk a lot of piss
> You're the nation's sweetheart, the nation's pride
> But your bloody big mouth is far too wide
> That's from the D-Day Dodgers out in Italy
>
> If you look around the mountains in the mud and rain
> You'll find the scattered crosses…

[He coughs and breaks down]

DH: I'm sorry, you see there it goes, I'm afraid—I get too moved by these things. Ach … [starts singing again]

> If you look around the mountains in the mud and rain
> You'll find the scattered crosses, some which bear no name

Heartbreak and toil and suffering gone the lads beneath
  them slumber on
For they were the D-Day Dodgers who'll stay in Italy.[19]

You know, that sort of poetry may not stand up to Palgrave's *Golden
Treasury*, but there's genuine feeling there. And you can get it, don't
you think?

JH: But the 'D-Day Dodgers' didn't just miraculously spring into
being, Hamish Henderson composed it, and it comes directly out of
his war experience, and that of his fellow soldiers.[20] Behind it too lies
a centuries-old tradition of popular song which allows many people
to speak their hearts and minds, whom a more literary and elitist
culture would keep forever silent. The fight is for the peace, in which
true freedom for all might yet be found.

HH: Ye know, 'Ah, Fredome is a noble thing/ Fredome mays man to
haiff liking.'[21] This is an idea, and a resonance from the middle ages in
Scottish literature and life, which is a reality and, you know, insofar as
I have found myself in the position there, in the Second World War, of
trying to fight fascism, this was, and remains, a dominant idea of mine
that freedom in some way has to come out of all this horror.

JH: And what better than to have now 'The Freedom Come-All-Ye',
which is your great poem of peace…

HH: Do you want me to sing it?

JH: Yes, I do, very much. I'll join in.

HH: All right… (wee laugh) very good…

Solo

Roch the wind in the clear day's dawin.
Blaws the cloods heelster-gowdie ow'r the bay,
But there's mair nor a roch wind blawin
Through the great glen o' the warld the day.
It's a thocht that will gar oor rottans
A' they rogues that gang gallus, fresh and gay –
Tak the road and seek ither loanins
For their ill ploys tae sport and play.

JH joins in

Nae mair will the bonnie callants
Mairch tae war when oor braggarts crousely craw,
Nor wee weans frae pithead and clachan
Mourn the ships sailin' doon the Broomielaw.
Broken families in lands we've herriet,
Will curse Scotland the Brave nae mair, nae mair;
Black and white, ane til ither mairiet,
Mak the vile barracks o' their maisters bare.

So come all ye at hame wi' Freedom,
Never heed whit the hoodies croak for doom.
In your hoose, a' the bairns o' Adam
Can find breid, barley-bree and painted room.
When Maclean meets wi's freens in Springburn
A' the roses and geans will turn tae bloom,
And a black boy frae yont Nyanga
Dings the fell gallows o' the burghers doon.[22]

JH: I venture to suggest, mischievously, that Palgrave's *Golden Treasury*, if it defeats the 'D-Day Dodgers', falls down helpless in the face of 'The Freedom Come-All-Ye'—an international anthem for peace. I suggest also that this body of Scottish war poetry, which we've only sampled here, in its sheer quality, its intellectual power, in its sympathetic imagination which embraces all classes, creeds, races and ranks—and its grasping of the political and moral nettle—is unique, in British literature at least. And, in two minority languages whose speakers number in thousands rather than millions. These Scottish poets have advanced our understanding of war and our aspirations for peace. They try to ensure that, in Heine's words, 'Freedom Becomes People'—a spirit we've seen recently in China and Eastern Europe. And our last poem, 'Yes' by Norman MacCaig, reminds us that this is a never-ending struggle:

NM:

'Yes'

You must say Yes, said the Commissioner
and the Gauleiter and the Priest and
their wet-lipped toadies.

They said it to the writer burying his poems,
to the woman going mad in a pink suburb,
they said it to the firing squad.

They said it to technology,
to philosophy, to stubborn science.

They even said it to the child
walking hand in hand with his mother.

And God trembled
like a man caught
with imprint of the gun butt
still on his palm.[23]

References:

1   Tom Scott, *The Dirty Business* (Barr, Ayrshire: Luath Press Ltd (The Blew Blanket Library), 1986), p. 1.

2   Sorley MacLean, *Seventeen Poems for Sixpence*, (Edinburgh: The Chalmers Press, 1940), reprinted in *Spring tide and Neap tide* (Edinburgh: Canongate, 1977), p. 13.

3   Robert Garioch, *Collected Poems* (Loanhead, Midlothian: Macdonald Publishers, 1977), p. 68.

4   Sorley MacLean, *Poetry Scotland*, No. 1. (1944), reprinted in *Spring tide and Neap tide* (Edinburgh: Canongate, 1977), p. 120.

5   Hamish Henderson, 'Fourth Elegy (El Adem)', in Hamish Henderson, *Elegies for the Dead in Cyrenaica*, (first published London: Lehnmann, 1948; Edinburgh: Polygon, 2008), pp. 27-28. As if 'on cue', in the natural silence which followed Hamish's reading of the poem, there was a sudden, and incredibly loud and protracted gust of wind. Everybody froze, amazed and, yes, a little frightened. We were all shaken by it, as if we had to keep silent to listen to the voice of God, giving his assent to Hamish's words. It was a moment Julian May (the producer) and I shall never forget. We had to work hard to reproduce the wind noise for radio.

6   George Campbell Hay, 'Mefta Babkum Es-Sabar?', in George Campbell Hay, *Mochtar and Dougall*, (Glasgow: University of Glasgow/Department of Gaelic, 1982), p. 46.

7   Maurice Lindsay (ed.), 'George Campbell Hay' in *Modern Scottish Poetry* (London, 1946), reprinted in *Collected Poems and Songs of George Campbell Hay*, edited by M Byrne (Edinburgh: Edinburgh University Press, 2003), p. 176.

8   *Spring tide and Neap tide*, p. 114.

9   Hamish Henderson, 'Interlude: the Jocks', in *Elegies for the Dead in Cyrenaica*, pp 32-33.

10 J K Annand, *Selected Poems 1925-1990* (Edinburgh: Mercat Press, 1992), p. 9.

11 Cut in the original programme.

12 Douglas Young, in *Auntran blads: an outwale o verses* (Poetry Scotland Series, No 1) (Glasgow: Maclellan, 1943), reprinted in Clara Young and David Murison (ed.), *Douglas Young: Poet and Polymath* (Loanhead, Midlothian: Macdonald Publishers, 1977), p. 41.

13 Norman MacCaig, *Surroundings* (London: Chatto & Windus, 1966), reprinted in *The Poems of Norman MacCaig*, edited by Ewan McCaig, (Edinburgh: Polygon, 2009), p. 165.

14 Norman MacCaig, *Rings on a Tree* (London: Chatto & Windus, 1968), reprinted in *The Poems of Norman MacCaig*, p. 185.

15 Tom Scott, *The Dirty Business*, pp 29-30.

16 *Ibid.*, pp 33-34.

17 *Ibid.*, p. 30.

18 *Ibid.*, p. 31. The reference is to Peggy, Garioch's wife.

19 BBC News Broadcast with Dennis Healey, 1989. Healy was promoting his newly published memoirs, but I doubt if anyone witnessing it could think that his emotion, evoked unexpectedly by the song, was anything other than utterly genuine.

20 John Barbour, 'The Brus', in *The Oxford Book of Scottish Verse*, edited by John MacQueen and Tom Scott (London, Oxford University Press, 1966), p. 10.

21 Hamish Henderson, 'The D-Day Dodgers', in *Collected Poems and Songs*, edited by Raymond Ross (Edinburgh: Curly Snake Publishing, 200), p. 94.

22 'The Freedom Come-All-Ye', in Hamish Henderson, *Collected Poems and Songs*, edited by Raymond Ross (Edinburgh: Curly Snake Publishing, 200), pp 143-44

23 Norman MacCaig, 'A World of Difference', in *The Poems of Norman MacCaig*, edited by Ewan McCaig (Edinburgh, Polygon, 2009), p. 397.

HAMISH HENDERSON AMONG THE PARTISANS

Pino Mereu

Where do I begin? My thoughts immediately go to the first volume of Timothy Neat's biography *Hamish Henderson: the Making of the Poet*.[1] This book brims over with such a rich collection of tales about Hamish's time in Italy that I wonder what I can add but a small memory, one of his personal stories or one of his edited or unpublished poems which have influenced us all, hoping in this way that I can leave something new, something to conserve in a small corner of the heart.

Hamish Henderson identified Rome and Italy with the Casina Valadier; a restaurant with a stunning view down from the Pincio hill over Rome: 'Even though I've been away for ages,' he would say to us, 'it seems that time has not passed. It's as if I've always been here. The sign of time passing is in me, as I get older, but I don't see this passing of time in things. And every time that I thought about Italy and Rome I thought about the Casina Valadier, in its place.'

I believe that Hamish had his own personal vision about Rome. He loved going back to the places he had already visited: he looked out for his favourite spots, like a vagabond wandering around his past.

I recall vividly the last time he came to Rome in October 1990: he asked me if I knew of a 'pensione' (little hotel) near Via del Gesu, right in the city centre. He had stayed there in the days following the liberation. He wanted to see it again, to see if he recognised it. It was not just nostalgia but simply a way for him to feel at home once more. He always left a piece of his heart each time he left Rome. But it was always just an 'arrivederci' to those places and to his dear partisan friends: from Amleto Micozzi who he got to know in July 1944 right at the Casina Valadier to the senator of the Italian Republic, Adriano Ossicini. Each one of their reunions was such an indescribable joy and an excuse for a party! They would spend lots of time round the table telling stories, singing, and drinking wine. But time did not stand still: each discussion had its meaning in time, and I remember that the last time we talked it was about the imminent American invasion of Iraq, with Hamish ever ready to give his pointed opinion on the issue. But we would end up after every dinner singing, especially partisan songs ('Bella Ciao', 'Bandiera Rossa', songs of the Italian Alpine troops), and the best amongst us was Hamish, not only because he knew the words so well but also because he had a great voice and spoke perfect Italian.

Hamish had loved the Italian language since he was young and had read Dante (whoever understands Dante can understand everything in Italian!). Then, later, during World War Two, he was an intelligence officer with the task of interrogating prisoners of war, and he picked up many of the popular songs directly from those prisoners because after each interrogation session he always tried to strike up some kind of human contact.

Hamish had landed in Italy for the first time at the dawn of 10 July 1943 in Portopalo, in Sicily, following the 154 Brigade of the Fifty-First Highland Division. The Sicily campaign was Hamish's first contact with our country, and songs like 'Ballad of Simeto' and 'The Banks of Sicily' remain some of the most beautiful he ever wrote.

And it was precisely 'The Banks of Sicily' which brought me close to Hamish for the first time, without knowing anything about his past. At the beginning I thought he was just a song writer when I listened to the version by singer Dick Gaughan. It was 1982 and the record was *Kist O' Gold*. I was immediately fascinated by the melody, but what really aroused my curiosity was that weaving of words. Reading the text more carefully, I understood that this was not only an anti-war song, against all wars but it was also a fusion between the Scottish soldiers—not considered as occupiers—and the Sicilian people. The idea came to him from a sergeant who exclaimed, after seeing an old woman dressed in black with a shawl over her head: 'My God, we might be in Lewis.'

It was only to be a few years after this first impact that I was to begin exchanging letters with Hamish, the author. And since at that time I had just begun to publish a little folk magazine called

Kilmarnock Edition—a homage to Robert Burns—and as I had obtained his address, I decided to write him a letter and send him a few copies. He replied almost immediately in Italian and sent me a copy of the *Elegies*, a special edition of the *Chapman* magazine dedicated to him which contained lots of previously unpublished work[2] and a few copies of *Tocher* magazine, containing some of his articles on Scottish folklore and folk singers.

Reading the *Elegies for the Dead of Cyrenaica*, his cycle of poems about endurance and passive suffering, and 'Freedom Becomes People' opened up a new world for me. And when I finally met up with him the following year in Edinburgh, I embarked upon my voyage into his kingdom.

I have been on this voyage for 25 years now, and the fruits have matured into my recent theatre piece called *La Ballata degli Imboscati* (*The Ballad of the D-Day Dodgers*). It is a ballad in three acts, inspired by the poems and songs (some of which are unpublished) that Hamish composed in Italy during the war, side by side with his fellow soldiers and partisans. But the *D-Day Dodgers* is also the fruit of his stories, his memories about those young soldiers from Banffshire who had come to Italy to bring us freedom and to die with honour. My task was to research and unite all the traces that Hamish had left behind him, and the story slowly emerged, starting from the African dead in the desert, to Sicily and then on the River Po which can be summed up in these verses.

'La ballata degli Imboscati'

We are the D-Day Dodgers, out in Italy
Always on the vino, always on the spree.
        8th Army scroungers and their tanks
we live in Rome among the Yanks
We are the D-Day Dodgers, way out in Italy.

We landed at Salerno, a holiday with pay (…)

Naples and Cassino were taken in our stride,
We didn't go to fight there. We just went for the ride .
        Anzio and Sangro were just names,
        We only went to look for dames (…)

On the way of Florence we have a lovely time
We run a bus to Rimini right through the Gothic Line (...)[3]

What a great ballad! Who could ever have imagined that a tune like 'Lili Marlene' could carry such a vibrant denunciation, so full of irony. It is a song written not only with the pen, but with the blood, sweat and tears of those who lived through that time. And they were those Banffshire lads—bagpipe players, fishermen, crofters—who became the protagonists through the voice of Seumas (the damned poet). There's Phil, Calum, Red Irish, Kenny, Donnie, Tam, Red Neill and the fondly loved Anzio Pipe Band.

Hamish often liked to recall how he had managed to ferry over an entire band of pipers to the island of Capri (at that time in the hands of the Americans). They set sail from Naples and, once on the island, played for the islanders' delight! Hamish chose the name of this band in memory of those who had lost their lives in the long battle of Anzio. And it is certain that Anzio and Cassino remained an open wound for those soldiers returning home, never to forget their fallen companions. And I think that they, like Hamish, would always remember them. It should be said that, in order for the Americans to enter Rome first without losing any men, the Scots were left to fight at Anzio. It reminds us of what happened in Gallipoli during World War One: a complete and utter waste of young lives. And Hamish was never to forget those lads 'who fell to the sound of 'The Siege of Delhi'':

Look around the mountains, in the mud and rain –
You'll find the scattered crosses –
(there's some which have no name).
Heartbreak and toil and suffering gone,
The boys beneath them slumber on.
Those are the D-Day Dodgers who'll stay in Italy.[4]

The Partisans and the Resistance

Ihave already mentioned that Hamish first came into contact with the partisans in Rome: Don Paolo Pecoraro, Adriano Ossicini, Piero Nelli, Adriano Paggetti. He became an enthusiastic regular at the 'Trionfale' district section of the Communist Party. Many were to remember Hamish dancing reels and jigs in the street, even trying some steps of our 'saltarello' dances. And then of course he met Liana and Amleto Micozzi in Rome too, as described in Timothy Neat's biography.

Rome became Hamish's base for any trip he would make in his jeep, with 'Bandiera Rossa' ('Red Flag') clearly written upon it. He drove up and down, from Naples to Perugia, and then went to join the partisans fighting for the liberation of Florence from the Nazi fascist troops. And this was the first battle in which he fought beside the communist partisan troops under the command of Aligi Barducci, known as 'Potente' (The Powerful One). There were four partisan brigades: *la Sinigaglia, la Lanciotto, la Caiani* and *la Fanciullacci*. Hamish immediately became a friend of Barducci's and fought at his side. Aligi Barducci died in combat during those days, and the four brigades immediately took the name of 'Divisione Potente dell' Arno'—'The Powerful One's Arno Division'—in his honour.

Hamish fought beside the partisans in the Apennine mountains, too, and during the conflict heard the story of Corbara the partisan. Corbara had already become a legend because he had led his men courageously in the fight against the German troops and the reorganisation of the fascist troops of Mussolini's newly founded Republic of Salò. Corbara and his men operated around the areas of Rimini, Forli, Faenza, and Colle della Futa. Hamish took these stories as the departure point for his beautiful poem 'The Ballad o Corbara', which remains not only original but unique in his entire work.[4] It could almost be the screenplay of a film. It is not just a homage to a partisan leader but to all of those who took up arms to chase out the invaders and bring freedom to the whole population. The images in this ballad follow each other in a frantic rhythm (determined by the fluidity of the languages: a mix of Scots, English, German and Italian) especially in the verses that deal with Corbara's capture: 'Senta! Sei matto? [...] Rendati... porco... Prendete quel bastardo!').

They went to kill him at night. And how can we forget the pained and angered cries of his companions—Uragano (Hurricane), Lupo (Wolf) and Sangue (Blood)—on seeing their leader murdered beside his companion Ines (who was pregnant) and his lieutenant. Then their corpses were brought to the main square in Forli to be hung up for all to see. And the image Hamish leaves us with of Corbara is: 'in his haun the biretta/ in his cap the Reid Star.'[6]

The Fosse Ardeatine massacre

Now I would like to touch upon two episodes of Hamish's time in Italy which I think he carried with him for the rest of his life.

If the Casina Valadier left happy memories for Hamish, there is a darker side to Rome. It is also the city where one of the most terrible war crimes was carried out. This massacre has come to be known as 'The Fosse Ardeatine massacre'. Every time Hamish visited Rome he never once missed going to pay his respects to the three hundred and thirty five hostages killed by the SS under the orders of commandant Kappler.

> Before I had time to cry out—
> Stop!
> Put him down! That's my son.[7]

These are a few lines from the poem 'Lament for the Son', one of Hamish's lyrics that I love best. In his free and sincere translation of the poem 'Aladino', written by the poet Corrado Covoni in remembrance of his son, one of the victims of that massacre, Hamish managed to portray all the drama, the essence of the sense of emptiness and uselessness of a human being (especially speaking as a father) when confronted with the death of his beloved son.

Govoni composed a collection of one hundred and twenty pieces: in one hundred and nineteen of these, Govoni railed against the Nazis, the fascists, God, the Pope, Rome, the entire universe, himself. Only in one piece did he rail against the partisans: he accused them of being responsible for the attack in Via Rasella and therefore the cause of the Germans' act of retaliation in the Fosse Ardeatina massacre. But let me make it clear that the partisans were not guilty of this. The partisans fought against the Nazis and fascists who, in their role as occupiers, applied 'reprisals' as an ignoble weapon to blackmail the entire Italian population into betraying their compatriots for fear of being arrested, deported or killed. This was not the first vile and atrocious reprisal that the Germans had carried out (for every German soldier killed, ten Italians were put to death) but the reprisal of the Fosse Ardeatine reveals today, after much research, a much wider and complex split— be it social or political—than all the others before and after it.

It is enough just to consider the choice of the victims—from Colonel Cordero Lanza di Montezemolo to the rag and bone men from the Jewish ghetto, from the Red Flag communists to the monarchists, not to mention a quantity of non-political figures: Jews, freemasons, atheists, Catholics, priests. There was even a former minister of Mussolini's government who was Jewish. They were seized from Regina Coeli and Via Tasso prisons or even directly from the streets, loaded onto trucks and transported to the Ardeatine quarry, on the outskirts of Rome, where they were barbarically assassinated with a pistol shot in the neck or in the face.

Talking about this atrocity, I cannot omit to mention Hamish's memory of his meeting with Kappler in the prison at Cinecittà where he was incarcerated. Hamish went there one morning with a copy of the partisans' magazine *Mercurio* in his bag. In that copy the poem by Govoni I mentioned earlier for his son Aladino had just been published. Hamish describes the meeting like this:

I wanted to see this man, Kappler, a man capable of such an atrocious crime. I spoke German well enough not to need an interpreter. We spoke for over two hours. He appeared very polite, like all German officials.

I asked him: 'Are you a fervent Nazi?'

'Yes' he replied without any hesitation. He was a fanatical Nazi, completely convinced about the Nazi idea.

At that point I took out Govoni's poem from my bag. I showed it to him saying 'This is a beautiful poem'.

And he said to me 'An old father's grief is something sacred for me'.

I was speechless. If in some other moment in time these words had been reported the listener might have felt some sympathy for this ferocious criminal. Now I can say these were the most obscene words I have ever heard spoken. I repeat: I had never in my life heard such an obscene and wicked thing.[8]

Hamish, Gramsci and Sardinia

Hamish first heard the name of Antonio Gramsci when he was in Florence during the liberation of the city. It was a lad from the Lanciotto brigade who told him about the formation of a Gramsci brigade. 'But who was this Gramsci?' asked Hamish. 'He was the leader of our communist party and a great thinker,' came the reply. During the following days Hamish heard lots of stories about him and got the message that Gramsci was indeed a great philosopher, 'il grande pensatore', even though he had never read anything by him.

We all know how important Gramsci was to become for Hamish — the political champion of the Rossa Bandiera: in this setting Antonio Gramsci resembled John MacLean, hero and martyr — whose ideas, articulated in the solitude of his prison cell, are still working away like yeast in the consciousness of the West. As you well know, Hamish finished translating Gramsci's *Lettere dal carcere*, (*Letters from a Prison Cell*) immediately after the war, but had to wait almost thirty years to see the work published.

Hamish, like no other, succeeded in penetrating into the intimate soul of Gramsci and this led him to love Sardinia. He studied the vocabulary and researched the spirit of the place. He admired the popular traditions that he discovered from reading Gramsci in his extraordinarily beautiful descriptions of his island. And it is therefore not a coincidence that the cover of the first edition shows the text and musical score of a Sardinian 'mutos' written for tenor voice by the late shepherd poet and singer Peppino Marotto, from Orgosolo, near my own village, who, like Hamish, dedicated his life to raising awareness about Gramsci and promoting his ideas all over his beloved land of Barbagia. And it is no coincidence either that my own tribute to Hamish was *Quadernos Iscrittos* (*Written Notebooks*) — a musical, poetic work which was a meeting point and fusion between Hamish's, Peppino's, Antonio Gramsci's and John Berger's writings.

Hamish loved Sardinia and its people with a deep passion. I remember once returning to Rome from Genzano in October 1990 after having been at dinner with some of his partisan friends. He asked me if I could teach him some 'mutos' — 'a sa sarda' — as we say in Sardinia. I told him that it was difficult even for me, even though they were songs from my land, in the language of my parents. However, thanks to Hamish, I started studying the Sardinian dialect again and began to speak it, sing it and translate it. So now I am in a position to tell you that Hamish's poetry sounds wonderful in our Sardinian language. This is the first verse of 'The Flyting o' Life and Daith':

> Narat sa vida, su mundu meu est
> Sas frores e sos arbores, tottu mi appartenet
> Deo seo sa die e sa luche de su sole
> Narat sa vida, su mundu meu est.

Conclusion

Our purpose today is to move forward and hand down to young people what we have learned, helping them with our unconditional support and experience so that they, in turn, can one day take up our history. Let these young folk carry on keeping Hamish Henderson's voice alive so that it will still be heard in one hundred years time as vibrantly as it is now. As alive as when he sang a song of the Partisans —like:

'Under the Bridge of Bassano' ('Sul Ponte di Bassano')

> Sul ponte di Bassano
>   Bandiera Nera
> è lutto fra gli alpini
>   che vanno alla guerra

> E' lutto fra gli alpini
>   che vanno alla guerra
> è la migliore gioventè
>   che va sotto terra.

> Nell' ultimo vagone
>   c'è l'amor mio
> col fazzoletto bianco
>   nel far la guerra.

> Lassù sulle montagne
>   bandiera nera
> è morto un partigiano
>   nel far la guerra

E' morto un partigiano
nel far la guerra
un altro italiano
va sotto terra.

Tedeschi traditori
l'alpino è morto
ma un altro combattente
oggi è risorto

Combatte il partigiano
la sua battaglia
tedeschi e fascisti
fuori d'Italia

Tedeschi e fascisti
fuori d'Italia
gridiamo a tutta forza
pietà l'è morta !

What Hamish taught us was to search for the spirit in every song or story, and he carried out his research on a tradition in continuous, creative fermentation. He loved young people who started developing an interest in folk music, encouraging them and making them feel worthy. In this context, I must mention the late Martyn Bennett: just thinking how much he left us in his brief, but intense life ('Floret Silva Undique', 'Hallaig', 'Glen Lyon') together with his mother Margaret, and *Grit*, his musical testament.

Hamish showed us the path we should follow, step by step, to understand the evolution of a story or a song. How a fragment can, over time and with determination, be rebuilt, give new light and energy to something that Hamish never considered an object to be conserved and placed in a museum. Author's rights on these works would have meant a kind of cultural cul-de-sac, making it difficult to pass them on freely from generation to generation.

References:

1   Timothy Neat, *Hamish Henderson: A Biography. Volume 1, The Making of the Poet (1919-1953)* (Edinburgh: Polygon, 2007).

2   Hamish Henderson, 'Freedom Becomes People', special issue of *Chapman* magazine), *Chapman*, 42 (1985).

3   Hamish Henderson, 'Ballad of the D-Day Dodgers', in Hamish Henderson, *Collected Poems and Songs*, edited by Raymond Ross, (Edinburgh: Curly Snake Publishing, 2000), p. 94.

4   *Ibid.*, p. 95.

5   Hamish Henderson, 'The Ballad o Corbara', in *Collected Poems ad Songs*, pp. 86-92.

6   *Ibid.*, p. 92.

7   Hamish Henderson, 'Lament for the Son', in *Collected Poems and Songs*, pp. 107-08.

8   Hamish was interviewed by an Italian journalist, Costanzo Costantini. This interview was published in the Italian daily paper *Il Messaggero* on 19 January 1979—a long interview in which Hamish talks, towards the end, about his visit to Kappler. This excerpt is my translation. At that time, Hamish was in Rome for the filming of *The Dead, the Innocent*.

'GRAMSCI IN ACTION': ANTONIO GRAMSCI AND HAMISH HENDERSON'S FOLK REVIVALISM

Corey Gibson

Following his demobilisation after World War Two, Hamish Henderson dedicated the years between 1948 and 1951 to the translation of Antonio Gramsci's *Prison Letters* (*Lettere dal Carcere*). The lasting influence of this period of scholarly activity is apparent throughout Henderson's later work in a vast network of implicit, and explicit, references to the life and thought of Gramsci. As the principal strategist and most vocal defender of the Scottish folk song revival, Henderson negotiated with the implications of Gramsci's theoretical structures within the tangible sphere of this popular cultural revival. This essay will consider the nature of Gramsci's influence on Henderson, firstly, in the context of his introduction to the figure of Gramsci and his subsequent translation work, and in relation to Henderson's ideas of folksong and revivalism. The tensions that Henderson inherited from Gramsci in his understanding of the function and potential of popular folksong will also be explored with reference to Henderson's public 'flytings' with Hugh MacDiarmid. Finally, the folk song revival in Scotland will be considered as a movement that exemplified 'Gramsci in Action', as Henderson later suggested.

Henderson's relationship with Gramsci and his work is characterised by a deeply and personally felt affinity. The philosopher looms heavily over Henderson's writings, yet the recognised terms of Gramsci's political philosophy, terms such as 'cultural hegemony', 'traditional and organic intellectuals' and 'the national-popular', are conspicuous in their absence. Rather, Henderson generally absorbed

Gramsci's teachings into the body of his work without acknowledging their source, or else he attached himself to the historical figure, and to the imagery of the great intellectual, the imprisoned father, and the political martyr. The selective focus that Henderson applied to Gramsci, fuelled by his own value-system, saw not only an expansive mind capable of great syntheses, but a figure formed by his native heritage and folk-culture: a Sardinian as he was a Scot.

Introduction to Gramsci and the translation of the letters

Henderson was introduced to the celebrated name of Gramsci in Florence in 1944, whilst serving as an officer in the Intelligence Corps. The Communist Partisans of the Italian *Resistenza* acquainted Henderson with the political-philosopher as a hero and a martyr, and as the co-founder and former Secretary-General of the Italian Communist Party. They told Henderson of the hardships of Gramsci's life, of his incarceration in Mussolini's prisons, of his fragile physical condition, and of his consequent early death. They also made the young officer aware of the growing currency of the idea—which had already taken root on a localised scale—of Gramsci as *un grande pensatore*, that is, 'a great thinker'.[1] Henderson engages with Gramsci's legacy from this foundation, rooted in the veneration of the Italian anti-fascist combatants. The translation of the letters was undertaken at a time when only a small portion of Gramsci's works had been published, and that only in Italian. In this sense, Henderson first approached Gramsci with little more than his own prerogatives, and the admiration of the Partisans, to inform his reading.

Henderson could not help but project his own cultural-political perspectives onto his translation of the prison letters. This tendency could of course be applicable to any scholar working on the ideas of another; however, Henderson's case is distinctive in this respect, as he makes no effort to resist the process, to conceal it, or even to defend it. He writes of Gramsci without intimating the tone of critical distance that would ordinarily be expected. This aspect is made clear in Henderson's introductory essay for the *Prison Letters*.[2] Beginning with a reference to a painting in the National Gallery of Modern Art in Edinburgh—*The Self-Taught Man* by Ken Currie—depicting a Clydeside worker reading Gramsci under a bare light bulb, Henderson states: '...that a Scottish working-class intellectual – a stubborn survivor in Thatcher's Britain – should be interested in Gramsci's political thought in the 1980s is readily comprehensible'.[3] He goes on to draw upon all sorts of other relatively tenuously connected sources, but the focus of the introductory essay rarely strays far from what can be identified as his three primary contexts: the cultural and political parallels between Gramsci's native Sardinia, and Scotland; Gramsci's conception of folklore and its particular legacy; and finally, the tragic imagery of Gramsci's prison life.

Though this introductory essay was written for the 1988 edition of Henderson's translation of the letters, a similar view is also expressed in an early letter from Henderson to the prospective publisher of the translations, in 1949:

> ...he [Gramsci] has a strange (Scottish) mixture of hardness and softness... Sardinian is not really a dialect at all but a language, like Provencal and Lallans (no word can so well translate the Italian expletive 'Beh' as the vigorous Scots and Irish 'och'). There is a Celtic aspect to Gramscian culture—oral—casual—deep—he was the islander, 'l'isolano''. [4]

Given the persistence of Henderson's own critical perspectives of Gramsci, it is clear that though the 'great thinker' offered Henderson theoretical foundations that he had quite possibly lacked until then; this influence did not displace the beliefs that had already begun to crystallise before this period through his socialism and his established passion for languages, poetry and folksong; rather it vindicated them.

Henderson's own interpretative contexts are also extended to the translations themselves. Even his tendency to pepper his writing with conversational Scots is retained. 'Wee' appears countless times, making especially frequent appearances in the more playful letters addressed to Gramsci's children.[5] Henderson uses terms like 'daft',[6] where another translator writes 'stultified',[7] he renders Gramsci's description of the 'Italian Jacobin' Carlo Cattaneo, as having 'bees in his bonnet',[8] where others employ 'having too many fanciful ideas',[9] and 'too full of chimeras'.[10]

Henderson also retains Sardinian terms in their original. As he makes clear in his introduction, Gramsci's conception of his Sardinian heritage is of central importance in understanding his world-view,[11] and this can be seen as, at least in part, a validation of Henderson's own cultural nationalism. Henderson's explanatory notes also set the text within a framework of Scottish folk and literary culture. In a note explaining the Sardinian term *moro cabbaru*, for example, Henderson writes: 'Literally 'black man wearing the hood', a macabre figure resembling the Devil in Scottish folklore (cf. Stevenson's *Thrawn Janet*)',[12] and there are countless other examples concerned with comparative folklore studies; with Hugh MacDiarmid's 'First Hymn to Lenin' (1931) (even citing a stanza); with Allan Ramsay's *The Gentle Shepherd* (1725), and with articles from *Scottish International* (1968-1974).[13]

The key to understanding the textual voice of Gramsci in Henderson's translation is perhaps evident in one of the letters addressed to his wife:

> ...for me literary expression... is a relationship between form and content: analysis shows me, or helps me to understand, if there is complete adhesion between form and content, or if there exist gaps, fissures, disguises etc. It's possible to be mistaken, especially if one tries to deduce too much, but if the critic has a certain criterion to judge by, he can comprehend a good deal—at any rate the general state of mind [of the writer].[14]

Though this passage is directed at his wife's inclination towards concealing the problems and misfortunes of life at home in her letters, or so Gramsci suspected, it can also be applied to the practice Henderson seemingly undertook in modelling his tone in the translations. The playful uses of 'wee' and the retention of Sardinian terms, for example, would suggest a mindfulness of the conscious, or imagined, registers of Gramsci's letters. Henderson's is a successful translation in so far as it contains within it such careful modulations of character and attitude.

Translation is of course complex, and any consideration of 'fidelity' to an 'original' raises questions over what it is in the 'original' that demands the faithfulness of a translation. In this case it seems that Henderson was loyal to the only impression of Gramsci's letters that he could truly conceive of—that is, his own. Though this means that Gramsci's sentiments—when approached through Henderson's translation—are ripe with referential frameworks and linguistic ticks that are perhaps not evident in the original Italian, the result is a strikingly honest translation of one man's personally informed interpretation of the letters and the man behind them.

Gramsci's folklore

Gramsci's observations on folklore were of particular importance to Henderson. Though they only constitute around five pages of the vast *Quaderni del Carcere* (*Prison Notebooks*), they can be seen to account for a large part of the foundations of Henderson's conception of folk-culture, and to represent crucial assertions that were to be reified throughout his long investment in Scottish folksong revivalism.

Henderson celebrated folksong as a 'process'.[15] The transmission of folk songs, and the inferred qualities of those songs that are able to survive, to adapt and to disseminate among people was, for Henderson, the basis of the political potential of folk-culture's 'underground' quality. In an early article, asserting the status of a given example of 'contaminated' song as a *folk song*, Henderson explains that it warrants the categorisation 'because the people have taken it, possessed themselves of it, gloried in it, recreated it, loved it. That is the only test worth a docken'.[16] Gramsci sets out a definition of 'popular song' on similar terms:

...those written neither by the people nor for the people, but which the people adopt because they conform to their way of thinking and feeling... since what distinguishes a popular song within the context of a nation and its culture is neither its artistic aspect nor its historical origin, but the way in which it conceives the world and life, in contrast with official society.[17]

The most distinctive quality of Gramsci's understanding of 'folklore' is the expansive definition that he supposes for the term, and, consequently, the broad range of applications it gains outside of what might be called the 'traditional' conception:

One can say that until now folklore has been studied primarily as a 'picturesque' element... Folklore should instead be studied as a 'conception of the world and life' implicit to a large extent in determinate strata of society and in opposition... to 'official' conceptions of the world that have succeeded one another in the historical process.[18]

In Gramscian terms, 'folklore', as a world-view, is necessarily 'subaltern' rather than 'hegemonic'; existing 'in opposition to "official" conceptions of the world' and offering a counterpoint of perpetual resistance, due to its very existence. Henderson reiterates this view in various adaptations. In his notes for a Workers' Education Association lecture from 1949, entitled 'The Role of the Artist in Society', he writes:

> The real study of folk art—the art of the labouring classes, the work-songs of the community—how they come about, how they grow, what their energy and aesthetic force consists of—is still in its infancy; for the very good reason that is has not suited the powers that be to further such studies. Folk art is an *implicit*—and in many aspects an explicit challenge to the ruling class way of looking at the world.[19]

Similar constructions reappear throughout Henderson's work. He saw the folk-arts as the creative expression of a rebel 'underground', and often used the image of this 'underground' to infer a counter-cultural, politically resistant folk-culture:

> …whether it be the love-songs which reject the values and prejudices of a money-minded bourgeois society, or a hypocritical puritan religious set-up; the bawdy songs which frankly rejoice in the fun and comedy of sex; the 'Ding Dong Dollar' CND songs which pillory the antics of military bigwigs and the bonzes of imperialist power politics; the 'Sangs of the Stane' which send up the pretensions and absurdities of a stuffy royalist Establishment; the bothy songs which put on record the cheese-paring niggardliness of skinflint farmers— all share to a greater or lesser extent this rebel élan.[20]

Henderson emphasised this 'underground' element throughout the development of the Scottish folk song revival in the 1950s and 1960s. In an article for the *Spectator* in 1956 Henderson set out the role of Scottish folksong as 'part of the submerged resistance movement which reacted against the tyranny of John Knox's Kirk'. In 1963, in the *Scots Magazine*, he explained that the folk-singer represents 'a sort of 'anti-culture' and embodies ideas, predilections and values which are not those of learned culture, and which in the sterner Puritan societies of the past were ruthlessly put to the horn'.[21] Although the elaboration of such examples can be seen as an extension of Gramsci's idea of folksong as 'a conception of the world and life' in opposition to an inflexible and self-serving 'officialdom': it must be noted that Gramsci's original assertion is based on broader philosophical foundations.

Gramsci's conception of folklore as a world-view stands upon the premise that 'all men are intellectuals... but not all men have in society the function of intellectuals'. In his work on the study of philosophy, Gramsci contends that all men are also 'philosophers' due to what he calls the 'spontaneous philosophy' exercised by everyone, at all times. This 'spontaneous philosophy' is, he explains, contained in:

1. language itself, which is a totality of determined notions and concepts and not just of words grammatically devoid of content. 2. 'common sense' and 'good sense';[23] 3. popular religion and, therefore, also the entire system of beliefs, superstitions, opinions, ways of seeing things and of acting, which are collectively bundled together under the name of 'folklore'.[24]

Gramsci's 'folklore' is then defined as a pervasive, all-inclusive, collective term for the diverse complexities of those interpretative structures that one inherits from social and cultural contexts, and through historical 'processes'.[25]

Gramsci insisted that folklore 'can be understood only as a reflection of the conditions of the cultural life of the people'.[26] Such discourses on the nature of 'folklore' are reflected on two distinct levels in Henderson's work. Firstly, the 'conditions of [the] cultural life of the people' are, in a literal sense, always at the heart of Henderson's writings about folksong.[27] The recordings and transcriptions of his field research trips are among the most explicit and comprehensive illustrations of this aspect. Song performances and folktale renditions are interspersed with Henderson's conversational rapport with informants, always characterised by a clear and direct investment in the 'ways of life' of his source-singers, and by the social-historical bent of his questioning.[28]

The second level on which Henderson can be seen to conscribe to the idea of 'folklore' as a 'conception of the world and life,' is in a personal and reflexive sense. Henderson appears to have purposefully stepped inside Gramsci's 'conception' of folklore by choosing to establish his 'view of the world and life' as one persistently framed by, and formulated through, folk-culture. Henderson's appreciation of F Marian McNeill's methodology in *The Silver Bough* (1957) reflects something of his own practice: '...[she] enters into the spirit of the customs and events she is describing, and (as it were) dons guising gear herself to communicate the fun of the fair. Her books convey vividly the eager joy of the participant...'[29] As a celebrated songwriter as well as song-collector, Henderson commented upon folksong revivalism from the perspective of the insider. Henderson's referential touchstone is always folksong in one form or another, a point illustrated by his centralising of folk-culture in the introduction to the *Prison Letters*. It seems that regardless of the remit of a given article, interview, or public dispute; folksong, as an expansive and absorbent conception of the world, bears upon him and finds its own significance.

Gramsci's folksong paradox

Gramsci fostered a broad construction of 'folklore' that could be mobilised as an interpretative framework for understanding the ways in which people conceive of their own lives, and the world around them. However, in some passages, he also discerned a reactionary element of folklore that revealed itself as definitively 'subaltern', inherently defensive, and in perpetual opposition to the dominant hegemonic forces in society, regardless of whether those forces are revolutionary and progressive and aim for a new society couched in the interests of the proletariat, or not:

> ...the state competes with and contradicts other explicit and implicit conceptions, and folklore is not among the least significant and tenacious of these; hence it must be 'overcome'. For the teacher, then, to know 'folklore' means to know what other conceptions of the world and of life are actually active in the intellectual and moral formation of young people, in order to uproot them and replace them with conceptions which are deemed to be superior...[30]

This is a process that occurs at any given historical juncture; just as Gramsci envisaged a socialist revolution that must be aware of the need for 'coercive' and 'consensual' strategies, so too must those who, for example, conscribed to Mussolini's model of government.

Essentially, the folklore 'paradox' is exposed when we recognise the friction between ideas of folklore as a fundamentally *conservative* or *progressive* force, as it is portrayed in Gramsci's work.[31] In his introduction to the *Prison Letters*, and following a review of the ways in which Italian folklorists had dealt with Gramsci's views on folklore, Henderson recognises that there is an 'unresolved but creative clash of contradictions in Gramsci's approach.'[32] Moyra Byrne summarises the anthropologist Ernesto de Martino's methodological perspective of this 'paradox':

> On the one hand, their Gramscian-Marxist aim would be to determine the best means of accelerating the disappearance of this cultural relic [folksong] which is so 'disorganic' in relation to the modern world. On the other hand, an ethnographic operation aiming at a historico-religious reconstruction of a phenomenon depends on that phenomenon's persistence, and cannot *at the same time* be concerning itself with the means of eradicating it.[33]

However, if this 'creative clash of contradictions' is based on Gramsci's comments on the diversity and heterogeneity of folklore and on the need for folklore to be 'overcome', it seems that the 'contradictions' can be dissolved with relative ease. If 'folklore' is the broad network of various 'conceptions of the world', shared, yet adapted and manipulated, by people within and between social groups, then the *progressive* and *conservative* elements can comfortably coexist within the territory of 'folklore'. There are conceptions that must be 'overcome', and there are those that might be harnessed and developed, from any given point of view, all within the broad forum of 'folklore'. The tensions that bring about an apparent paradox in folklore can therefore be understood as its dialectical nature—at once progressive and conservative, flexible and static, timeless and anachronistic. In a series of notes addressing the problems of criticism Gramsci writes that:

> ...critical activity must be based on the ability to make distinctions, to discover the difference underlying every superficial and apparent likeness, and on the ability to discover the essential unity underlying every apparent contrast and superficial differentiation.[34]

It is in this spirit that Gramsci conceives of folklore. In the introduction to the *Prison Letters*, Henderson writes that:

> ...[passages from these letters] served to a large extent to neutralise the effect of the long series of negative attributes which passages in the *Quaderni* attribute to folklore. In the past decade a certain equilibrium, a synthesis of speculation and experience, has been achieved in this whole disputed area, and some of the lesser-known remarks of Gramsci have acquired a fresh relevance. In addition, folklorists outside Italy have begun to tackle the job of examining their field of study from a class perspective, and the fresh controversies and 'flytings' which will inevitably surface can only benefit from the vigorous intellectual battles already fought.[35]

The legacy of debate around Gramsci's views on folklore is one that Henderson maintained in one such series of 'flytings' with Hugh MacDiarmid. In a series of correspondences that became known as the 'Folksong Flytings', published in the letters columns of the *Scotsman* newspaper throughout 1964, MacDiarmid attacked the folk revival's political and cultural credentials, contrasting them with his own in an effort to promote his conception of the social and political responsibilities of literature. MacDiarmid confidently stated that 'the demand everywhere today is for higher and higher intellectual levels', and asked, 'why should we be concerned then with songs which reflect the educational limitations, the narrow lives, the poor literary abilities, of a peasantry we have happily outgrown?'[36] In response, Henderson assured that 'we are again in a period when folksong and art-poetry can interact fruitfully, and that it is in and through the present movement [the folk song revival] that this will come about'.[37] Gramsci was, at various points, wielded by both Henderson and MacDiarmid in efforts to validate their respective positions. In response to one of MacDiarmid's evocations of Gramsci, Henderson writes:

> Gramsci, friend and antagonist of Croce, was a polymath who, ranging as widely as MacDiarmid (and digging far deeper), was always ready to learn from, and appreciate, popular culture. He was one of the few men in this century in connection with whom one can meaningfully use such a term as 'universalization'... Yet,

far from despising the folk arts, this universal genius devoted much of his time to their study.[38]

The tension between Henderson and MacDiarmid was largely based on the opposition of the 'individual' and the 'communal' as cultural-political agents, and it was manifest as an interrogation of the relationship between the literary arts and the folk arts. In fact, these debates can be seen to mark out the very points between which Gramsci sought to synthesise the cultural focus of his writings: 'Marxism crowns the whole movement for intellectual and moral reform dialecticised in the contrast between popular and higher culture.'[39] In this sense, Henderson and MacDiarmid's disputes literally enact the dialectical engagement that Gramsci saw as necessary to realise the potential of a cultural Marxism.

Gramsci's concept of 'contradictory consciousness' is useful in illustrating this point:

> We can almost say that [the active man of the masses] has two theoretical consciousnesses (or one contradictory consciousness), one implicit in his actions, which unites him with all his colleagues in the practical transformation of reality, and one superficially explicit or verbal which he has inherited from the past and which he accepts without criticism… this contradictory consciousness can result in a state of moral and political passivity.[40]

Henderson and MacDiarmid were, in their different ways, looking to resolve this 'contradictory consciousness'. MacDiarmid rejected the idea of appealing to the tastes of the masses as the patronising work of an 'interpreting class', and called for a 'monumental' art that aimed for nothing less than a 'grand syntheses' for the times.[41] Accordingly, his own later poetic works are largely set at a level that refuses to conceal their complexity. Henderson on the other hand sought to harness the inherent power of folk-culture, to synthesise it with the progressive elements of literary practice in Scotland in an effort to mobilise, and politicise popular culture.

The Scottish folk song revival as 'Gramsci in action'

Gramsci's influence on Henderson's understanding of folk culture has implications that extend beyond the ideas articulated in Henderson's various writings. In the early 1950s, Henderson was involved in the Edinburgh People's Festival (1951–1954) and played a prominent role in the organisation of the associated People's Festival Ceilidhs. These events were, according to his own retrospective accounts, instrumental in the development of the folk song revival in Scotland.[42] As a panel member on a televised debate on the significance of Gramsci in contemporary Britain, aired in 1987, Henderson referred to these events as a realisation of 'Gramsci in action'.[43] He explains the theoretical connection with the People's Festival: '…it [the Festival] was an attempt, in fact, to carry Gramscian ideas of infiltration, to put it bluntly, into the body politic'.[44] The Festival was, in Henderson's words, about Scottish culture, not 'high heid yin culture'.[45] Its objectives, as set out in the first programme of 1951, were:

> To initiate action designed to bring the Edinburgh International Festival closer to the people as a whole and to make it serve more fully the cause of international understanding and good will; and also to initiate action such as will more generally make what is best in the cultural life of our country more accessible to working people, and will secure further facilities for the development of the cultural activities of working people.[46]

The programme for the first Festival Ceilidh in that inaugural year articulates a desire to 'restore Scottish folksong to the ordinary people, not merely as a bobby-soxer vogue, but deeply and integrally'. [47]

The ceilidhs brought together and, importantly, brought to Edinburgh and to the urban central belt, many of the artists and source-singers that Henderson 'discovered' on his early recording trips, including that with Alan Lomax in 1951. As Henderson stated in many of his accounts of the period, these recordings, and the ceilidhs themselves, played a vital role in energising a new generation of folk-singers and song-collectors, many of whom—such as Norman Buchan—were then inspired to take the material to schools, folk workshops and, in later years, folk-clubs, in an effort to disseminate previously unheard examples of an invaluable indigenous folk-culture.[48]

Henderson saw the revival as an attempt to put into practice Gramsci's understanding of the capacity of 'folklore' to 'bring about the birth of a new culture among the popular masses, so that the separation between modern culture and popular culture of folklore will disappear.'[49] The momentum of the revival was realised in many ways; through traditional 'oral transmission', at ceilidhs and at folk-clubs; the passing around of field recordings among interested parties; articles such as those written by Henderson exploring folk-song threads and defending the programme of revivalism; the establishment of folk-music festivals, and through the formation of bodies like the University of Edinburgh's School of Scottish Studies. All of these elements can be seen to represent prime examples of what Gramsci infers when he writes:

> The creation of a new culture does not only mean individually making some 'original' discoveries. It means also and especially the critical propagation of truths already discovered, 'socialising them' so to speak, and so making them become a basis for live action, and element of co-ordination and of intellectual and moral order.[50]

The 'socialisation' of the 'truths' of the folk revival was, if anywhere, realised in these capacities. Such examples of the outward manifestation of Gramsci's principles can perhaps be called upon to extend Henderson's description of the Edinburgh People's Festival as 'Gramsci in action', to account for the whole of the movement of Scottish folk song revivalism.

Henderson's Gramsci

Gramsci's influence on the strategies of folk-revivalism in Scotland went largely unacknowledged, as it does in much of Henderson's writings on the 'folk process' and the political character of folksong. Nevertheless, the capacities in which Henderson directly addressed Gramsci are indicative of the precise nature of his relationship with the philosopher and his work, and can be seen to set Henderson apart from the general movement of Gramscian scholarship, particularly in the UK. As discussed above, it is clear that Henderson looked upon Gramsci in a very human light: as a Sardinian, and a father, one incarcerated for his beliefs and thrust back upon the traditional cultures of his home, to help him through the darkest nights of that 'long prison Calvary'.[51] The introduction to the *Prison Letters*, and the suggested reading list therein, reveal that Henderson was well acquainted with the work of Gramsci scholars that had arisen in the years following his original translation work. He directs the reader towards the critical introduction by James Joll, the translation work of Quintin Hoare and Geoffrey Nowell-Smith, and the uses and applications of Gramscian thought proposed by Stuart Hall and Tony Bennett.[52] He also expresses a great empathy for the plight of those Italian folklorists who sought to square their work with the theoretical structures of Gramsci's political-philosophy.[53] However, the character of Henderson's relationship with Gramsci is distinct from the work of these figures. Not only does Henderson invest whole-heartedly in a conception of folklore as a world-view, as this essay has posited, but Gramsci, the man, also offered Henderson a more conceptual inspiration. Henderson compared Gramsci to John MacLean, Rosa Luxemburg and Karl Liebknecht, in terms of his historical significance.[54] The common factor between them, and that which was so inspiring for Henderson, is a symbolic unity of theory and practice. In the letter cited above, to the prospective publisher of his translations of the letters, Henderson concludes:

> Gramsci's humanist vision was beyond party, law or imposed power —and he would not compromise the union he had constructed between his inner vision and external human need… Thus amongst the last sentences uttered by Gramsci [in the letters] some are very like those uttered by Christ on the cross: 'I have destroyed my own existence!'[55]

Gramsci is shrouded in Christological qualities, as the model of a perfect confluence of philosophy and life-course. The implication is that Gramsci's example offers a message of sacrifice and redemption, a message that should be maintained and carried forward, free to adapt and reengage with changing historical circumstances, like a folk song.

The most noticeable aspect of Henderson's work—heavily influenced by Gramsci as it is—is the conspicuous absence of the terms of those theoretical constructions celebrated by so many other scholars; concepts such as 'hegemony', 'war of position', 'traditional and organic intellectuals' and the 'historic bloc'. Gramsci's influence on Henderson is, rather, coded into the texture of his work, and invested in his own referential frameworks. In his prison notebooks Gramsci writes that 'if the cultural world for which one is fighting is a living and necessary fact, its expansiveness will be irresistible and it will find its artists'.[56] The same might be said of Gramsci's influence on Henderson: Gramsci and his legacy bore down on Henderson as a 'living and necessary fact' and found its realisation, its art, in his work.

References:

1 Henderson's experiences with the partisans and his introduction to Gramsci are detailed in an article written for *Cencrastus* in 1996, 'Gramsci and the Partisans', reprinted in *Alias MacAlias: Writings on Song, Folk and Literature*, edited by Alec Finlay (Edinburgh: Polygon, 2004), pp. 339-44. His time among the Partisans and his later work translating Gramsci's letters are explored in detail in the first volume of Timothy Neat's biography of Henderson, *Hamish Henderson, A Biography: Volume 1, The Making of the Poet (1919-1953)* (Edinburgh: Polygon, 2007), pp. 143-60 & 242-55. See also Pino Mereu's essay in the present volume.

2 Henderson's translation of the letters finally achieved independent single-volume publication with Zwan in 1988, and the introductory essay was written for this volume. It was reproduced in the Pluto Press reprint in 1996, and it is to the latter edition that this essay will make reference.

3 Antonio Gramsci, *Prison Letters*, translated and introducted by Hamish Henderson (London: Pluto Press, 1996), p. 1.

4 Letter to John Lehman, as cited by Neat (2007), p. 246.

5 Antonio Gramsci, *Prison Letters*, translated and introduced by Hamish Henderson (London: Pluto Press, 1996), pp. 143, 177, 239, 282, 285, 288.

6 *Ibid.*, p. 218.

7 Antonio Gramsci, *Letters from Prison*, edited by Frank Rosengarten, translated by Raymond Rosenthal, (New York: Columbia University Press, 1994), p. 175.

8 *Prison Letters*, p.162.

9 *Letters from Prison*, p. 67.

10 *Ibid.*, p. 205.

11 *Ibid.*, pp. 4-6.

12 *Ibid.*, p. 127.

13 *Ibid.*, pp. 188, 154, 49, 227.

14 *Ibid.*, p. 125.

15 In a previously unpublished notebook, cited by Neat (2007), Henderson explains the 'folk process' quite succinctly, as: '…a useful shorthand phrase for what happens to folk songs when they begin to take on a life of their own – start shedding some things, accruing others – generally taking on a new and changing form', p. 368. This 'process' is intimated and explored throughout Henderson's critical writings and his correspondences.

16 Hamish Henderson, 'Enemies of Folk-song' (1955), reproduced in *Alias MacAlias*, p. 50.

17 Antonio Gramsci, *Selections from Cultural Writings*, edited by David Forgacs and Geoffrey Nowell-Smith, (London: Lawrence & Wishart, 1985), p. 195. Though this quotation is concerned with 'popular song', rather than 'folksong', its relevance for Henderson is made clear in his work. In his essay 'It Was In You That It A' Began' (Edward J Cowan, ed., *The People's Past: Scottish Folk, Scottish History*, Edinburgh: Polygon, 1980), Henderson translates it as 'folksong' rather than 'popular song', p. 13). In an interview with Jennie Renton in *Textualities* in 1987, Henderson refers to these lines as Gramsci's 'most suggestive remark' and 'most pregnant insight' into folksong.

18 Antonio Gramsci, *Selections from Cultural Writings*, pp. 188-189.

19 As cited by Neat (2007) pp 235-6.

20 Henderson, ''It Was in You That It A' Began': Some Thoughts on the Folk Conference.' Ted Cowan (ed.), *The People's Past: Scottish Folk, Scottish History* (Edinburgh: Polygon, 1980), p. 8.

21 Reproduced in *Alias MacAlias*, pp. 28, 34.

22 *Selections from the Prison Notebooks*, p. 9.

23 'Common sense' is explained by Gramsci elsewhere in the *Prison Notebooks*: 'Every social class has its own 'common sense' and 'good sense', which are basically the most widespread conception of life and man. Every philosophical current leaves a sedimentation of 'common sense': this is the document of its historical reality. Common sense is not something rigid and stationary, but is in continuous transformation, becoming enriched with scientific notions and philosophical opinions that have entered into common circulation. 'Common sense' is the folklore of philosophy and always stands midway between folklore proper (folklore as it is normally understood) and the philosophy, science, and economics of the scientists. Common sense creates the folklore of the future, a relatively rigidified phase of popular knowledge in a given time and place'. *Selections from Cultural Writings*, p. 421.

24 *Selections from the Prison Notebooks*, p. 323.

25 *Ibid.*, pp. 325-26.

26 *Selections from Cultural Writings*, p. 190.

27 See articles 'Folk-song from a Tile' (*Alias MacAlias*, pp. 104-109)and 'An Aberdeen 'White Paternoster'' (*Alias MacAlias*, pp. 110-114) for good examples of Henderson's work in tracing folk-songs through their historical trajectories. Other articles, more directly concerned with the social history reflected in folksong, include 'A Colliery Disaster Ballad' (*Alias MacAlias*, pp. 119-124) and 'Scottish Songs at Work' (*Alias MacAlias*, pp. 129-131).

28 For an example of this practice, see the transcription of Henderson's recordings with Willie Mathieson, 'Willie Mathieson's Young Days', *Tocher*, 43 (1991), pp. 22-25.

29 *Alias MacAlias*, p. 263.

30 *Selections from Cultural Writings*, p. 191.

31 Moira Byrne, 'Antonio Gramsci's Contribution to Italian Folklore Studies', *International Folklore Review*, Vol. 2. (1982), p. 72.

32 *Prison Letters*, p. 15.

33 'Antonio Gramsci's Contribution to Italian Folklore Studies', pp. 72-73.

34 *Selections from Cultural Writings*, p. 134.

35 *Prison Letters*, p. 17.

36 Letter to the *Scotsman*, reproduced in *The Armstrong Nose: Selected Letters of Hamish Henderson*, edited by Alec Finlay, (Edinburgh: Polygon, 1996), p. 118.

37 *Ibid.*, p. 124.

38 *Ibid.*, p. 131.

39 Antonio Gramsci, *The Modern Prince and Other Writings*. (London: Lawrence and Wishart, 1957), p. 86.

40 *Ibid.*, p. 66.

41 Letter to the *Scotsman*, reproduced in *The Armstrong Nose*, pp. 127-128.

42 Hamish Henderson, 'The Edinburgh People's Festival, 1951-1954', in: Andy Croft (ed.), *A Weapon in the Struggle: The Cultural History of the Communist Party of Great Britain* (London: Pluto, 1998), pp. 163-170.

43 *Ibid.*

44 *Gramsci: Here and Now*, directed by Les Wilson. Participants: Hamish Henderson, Stuart Hall, John Reid, Lidia Curti. STV (1987).

45 *Ibid.*

46 As cited by Henderson, 'The Edinburgh People's Festival', p. 165.

47 *Ibid.*, p. 168.

48 *The People's Past*, pp. 14, 97; *Alias MacAlias*, pp. 1-2, 16, 213; 'The Edinburgh People's Festival', pp. 163-70.

49 *Selections from Cultural Writings*, p. 191.

50 *Ibid.*, p. 60.

51 'Introduction', *Prison Letters*, p. 65.

52 *Ibid.*, pp. 10-12, 23-24.

53 *Ibid.*, pp. 13-15.

54 *Ibid.*, p. 6; Hamish Henderson, 'Antonio Gramsci', *Cencrastus*, (Winter 1987/1988), p. 23.

55 As cited by Neat (2007), p. 246.

56 *Selections from Cultural Writings*, p. 109.

A HEADFUL OF HIGHLAND SONGS: JOURNEYING HOPEFULLY THANKS TO SEUMAS MÒR[1]

Rob Gibson

Around the walls of Porterfield Prison in Inverness, bagpipes played, slogans were shouted and then a ringing rendition of 'The Freedom Come-All-Ye' tried to reach Donnie Macleod, the GM Martyr incarcerated therein. He had been sent down for twenty-one days, following his refusal to reveal the names of others who had protested with him on UK Election Day, 7 June the previous year. Before the polls officially opened, the protesters had cast the first vote of the day with a huge X trampled across a trial planting of genetically modified oil seed rape in a field at Rhives in the Black Isle.

Hundreds more people were inspired by this most modern cause of the threat to bio-security, and organic food an issue that was undreamed of in the days of the Knoydart Land Raid in 1948. But the spirit of Hamish Henderson filled the protesters' lungs and inspired new songs to keep Scotland GM free. During the previous summer six hundred folk had marched through Inverness ahead of the second proposed GM trials in the Black Isle. A GM Vigil was set up for eleven months in a lay-by at Roskill Farm using a yurt and a small caravan. To support the vigileers many fund-raising ploys drew cash from a' the airts.

Anti GM songs had already been composed locally, performed to raise funds and boost morale in the vigil's yurt. That gave me the idea we could reach a far wider audience by making a CD. The resulting five tracks were laid down courtesy of Allan Harfield's Walled Garden Studio near Auldearn. Under the banner 'Oilseed Raped?', over £600 was raised for the Munlochy Vigil and prompted local reviewers to praise the album for its 'clever balance of traditional Scottish music and a funky, Paul Weller meets Peter Gabriel kind of sound.'[2]

Our squibs were a potent mix, robust old tunes, some new and pithy words, plus modern vibes. They prove that the carrying stream expands horizons in multicultural twenty-first century Scotland. The activist/artists were BB Blacksheep and the Horny Diddlers, me, Joost and Donald Jack with Champin' at the Bit. We could not have asked for a better local response than the *Highland News* reviewer who concluded that a Scottish Executive minister should tune in, for he had defied local opinion that opposed the GM trials. 'Let's hope someone sends a copy to Ross Finnie because he is bound to enjoy it. After all he seems to be very good at dancing to other people's tunes...'[3]

Hamish Henderson wrote a foreword to *The Democratic Muse* by Ailie Munro. In it he noted that 'anyone even vaguely familiar with the bountiful heritage of radical poetry in our tradition will readily comprehend what wonderfully fallow ground Scotland was— and is—for this invigorating demotic influence.'[4] I would argue that the Highlands and Islands have added their fair share towards the Scottish total. However too many real campaigns in the north are less well known. I am taking the Knoydart Land Raid as a starting point when Hamish triggered wider Scottish sympathy for the would-be crofters and sowed the seeds of protest and happy defiance across the north down to the present day.

From prolonged personal involvement I believe that Highland hot topics contain the same elements as political songs elsewhere. I will include land campaigns; threats of nuclear dumping; nuclear accidents such as the fallout from Chernobyl; NATO military colonialism; the coming of TV; the sudden closure of the aluminium smelter at Invergordon; resistance to tolls on the Skye Bridge; the tragic decline of fish stocks; responses to klondikers and wider environmental themes like GM crop trials.

I have been involved for over thirty years as a political activist, singer, collector and music organiser. For example, I led the team which ran the annual Highland Traditional Music Festival [HTMF] in Dingwall during its twenty-year life until 2002. This gave a platform to new songs and coincided with the rise of Feis Rois as the leading agent for Gaelic music development in the Highlands. The wider backdrop included the oil boom and betrayal of devolution in '79, resistance mode during the Thatcher years, the dawn of New Labour, followed by the belated but popular arrival of the Scottish Parliament. Political action in the Highlands sat naturally alongside solidarity with national and international peace and anti-apartheid campaigns. That is why I started this story with the anti-GM stance that made us think global and sing local.

The abolition of oppressive landlordism is still a key part of the long quest for Scotland's freedom. Yet for many years our scenery was draped in a 'tartan' world view full of longing for fictitious scenes of sheilings and glens that were staple fare for music hall audiences. One of the classics of the genre, Jim Copeland's 'These are my Mountains' as sung by the Alexander Brothers, was heard here and across the globe. It plays on the romantic hopes of the wandering Scot:

> For these are my mountains
> And this is my glen
> The braes of my childhood
> Will see me again
> No land ever claimed me,
> Thoough far I did roam
>
> For these are my mountains
> And I'm coming home.[5]

In 1973 John McGrath used the original to warm up his audiences before curtain up on his ceilidh play *The Cheviot, the Stag and the Black, Black Oil*. Actor Allan Ross played the tune on his fiddle, encouraged audience participation and proceeded to the stage. But a sinister twist in the story line came from the character playing Queen Victoria:

> These are our mountains
> And this is our glen
> The braes of your childhood
> Are English again
> Though wide is our Empire
> Balmoral is best,
> Yes these are our mountains
> And we are impressed.[6]

McGrath combined this artifice with traditional songs in both English and Gaelic to carry his story of expropriation that fired up audiences across Highlands and Lowlands in 1973, so much so that a TV version appeared soon after.

Art had imitated art or, alternatively, satire borrowed from music hall, then life imitated art when the Assynt Crofters made a bid for the North Lochinver Estate in 1992. At fund raising ceilidhs, such as the one I sang at in Achiltibuie hall, the women land campaigners unrolled their chorus written on large sheet and sang the Assynt Crofters Song, with new words written by Issie Macphail:

> For these are my mountains and the crofts we all ken
> The land's for the people, not for sale, yet again.
> So the crofters of Assynt all met in the school –
> The land's for the people, not for landlords to rule.[7]

They won their land in December 1992 and boosted national morale and underlined the urgent need for land reform through the TV and media coverage Assynt generated. This produced new songs such as 'Anthem for the North Assynt Crofters Trust' by Norman Stewart and Stuart Palmer.[8] Meanwhile, Ullapool-based singer songwriter Andy Mitchell caught the germ of an idea from land historian James Hunter who foresaw new lights in the glens. Apologising for the song's late arrival several months after the handover of Assynt in February 1993, Andy captured in four verses and a new melody the saga from clearances to buyout in 'New Lights Shining in the Glen'. His performance and encore at the HTMF in June 1993 was well worth the wait. It concluded:

> The spirit once was daunted but it never ever died,
> A whole new generation has found a newborn pride
> We hope that others like us will also learn to see
> That destiny is ours to choose and we choose to be free.
>
> New lights are shining, new lights are shining,
> New lights are shining in the glen.

In the 1950s and 1960s topical songs were rife. Mostly they went from mouth to mouth rejoicing the retrieval of the Stone of Destiny, exploding EIIR pillar boxes, laughing at the Royal Family and the mobilising against Polaris. The rising SNP spawned more songs with the election of Winnie Ewing at the Hamilton by-election in 1967. Already Morris Blythman, a close collaborator with Seamas Mòr, had tackled the above subjects and added the successful land raid in North Uist in 'The Ballad of Balelone', following the Knoydart debacle.[9] To many of these issues Highlanders contributed. Naturally, Gaelic songs covered some of them, for there had been land raid songs from the 1920s which were still sung.

'Oran Na Cloiche'—a humorous song of the Stone—was composed by Donald MacIntyre (1889-1964). It gained much local celebrity through the singing of Captain Donald Joseph MacKinnon of Barra. The return of the Stone of Destiny to austerity Scotland was a national tonic. The song resurfaced when Kathleen MacInnes took the part of Kay Matheson in the 2000 TV drama An Ceasnachadh— the interrogation of a Highland lassie.[10] Kay had been one of the four reivers. Led by Iain Hamilton, they delivered the surprise 1950 Christmas Day present which delighted many patriotic Scots such as Gaelic poet Sorley MacLean.

Earlier in the century, Marjory Kennedy Fraser had, arguably, bowdlerised many island songs. In contrast, the pawky humour of Compton MacKenzie's books was enjoyed in their comedy treatment of the wartime Whisky Galore and its Ealing Studios sequel Rockets Galore. However, real life dealt a potential threat to townships around Stornoway in 1979 when the Ministry of Defence made a surreptitious announcement. The local airport was to be upgraded for operational use for Cold War surveillance of Soviet naval and air forces in the Iceland Faeroes Gap. The Keep NATO Out [KNO] campaign quickly gained local support.

Among its most ardent activists was Murdo MacFarlane, the 'Melbost Bard', whose township, near the airstrip, seemed most likely to lose even more of its good land than it did in 1939. Murdo had been loved for his life affirming songs for decades. At an action meeting of KNO in Stornoway Town Hall he recited his song 'Leag Iad Am Bom an Raoir'—a mother's lullaby to her child in the year 2050 after the bomb has been dropped. It received a standing ovation, and in 2007 it was a cert for the recording of The Murdo MacFarlane Song Book.

Alyth chose to sing it, which she did beautifully. She is the daughter of the then KNO chairman Angus McCormack.[11] Fortunately, the Berlin Wall came down in 1989 and ended the Tory Government interest in Stornoway airport. The quality and range of Murdo's songs for over fifty years are gems of the modern Gaelic song tradition.

Around the North West, Andy Mitchell began to ply his day job as a radar engineer repairing electrical equipment on fishing boats up and down the Minch in the 1980s. The range of his material is extensive. He happily uses both Doric and Highland English in his lyrics, having been born of Highland parents in Ellon, and explained that so many East Coast men fished the Minches.

Andy was writing every week in the heyday of the Ullapool Folk Club in the '80s and early '90s. One piece concerned the Klondikers, fish processing ships, moored in the bay. Soon after the election in 1983 of Charles Kennedy, the new Social Democrat MP for Ross, Cromarty and Skye backed increased numbers of customs men to police the Ullapool area, seeing these eastern Europeans as a security risk.

In reality, during the Cold War, a peaceful, law-abiding multinational community evolved between locals and the Eastern bloc fishers. The imagined Russian spy with the improbable name of Van Lyker explains:

> At disguises nobody can match me
> On the lifeboat they did dispatch me
> I was decked out in tartan as we sailed round Isle Martin
> I was sure that nobody would catch me…[12]

The fish trade changed and the Klondikers left as peacefully as they had arrived.

Vin Garbutt covered Andy Mitchell's 'Calum Mor', a sad tale of wife beating in a west Highland town. Andy Irvine famously included Andy's 'Indiana' in the first album by Irish supergroup Patrick Street. 'Indiana' is a powerful anthem to reverse emigration, a beam of light in the 1980s. It tells of Scots couple Tom and Valerie Bryan who met in Scotland, went to study in the USA and, determined to raise their family back in Scotland, returned to near Ullapool.

Driving the roads of the west coast gave Andy Mitchell lots of time for composition. He often passed Gruinard Island, which was contaminated with deadly anthrax spores in an MoD experiment during World War Two. He captured the beauty of Gruinard Bay in a spectacular midsummer afterglow and contrasted that idyll with the deadly legacy bequeathed by a distant military decision. The song received a memorable performance by Rita Hunter, who herself was brought up in Aultbea where her dad had been the local bagpipe playing GP. The event, a fund raising concert in Dingwall Town Hall in February 1988, was in aid of Ross-shire Against [nuclear] Dumping [RAD] because the UK Government agency NIREX had targeted areas such as Caithness, Easter Ross and Buchan for possible dump sites.

Rita, Andy and I shared the opening slot on a bill that night which included a Wick-based blues band, the Sutherland Brothers, Phil Cunningham and the Battlefield Band who generously gave their support for free to help fund a plebiscite that was to test public opinion in Easter Ross. Our set raised the political temperature against both civil and military nuclear threats.

For our second song we developed 'The Nuclear Dustbin Song' set to the tune of 'The Kelty Clippie'. I wrote an additional verse.

So all you people stand up now and fight the NIREX plan
Your children's lives and future jobs demand a nuclear ban
On radioactive transport for burial down below
Our united voice throughout the land's
    a loud resounding NO![13]

Next came Andy Mitchell's hilarious parody of the popular Highland ceilidh song 'Grannie's Heiland Hame'. It is a holiday complex sited in the village of Embo north of Dornoch to this day. After the Chernobyl accident in 1986, thoughts of being 'doonwind of Dounreay', the nuclear test station in Caithness, were very scary!

Away in the Heilands there stands a wee hoose,
And it stands by the back of the brae,
But the trouble with wee butt and ben,
It stands just doonwind of Dounreay,
I can still see auld Grannie a tear in her e'e,
That lights up the whole sky at night,
And I'll never forget these great mushroom clouds,
Each time Granda lights up his pipe.
    Oh the heather bells are glowing a bonny bright yellow green,

Rowan berries growing to the size of aubergines,
And there's white dust on the carpet that's no'
 dandruff or cocaine,
Oh I think it's time I left my Grannie's Heilan' Hame.

After our set that night Lorraine Mann, the RAD leader, asked Andy to let her have the song to sing on a radio programme. She had led the enquiry team opposed to the dangerous expansion of Dounreay in a hugely complex public enquiry, but was also another local folky.

Our finale was 'Song for Scotland', composed the previous year by Terry Leonino and Greg Artzner, who are the American eco-activist singing duo Magpie. They sang two verses for Andy whilst staying the night at his home after an Ullapool gig. It opens on a winter sea shore:

In the quiet of that morning my eyes were turned on high
By the sudden roar and rumble of a jet bomber
 across the sky…

So depressing was the picture of Scotland on the frontline between the USA and USSR 'caught in a struggle of terrible power of ideology,' that Andy pleaded with Terry and Greg to give us some hope. They duly composed verse three before breakfast. The final chorus goes:

Old friend a beacon in the Northern Sea
May you find your own safe harbour in a land that's
 strong and free,
Looking towards that morning when your destiny's your own,
I sing this song for Scotland and her people I have known.[14]

It is strong meat, even today, but encompassed that dread Cold War mood. We were pleased to give it a premiere at the RAD concert. Later that year, in locally run referenda Caithness, Easter Ross and Buchan all rejected overwhelmingly the idea that they should host a deep nuclear repository for British nuclear waste.

Social change and challenges in the community often provoke song writers. TV came late to the north—in some places not before the 1970s. A friend of mine collected a ditty on the subject sung to the tune of 'The Barnyards o' Delgaty'. It began:

> Och an Och the peats need cutting
> Not a bannock for the tea
> Not a tattie or a herrin'
> Since they gave the West TV...[15]

Big industry came north in 1967 when the first sods were cut at Invergordon on the only Class A agricultural land north of the Great Glen for the aluminium smelter which was to have a full working life of only ten years. Then the power deal unravelled and a thousand local workers got the sack at Christmas 1981. It was a black day that led to political recriminations in Westminster, protest meetings, threats of a factory sit-in, and it struck a huge blow to the self-confidence of Easter Ross.

As a guidance teacher in Alness Academy I was able to mobilise pupils and colleagues to help keep the community together. I wrote a defiant song, 'Save the Smelter', to the tune 'Wha Saw the Forty-Twa' or, as known locally, 'Wha Saw the Hilton Fishers'. At several events, along with my singing friend and teacher colleague Allan Thomson, we gave it laldy. Later in the year, Channel 4 TV was reaching Scotland, and a film maker won a commission to look at Alness and Invergordon a year after the closure. *A Guid New Year?*, filmed in Alness in November 1982, was screened at New Year 1983. However, it was only seen further south—as we did not have Channel 4 in the Highlands by then, so some friends sent us videos of the show. Here's a snatch of my song:

> But the men of Invergordon said the smelter will not die,
> Stand together we will show them, barricade and occupy!
>
> We make the metal of the future; world demand is on the rise,
> We have the power, so set a fair price; turn the
>   cell rooms on supply.

One result from the struggle was a new policy adopted by Ross & Cromarty District Council to promote 'quality of life' as a core aim. This included the founding of Feis Rois.

Throughout the 1980s and into the 1990s, new bands and song writers plied their trade. Capercaillie from Oban championed Gaelic song and chafed at the lack of a future for young Highlanders in songs like 'Waiting for the Wheel to Turn'.

Also heard at the Dingwall Festival was Iain MacDonald, who is from Stornoway and now living in Insch. His raging, committed self-penned songs ran the gamut of the personal, the travails of land and sea and onto the fight to free South Africa. At the 1986 festival he unveiled his song 'No Fun City' which included the Jerry Dammers chorus 'Free Nelson Mandela.' It rails against the bands that played in Sun City without acknowledging the shame of apartheid.

Following rapturous applause, a black man in the audience walked up to the stage. He thanked Iain and announced he was the British representative of the ANC on his way to Dundee to accept the freedom of the city on behalf of Mandela. The Seaforth Room of the National Hotel erupted and an encore was demanded. The set was being recording that evening for BBC Highland. So Iain's cousin, also Iain MacDonald, a radio journalist, took the clip and it was played on the eight o'clock Scottish news next morning.

Iain brought a new edge and rockier tone to the tradition. His LP and tape issued that year, *Beneath Still Waters*, included various memorable songs such as 'All Our Dreams', 'The Maid of Islay', 'Santiago Stadium', and 'The Iolaire', the last of which reworked the tragic sinking of an Admiralty yacht drowning over two hundred of servicemen, returning after the end of World War One, on New Year's Day 1919.[16]

Dougie MacLean has made a big impression on us with his sympathy for the aborigines of Australia and comparisons with what Scotland was also losing. In his song *Homeland*, he grabbed a key message of defiance:

Look to the south, I tell you, the black man has it
    cruel and hard,
But you don't have to look any further than the rumble of
    stones in our own back yard,

> And Oh sad the day and all that's left are a fading few
> Yes sir, you may have paid good money for it,
>   but no, it'll never belong to you.[17]

Further north, the doings at the atomic research station at Dounreay had produced their own glowing tributes courtesy of the Dounreay Strathspey and Reel Society. But Nancy Nicolson, an Edinburgh teacher who hails from Wick, was penning various feminist songs such as 'They Sent a Wuman'. However, her satirical pen captured the rather lax arrangement for security in the early atomic days in the 1960s.

> E'm E Man At Muffed id,
> E'm the man at boobed,
> E'm e man at lost the radioactive tube.[18]

Some years later, a protracted campaign got going to oppose the tolls proposed to pay for the cost of the new bridge to the Isle of Skye. This was to lead to a string of court cases and nights in prison at Dingwall Sheriff Court for some protesters. But that phase was preceded by a debate about whether a bridge was wanted at all. A Skye school teacher, Morag Henriksen, wrote 'The Skye Bridge Song', using the tune of 'The Erie Canal', which gave each side their say. The chorus goes—

> NO bridge to the Isle of Skye
> YES! A bridge or we'll know the reason why
> Oh! We all have our opinions and none of us agree
> Should we cross to Skye by a bridge or the sea?[19]

At the Battlefield Band Circus on the north coast at Bettyhill, in a song-writing workshop, Andy Mitchell met a shepherd from Strath Halladale, Colin F MacKenzie, who had penned 'No Man's Land, Welcome the Stranger' which used a Phil Cunningham tune and began with a warning:

> Ask your sons and your daughters how their
>   history made them
> How their future is shaped by other hands than their own

Will they ever be able in friendship and kinship
To welcome the stranger in a land that's their own?[20]

He was a singer/guitarist at ceilidhs and sessions around Melvich on
the 'Back Coast', also composing some new songs or putting tunes to
the words of his friend Willie Mackay, Reay, such as 'The Shell'. Andy
had suggested Colin would enjoy the Dingwall Festival which he first
attended in 1991.

Back in the winter of 1948-49 Hamish Henderson, having attended
a meeting of the Knoydart Defence Committee held in Glasgow,
took the overnight ferry to Belfast. On board he wrote a satirical
masterpiece, featuring the Nazi laird Lord Brocket and the failure
of the Labour government to back the 'Seven Men of Knoydart'. It
blended high farce with uplifting sentiments of demands for Scottish
self-government that followed World War Two.[21]

At that time Hamish worked for the Workers Education Association
in Northern Ireland, and he chose the 'rebel' tune to *Johnstone's Motor
Car* from the Irish Civil War for 'Knoydart'. In his mind, the causes
and cultures of Ireland and Scotland were intertwined.

An increasingly destructive succession of lairds ruled over
Knoydart after the land raid failed in 1948. Scottish Office indifference
had ignored the letter of the land settlement laws, despite the 'victory'
of the hated Lord Brocket, and the native population dwindled to
zero in the next ten years, while some outsider wilderness seekers
and holiday home buyers moved in. At one stage in the Thatcher era
it narrowly escaped returning to be used as a huge military training
ground as it had been in World War Two.

On the fortieth anniversary of the land raid in November 1988,
Archie MacDougall, one of the group who staked claims at Scottas, was
a gardener for Inverness Council. He told journalist Iain MacDonald
on BBC Radio Highland that he hoped that a monument to the land
raid could be put in place. I responded to Archie with a pledge to see
what could be done. Working with local Highland councillor Michael
Foxley, we gathered support from far and wide. But the hardest job
was getting a site for a cairn, as landowner Philip Rhodes forbade any
use of his estate. Finally, we made the breakthrough in 1991 when
the community council offered a site in front of the village hall. We
engaged stone mason Duncan Matheson from Kintail to construct the
cairn.

The unveiling took place on 14 September that year, accompanied by piper Iain MacDonald, youngest of the three piping brothers of Glenuig, and fiddler Farquhar MacRae, Glen Sheil, one of the survivors of the Moidart Ceilidh Band. When we all repaired to the bar at Inverie, I sang 'The Seven Men of Knoydart', but to a marked silence from locals. The sentiment of the words had, as yet, only remotely touched their consciousness.

Four years later, to coincide with the fiftieth anniversary of VE Day, we added a second plaque to the cairn with the raiders' names emblazoned there. Since relations between the latest laird and the locals had collapsed in a welter of unpaid wages, my rendition of 'The Seven Men of Knoydart' was met with warm applause. It was even more welcome at the celebration of the liberation day of Knoydart in March 1999.

The local community now controls 17,000 acres of 'The Rough Bounds', and various improvements are in hand. The wild peninsula attracts walkers, tourists and yachting crews to a remote and iconic place. Many times since then Hamish Henderson's masterful lampoon of the Nazi Lord Brocket has cheered a ceilidh. It undoubtedly kindled appetites for land reform, and the Scottish Parliament ended feudalism for ever in 2001, when freed from the House of Lords.

Since the abortive Knoydart Land Raid in 1948, a growing interest in our folk traditions has inspired performers, at folk clubs, festivals, to record albums and to feature on radio and TV programmes.

Through the years, through the medium of traditional songs set to airs that were borrowed, blue or new, our most pressing social messages have carried our concerns and gathered support for a multitude of causes. I believe that the health of our contemporary scene stems from the part played by our distinctive music. History is always a contest of conflicting views, yet invariably traditional song has sided with social, economic and environmental justice. This is manifest in the Highlands and Islands as it is throughout Scotland.

About fifteen years ago a plaque was placed on the steeple in Church Street, Inverness where the court house used to be. It honours Robert McKid, who unsuccessfully indicted Patrick Sellar, formerly sub-factor and potential sheep tenant, the brutal clearer of Strathnaver in 1814.[22] The Gaelic tag 'Se Firinn is Ceartas a Sheasas' translates as 'Truth and Justice Will Prevail'. Politicised songs in the Highlands continue to honour that clarion call.

References:

1   Seamus Mòr ('Big Hamish') is the Gaelic nickname for Hamish Henderson.

2   CD *Oilseed Raped?* Released 2001. Tracks included 'No to GMO', 'Munlochy Vigil', 'Trouble Ahead', 'The Aventis Salesman's Song' and 'Marches'.

3   *Highland News*, 26 January 2002, 'Sounding Out' — CD review.

4   Hamish Henderson, 'Introduction', in Ailie Munro, *The Democratic Muse: Folk Music Revival in Scotland* (Edinburgh: Scottish Cultural Press, 1996), p. x.

5   Questions to Jim McLean on the folk song websire www.mudcat.org explain the background. 'These are My Mountains' is published by Peers Music Ltd.

6   John McGrath, *The Cheviot, the Stag and the Black, Black Oil*, presented by 7:84 Theatre Company (first published 1974; London: Methuen Drama, 1981), pp. 37-38.

7   Quoted in John MacAskill, 'Introduction' to *We Have Won The Land* (Stornoway: Acair Publishig, 1999), p. 17.

8   The author holds a copy of the words.

9   Willie Kellock (ed.), *The Rebels Ceilidh Song Book*, second edition (Bo'ness: Bo'ness Rebels Literary Society, 1965).

10   Kathleen MacInnes, *Og-mhadainn Shamhraidh* (Summer Dawn), Greentrax, 2006. The TV show was replayed on BBC Alba on 28 December 2008.

11   Dhachaigh/Home, *The Murdo MacFarlane Songbook*, CD released by An Lanntair/HCF, 2007. The words were first published in *Islands at Risk*, a joint publication in 1980 by KNO and Hebrides Against Nuclear Dumping Joint Committee.

12   From a private recording made at the Ceilidh Place Clubhouse, Ullapool, July 1991.

13   'Nuclear Dustbin Song' by Angus Lyon and Chris MacLaren. Extra verse by Rob Gibson.

14   Private recording of the songs at the RAD concert, archived by the author; words by Magpie.

15   Words passed to the author by Liz Collie after a visit to Achiltibuie.

16   Iain MacDonald, *Beneath Still Water*, Greentrax. LP, TRAX 003.

17   Dougie Maclean *Real Estate*, LP, Dunkeld, 1988, DUN 008.

18   Nancy Nicolson, *Rhyme and Reason*, (cassette tape — soon to be reissued as CD). Nancy has continued to sing at ceilidhs and for children in her classes in her inimitable Caithness dialect of Scots. She has also played host to 'Homage to Hamish' at the Scottish Storytelling Centre, part of Edinburgh Folk Club's annual Carrying Stream Festival.

19   Morag produced these words for us to sing at a Feis Rois weekend.

20   Colin's sudden death in January 1998 was a sad loss. His family and many of his friends included a tribute to his life at the HTMF that June. I entered the final chorus of the song as a 'poem' to be displayed on hoardings around the new Scottish Parliament building site. The sponsorship by the *John o' Groat Journal* was successful.

21   Hamish Imlach sang 'Men of Knoydart' ('Ballad of the Men of Knoydart') on Transatlantic LP XTRA 1039; it is also recorded by Geordie MacIntyre on *A' the Bairns o' Adam: the Hamish Henderson Tribute Album*, Greentrax, 2003. Words reproduced in *The Rebels Ceilidh Song Book*, and in Hamish Henderson, *Collected Poems and Songs*, edited by Raymond Ross (Edinburgh: Curly Snake, 2000), p. 128.

22   Rob Gibson, *The Highland Clearances Trail* (Edinburgh: Luath Press, 2006), p. 71.

LIBRARIES OF LOVE AND PASSION: HAMISH HENDERSON'S LIBRARY

Donald Smith

Edinburgh is a bookish city. If the New Town represents classically ordered and catalogued shelves, then the Old is a profusion of volumes piled higgledy-piggledy ready to hand for the reader sunk in an armchair or in the snug of a Cowgate bar.

There are, of course, libraries aplenty, each with their devoted readers and researchers, but within the form and structure of the city are the private accumulations, the organic sub-soil of literate culture. These are the libraries of love and passion, brimful of manuscripts, pamphlets, old editions, and books marked and worn by life rather than by time alone.

A familiar sight in Edinburgh for many years was the tall gangling figure of Hamish Henderson, wandering between University and Sandy Bell's Bar, with the eponymous and beloved dog Sandy wandering in sympathy. Equally Hamish might cut out of the classical elegance of George Square to head for home across the Meadows, leafy or exposed according to the season. Regardless of temperature, however, this noted folklorist and cultural activist sported a capacious crinkly cardigan, largely unbuttoned.

Those inclined to smile on another Edinburgh eccentric knew nothing of Hamish Henderson's life experience or the library of passionate engagement which was breeding back in his top-floor Southside flat. That personal accumulation is now sadly dispersed yet, faithfully catalogued by Carmen and Gordon Wright, its poetry and passions live on.

A play written by Henderson for the Cambridge Mummers in 1939 reminds us that this Perthshire Scot grew up in a decade of political conflict and disaster. *The Humpy Cromm* is set at Speakers Corner, allowing the working class voices of Communists, Irish Nationalists, Spanish Republicans and British Fascists to be heard in discordant chorus. The struggle against Fascism was to swallow the best years of his youth, but not without protest.

In the library the Spanish poet Lorca was a significant presence,

> because we want our daily bread
> alder flower and perennial threshed tenderness,
> because we want the will of the Earth to be fulfilled
> that yields up its fruits for all of us.[1]

Thirty to forty years later Henderson was still celebrating Lorca and explicitly connecting him to Scotland. The *duende* or indefinable artistic power which Lorca perceived in Andalusian *cante jondo* became equivalent to the conyach acknowledged by the Scottish Travellers as the ground of their ballad-singing art, without which even a superb voice was hollow. It was not the text, the music, the performer or the audience that counted but what happened between them. Like Lorca, Henderson was never content with the mere publication of poetry.

I heard those lectures and I have the articles on my sprawling shelves. I have also memorably heard Sheila Stewart, the Scottish Traveller, sing with the conviction of the conyach. Yet perhaps Henderson's commentary would have lacked its carrying power had he not found his own poetic voice. The young Henderson, now a Cambridge graduate in modern languages, went to wartime service with the 51st Highland Division first in the North African desert and then in Italy. His *Elegies for the Dead in Cyrenaica* are among the great poems of World War Two—Scottish, European, and universal.

> There were our own, there were the others.
> Therefore, minding the great word of Glencoe's
> son, that we should not disfigure ourselves
> with villainy of hatred; and seeing that all
> have gone down like curs to anonymous silence,
> I will bear witness for I knew the others.
> Seeing that littoral and interior are alike indifferent
> and the birds are drawn again to our welcoming north
> why should I not sing them, the dead, the innocent?[2]

It is easy to forget the post-war impact of those poems because other aspects of Henderson's muse were to sound out so vibrantly. My slim copy of the *Elegies* sits alongside the expansive *Collected Poems and Songs* produced by Raymond Ross and published in Edinburgh in 2000. There was an eightieth birthday ceilidh in the Old Town and, if truth be told, the elderly poet remained impassive to the voicing of elegies, but came to life at the sound of lyrics which he had brilliantly conceived for the popular sung tradition.

> Then fareweel ye banks o Sicily,
> Fare ye weel ye valley and shaw.
> There's nae Jock will mourn the kyles o ye
> Puir bliddy sqaddies are wearie.[3]

Or one that gained the supreme accolade of 'anonymous' as an attribution, but was penned by Henderson to the tune of 'Lili Marleen':

> We are the D-Day Dodgers, out in Italy—
> Always on the vino, always on the spree.
> 8th Army scroungers and their tanks
> We live in Rome-among the yanks.
> We are the D-Day Dodgers, way out in Italy.[4]

These songs still echo in Edinburgh, in Scotland and elsewhere, but the library reveals a complex underweave of reflection and purpose. Henderson witnessed at first hand the resistance movement in Italy and the struggle to renew the left in post-war conditions. When the prison letters of Antonio Gramsci, the Communist leader who suffered ten years of incarceration under Mussolini's tyranny, were published in 1947, Hamish Henderson was the first to translate them into English. Here was a radical political vision that recognised the importance of popular culture and the national dimension.

That was Europe, but was Scotland part of the European dynamic? The library demonstrates Henderson's closeness to the Scottish Renaissance movement. Beside Gramsci was the libretto of Erik Chisholm's Celtic opera *Isles of Youth*. Chisholm championed modern music in Glasgow at a time when the painter J D Fergusson, dance artist Margaret Morris, publisher William MacLellan, poet Hugh MacDiarmid, and many others were creating a genuinely international movement in Scottish culture. Hamish Henderson became part of this movement but he brought his own distinctive contribution—art that was international, unrecognised and owned by the marginalised and oppressed.

The clues for Henderson were the songs of the 8th Army and the Italian partisans, Gramsci's Sardinian roots, and the work of the Irish Folklore Commission which had employed Calum MacLean to record Scottish Gaelic oral tradition. He took the road, beginning in his native Perthshire, to discover the extent of surviving folksong in Scotland. The result was, in his own image, like holding a tin pail under a waterfall.

Travelling people, crofters, agricultural labourers, former soldiers, and shepherds opened hearts and minds to Henderson and MacLean revealing an unsuspected treasury of artistic wealth and performative power. But Hamish's further political inspiration was to bring this scattered work of cultural survival home to Scotland's capital city, both in the founding of the School of Scottish Studies at Edinburgh University and in the People's Ceilidhs of 1951 and 1952. In this grand riposte to the Edinburgh International Festival trade unionists, the despised 'tinkers', and Gaelic tradition-bearers united to give public voice to what had previously been heard only within their own communities.

Edinburgh was not accustomed to such outbursts of radical passion and took notice. The city inclined solidly to order and, in the axiom of Odysseus Elytis approvingly quoted by Henderson, 'whenever you hear about order start smelling human flesh'. The oppressive contrasts of the capital city—the gibbet and the reveller—were now harnessed to the engine of protest, upearthing burghal dead weight with folksong spiced by Hamish's personal poetics:

> Reekie, tell me my true love's name.
> Edinburgh Castle, toun and tour
> The Gowans gay and the gilliefloor.
> Lovers daffin aneath the slae
> Floret silva undique
> The bonniest pair ye iver seen
> Fuckin aneath the flooerin' gean.
> Bairnies wankin abuin the clay
> Floret silva undique[5]

In 1952, the Peoples Festival Committee was banned by the Edinburgh Labour Party. But by now Henderson was unstoppable.

A folk revival had begun—but it was much more than an enthusiasm for folksong, and the nature of the 'more' is revealed in Hamish Henderson's library. Firstly there was the international scholarship positioning the past and present study of Scottish traditions in the contexts of European and American Romanticism, African independence movements, and worldwide literature. Hamish's one volume, ready reference edition of Francis James Child's *English and Scottish Popular Ballads* has now migrated from his shelves to mine. It is a well-thumbed, hard-worked book which Henderson radically reinterpreted through his knowledge of living folksong. Child's international classic has never been read in the same way since Henderson.

Secondly, or equally, there are the links to contemporary politics in Scotland and beyond. The folk song revival spun into CND, the anti-Polaris campaign, industrial protests and attacks on absentee landlords. Amongst the volumes of Henderson's passions and protests is the 1951 printed version of Ewan McColl's *Uranium 235,* dedicated to Joan Littlewood and introduced by MacDiarmid. This 'documentary play' was performed to huge audiences in Scotland and England, reinvigorating theatre as a political art, and paving the way for the 7:84 theatre company. Just as Gramsci's thinking opened up a possibility for Dario Fo in Italy, so the thinking behind the folk revival was to invade theatre in the seventies to dramatic effect in John McGrath's *The Cheviot, the Stag and the Black, Black Oil* (1973).

The stream of activism was then flowing freely from Henderson's library to mine, uniting culture and politics. There is an Edinburgh Festival broadsheet of 1973 in which the founding father is focused on forward momentum—'The revival will sink or swim by its capability to throw up new and constantly fresh thinkers and writers'. Then in 1979 came the re-established Edinburgh Folk Festival, the same year as the failed devolution referendum. It snowed across the city that Easter, but the passion came through. A major conference themed 'The People's Past' explored the relationship between folk traditions and Scotland's disputed histories. The political ground was shifting in Scotland, but Hamish Henderson was not seeking a new consensual centre:

> Folk—the Folk that matters—has always in fact something of the rebel underground about it; whether it be the love-songs which reject the values and prejudices of a money-minded bourgeois so-

ciety, or a hypocritical puritan religious set-up; the bawdy songs which frankly rejoice in the fun and comedy of sex; the 'Ding Dong Dollar' CND songs which pillory the antics of military bigwigs and the bonzes of imperialist power politics; the 'Sangs of the Stane' which send up the pretensions and absurdities of a stuffy royalist Establishment; the bothy songs which put on record the cheese-paring niggardliness of skinflint farmers—all share to a greater or lesser extent this rebel élan.[6]

Later that same year Odysseus Elytis won the Nobel Prize for Literature, and the Greek students in Edinburgh threw a party. At the centre of the action they put Hamish Henderson as both ceilidh master and a superb reader of Elytis translations. I still have the hand stitched booklet produced for the occasion, as did Henderson, but more important is the experience of Edinburgh transformed for one night into a true Athens of the north by this mantic declamation:

> Here then am I,
> created for the young Korai and the Aegean islands,
> lover of the deer's leaping,
> initiate in the Mystery of olive leaves,
> sun-drinker and locust-killer.
> Here am I, face to face
> with the black shirts of the ruthless
> and of the years' empty belly that aborted
> its own children, in heat![7]

To the Italian patriot then must be added the Hellenist, but still above all the apostle of Eros—'I'll unleash the old kisses canonized by my longing!'

The Henderson library re-affirms that with its attachment to the Alexandrian poet C P Cavafy, who brings us geographically full circle to the North African elegies. Disappointment is a word not easily associated with Hamish Henderson, yet the ageing radical had to thole seventeen further years of political stagnation in Scotland and the inevitable institutionalisation of his brainchild the School of Scottish Studies. The path to Sandy Bell's and the company of a new generation of enthusiasts brought congenial compensations, but it was Cavafy who offered consolation.

As you go on the journey to Ithaca,
Pray that your way may be a long one,
Full of adventures, full of knowledge,
Do not be afraid of Poseidon's anger,
The Cyclops or the Laestrygonians,
You will never find such things upon your journey
If your thoughts remain lofty, and if a fine
Feeling has touched your body and your soul...

Always have Ithaca at the back of your mind.
The arrival there is your objective.

But do not be in any hurry on your journey.
Better to let it last for years.
In old age you will anchor at the island,
Rich with all you have gained upon the way,
Not expecting Ithaca to give you riches.[8]

Hamish Henderson's library has been scattered now, but his voices live on in the city of loves and passions. We store them on new shelves and in new minds and voices. One of the poet's songs is the unofficial anthem of a new devolved Scotland—'The Freedom Come-All-Ye'—though for Henderson the Scottish Parliament was a milestone but not the final destination of an independent socialist country.

So come all ye at hame wi Freedom,
Never heed whit the hoodies croak for doom.
In your hoose a' the bairns o Adam
Can find breid, barley-bree and painted room.
When MacLean meets wi's freens in Springburn
A' the roses and geans will turn tae bloom,
And a black boy frae yont Nyanga
Dings the fell gallows o the burghers doon.[9]

Aspiration and protest join to affirm not what is but what should and could be. But the tone is ringing not shrill or hectoring. That is because the library has a ground note beneath its many variations. You catch it I think in an early Henderson poem, based on Holderlin:

He who has thought the most loves the fullest of life;
Highest virtue is prized by him who has looked on the world;

And often the wisest turn
To beauty in the end of all.[10]

That is an apt epitaph for Henderson, fit to be inscribed on the stones of Edinburgh City of Literature, but it is also a declaration of love. The *Collected Poems and Songs* has pride of place on my bookshelves, because it speaks to heart and mind. 'And often the wisest turn to beauty in the end of all.'

References:

1 Translated from Lorca's 'El poeta en Nueva York' by Paul Binding in his *Lorca: The Gay Imagination* (London: GMP, 1985), p. 131.

2 Hamish Henderson, *Elegies for the Dead in Cyrenaica* (London: Lehnmann, 1948; Edinburgh: EUSPB, 1997), p. 18.

3 *Ibid.*, p. 84.

4 *Ibid.*, p. 94.

5 *Ibid.*, p. 142.

6 Hamish Henderson, 'It was in You That it A' Began' in Edward J Cowan (ed.) *The People's Past: Scottish Folk, Scottish History* (Edinburgh: EUSPB, 1980).

7 Odysseus Elytis, *The Axiom Esti*, translated by Edmund Keeley and George Savidis (London: Anvil Press Poetry, 1980), p. 31.

8 Translated from Cavafy's 'Ithaca' by Robert Liddell in his *Cavafy: A Biography* (London: Gerald Duckworth & Co, 1974), p. 154.

9 Hamish Henderson, *Collected Poems and Songs*, edited by Raymond Ross (Edinburgh: Curly Snake Publishing, 2000), p. 143.

10 'Socrates and Alcibiades', *ibid.*, p. 29.

RICHES IN THE KIST: THE LIVING LEGACY OF HAMISH HENDERSON

Steve Byrne

He has given us something which we badly lack: a knowledge of where we have been; a building upon the edifice of the past.
Fred Freeman (writing on Robert Tannahill)

He gave a voice to those who could not speak for themselves, who could not be heard in the clamour of the twentieth century.
Michael Russell MSP[1]

Hamish Henderson's collecting activities began in earnest with the arrival in Scotland of Alan Lomax from the United States in 1951. Thus began what can only be described as the heyday of Scottish folksong collecting in the field, work that was to continue for Hamish for another thirty years or so.

Rarely would he recover those halcyon days in the berry fields and the bedazzling discovery of Jeannie Robertson. Nonetheless, the entirety of Hamish's collecting is still misunderstood, or perhaps less well-known than it should be, largely for the reason that he collected a vast amount across several decades, in a variety of different settings.

In this essay I will first consider some specific examples from Hamish's lowland Scots collecting, approaching some unusual items from a number of perspectives and addressing some of the the implications for our perceptions of the tradition. I will then comment on some aspects of Hamish's methodology, his role as a collector and disseminator in the folk revival, and his role in our view of Scottish traditional culture in the twenty-first century.

Hamish's collecting in the public eye

Until recently, material collected by Hamish has been published in sporadic and somewhat limited form, on commercially-released audio compilations such as the Tangent/Greentrax *Scottish Tradition* albums (although when originally released in the late 1960s, they were received enthusiastically given the relative dearth of material publicly available at that time), Mike Yates's *Hamish Henderson Collects* CDs, and in print in *Tocher* articles (invariably from Hamish's own hand), the *Alias MacAlias* anthology, and occasional academic journals such as *Scottish Studies*. Necessarily, many of the featured collected items have published in isolation, with audio tracks edited to exclude preamble and the valuable contextualisation of an entire collecting session.

To some extent, wider publication has been limited by the restrictions on access to the actual recorded materials within the School of Scottish Studies, for reasons mainly of the increasing fragility of the original material, and the lack of resources to field requests from extra-departmental and private scholars amidst the School's duties to its students, having moved to being primarily a teaching department in the 1970s. Attitudes and opinions on the School's dissemination policy are largely outwith the purpose and ken of the present writer, but are discussed widely, (including interviews with employees of the School, such as Hamish Henderson and Alan Bruford), in Ailie Munro's paper, 'The Role of the School of Scottish Studies in the Folk Music Revival', in the English Folk Dance and Song Society's *Folk Music Journal*.[2]

Tobar an Dualchais / Kist o Riches

As regards wider access to the School's archive material, things are happily on the turn. From 2007 to early 2010, I had the distinct privilege, with a small team of colleagues, of working on the landmark *Tobar an Dualchais/ Kist o Riches* project which, after some 15 years in the making, (including significant fundraising efforts and a pilot project), set about digitising and cataloguing materials in the School's sound archive systematically for the first time.[3] The project has benefits for all parties—the School in having its material safeguarded and catalogued, plus easier access for researchers, descendants of contributors to the archive, and the general public to the material therein.

Alongside issues of policy and practicality of access, the largely paper-based records of the School's archive and only partial-computerisation of them have, until recently, made a full cross-referenced picture difficult to obtain. Some initial work on *Tobar/ Kist*, before cataloguing began, involved the computerisation of nearly 30 Scots song index books, proving that there had been no set manner in which songs were recorded by title, or first line, or alternate title. Often the songs were noted under a title only known (subjectively) to the fieldworker.

This proved to be a recurring problem, as the School's tape archive is also recorded via typewritten register books and a card index. As more and more fieldworkers and register book editors, each with slightly differing approaches, made their mark on the School's records, many items have become confused or even lost, as a result of names of songs being given as first lines, or obscure, subjective titles. Such items can remain isolated, detached from similar versions of the same song, as long as cataloguing remains incomplete.[4]

While no slight is intended here to the efforts of fieldworkers and archivists past and present, it is clear from the paper records that the simple fact of lack of time to fully check all accessions against existing material without a complete computerised database, plus differences of approach across numerous fieldworkers, and cumulative human error down the decades have meant cross-referencing has been far from foolproof. The work of archivists and register book editors was also not made the easiest by the sometimes slapdash—or at best, inconsistent—manner in which tape boxes were annotated [see fig 1a and 1b]. In some cases this could be the only source of information on what was on a tape, sometimes in conjunction with notebooks from fieldworkers and educated guessing by the archive staff. Hamish was certainly not exempt! In a sense, one of the main benefits of *Tobar/ Kist* was actually to find out just *what* was on some of the tapes! As a result, full interpretations of the archive's holdings have proven very difficult without the kind of studious listening and cataloguing that *Tobar/ Kist* has afforded.

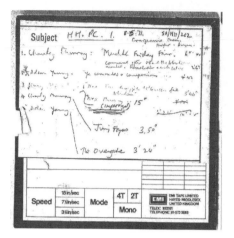

Fig. 1a–tape box of SA1971.202 in Hamish's handwriting. (School of Scottish Studies Archives)

Fig. 1b–tape box of SA1971.203 in Hamish's handwriting. (School of Scottish Studies Archives)

Along with Chris Wright and Sheena Wellington, I was employed as a Scots song specialist, and so it was that I had the privilege of spending many of my days with Hamish and a cast of many singers down through the years from across Scotland. A laptop, a pair of headphones, hours of tape processed into downloadable mp3s and a pile of songbooks, and my imagination picturing the room in which Hamish and the singer had sat, the background noises of a clock, a greetin bairn, cars rumbling by on the Rattray road, or a door clunking open as a round of refreshments was brought in. With this I began my own adventure into the world of Scots folksong, of which until then I had but scratched the surface. I had long wished to return to my *alma mater* at the School of Scottish Studies with an older head on my shoulders and a bit less daft laddie between my ears, and essentially I did just that.

From an objective standpoint too, I felt able to begin reassessing the contents of the archive as someone who did not know Hamish personally, and with a natural mild cynicism, questioning mind, and keen ear for detail through my professional experience in the recording studio, I attempted to interpret what was on the tapes along with what were usually sparse notes in the School's song index and register books.

Working on the tapes, Chris Wright and I would be regularly discussing, debating, even *flyting* spiritedly over the gems we would find, sending files back and forth, listening and re-listening, sharing snippets of information we would find whilst researching certain things and keeping mental notes for further down the line. We were, so we thought in our own conceited wee bubble, Henderson and Lomax for a while, gorging ourselves on raw song. But unlike many of our illustrious predecessors, *we* were fortunate enough to be armed with the internet.

From the earliest days of the cataloguing process, it took me some time to realise and feel comfortable with the synthesis of Hamish's work. Being able to piece together his collecting life by way of the live sound recordings and archive tape numbers was a very different experience to that gleaned from Hamish's writings, letters, biographies or *Tocher* articles. The measure of the man and his approach was gained more fully from the tenor of his enquiry, his local knowledge, and his own awareness that the songs and the singers did not stand alone in isolated communities but were part of a constantly shifting ocean of Scots folksong. But after the flood? Primarily, there was a reinforcement of our own personal beliefs of the strength, power and intrinsic value of our own tradition, yet an awareness that it is still very much on the margins and outwith the ken of the main Scottish populus. Even more so, it was clear that the gems within the archive were only known in part even by the most ardent folk enthusiasts, understandably, given the access issues previously mentioned, but also through incomplete indexing and cataloguing to date.

The strength of the tradition we were encountering outstripped even our own preconceived ideas and began to feel like a redoubtable tool with which to combat the naysayers, all too ready to do Scotland down and write off traditional arts as the domain of kilt-wearing, tartan shortbread tin-wielding harkers-back-to-the-past. Here on these tapes was, over many hours, across many miles from Campbeltown to Crichie, from Spey Bay to Stromness, evidence of an older Scotland, (but one still within reach and living memory), a somehow truer picture of the people than the one propagated on the airwaves in recent decades, a Hendersonesque vision of a multi-faceted Scottish *Kulturgut* that had long been absent from the minds of many, and *never* present in the minds of many more.

It became abundantly clear that Hamish's recordings—and those of his many talented colleagues, lest we forget—gave us more than a glimpse of a Scotland past, where the modern obsession with compartmentalisation and division of culture into marketable boxes was neither apparent nor important. While there was certainly a 'Scottishness', encompassing Scots and Gaelic, lowland and highland, with more mutual respect perhaps, this did not seem like an idealised, 'we are all one' fashion, but something approaching a 'federal' view of culture, where each component part has its own individual strength and uniqueness, whilst also recognising the shared commonalities; whether that be in content, such as the often overlooked influence of Gaelic on the Scots tongue, or that of Gaelic airs on songwriters like Burns. Perhaps a Scotland where, as Alec Finlay commented, 'the orthodoxy of a single homogenous nation is repudiated.'[5]

Hamish and the mythology of the oral tradition

> *All folksong kids us on. And why not? Folksong after all is largely myth, so why expect practitioners to stick to facts when they are dealing with one of the great unrealities of life?*[6]

The modern interpretation of Hamish's collecting, with some romanticising of the background of informants, in particular Scottish Travellers, and the folk revival's search for the 'authentic', has left a somewhat skewed view of reality. A close reading of Hamish's essays shows a man who was fully aware of the complex synthesis of book, broadside, gramophone record, radio and oral sources that made up the repertoires of the singers he was collecting. It seems to me that Hamish was under no illusion that there was a 'holy grail' of the pure 'oral tradition', but accepted the singers' wide-ranging influences with minimal bias, with, on the face of it, music hall and country music radio squib seemingly every bit as valid as other songs. Revivalists and scholars with hindsight forget that 'traditional' material formed but one part of widely varying repertoires of some of our most revered 'tradition bearers', at a time when fewer conscious repertoire choices were made by singers within the social context in which they lived and performed. It was only once they were discovered by the folklorists, and put on the pedestal of the concert stage that self-identification of themselves as 'folk singers' began and performance repertoires were considered more carefully. And thus began the cult of the singer, wherein the material was in some ways almost secondary to the persona and mystique of sometimes 'folked-up' back-stories to please the folklorists and the hungry folk music fan in the 1950s and '60s, tiring of mainstream attitudes and seeking something more 'real'. In reality, the handful of virtuosos does something of a disservice to the wide variety of rare material in the archive that may not have the benefit of being in the mouth of a particularly gifted singer—'Not all folk-singers are of equal merit,' wrote Hamish himself[7]—but there needs to be a closer look, I believe, at the material itself, overlooking the croaky, hoarse, pitch-varying singer, for some absolutely rare gems that may otherwise have passed us by in the twentieth century. In time, more and more people accessing *Tobar/ Kist* should help remedy that.

Hamish was, of course, highly instrumental in presenting Jeannie Robertson as an exotic 'tinker singer', particularly to the American market, with records such as *Songs of a Scots Tinker Lady*[8] appearing in 1960 under the guidance of American scholar Kenneth Goldstein, who had spent some time at the School collecting with Arthur Argo in Aberdeenshire. Indeed, James Porter and Herschel Gower state that Jeannie—Christina Jane Robertson, formerly Regina Christina Stewart, according to her 1927 marriage certificate—even had her 'stage name' suggested to her by Hamish.[9] Hamish's promotion of Jeannie could be seen as being for a number of different reasons. He certainly had a superb candidate with which to advance his cultural ideals for Scots folksong. He most certainly also would have been keen to help Jeannie realise a fair income for her talents, although this was with mixed results, as seen in letters between Hamish, Jeannie and others in *The Armstrong Nose*.[10]

These things said, the folklorists and the hungry public are not necessarily always the guilty party either. To my mind, there is evidence in the archive that, as they and their families became more famous and revered over time within the folk scene, and competition arose between 'tradition bearers', some informants developed a propensity for creating or embellishing back stories about themselves and their songs, that were misleading to say the least.

Jeannie sang it, it must be traditional!

The reverence with which certain tradition bearers are viewed has lead to problems in interpreting the entirety of their repertoire, particularly with regard to ideas of the *oral* tradition. Take the case of Jeannie Robertson's 'Hobo Song', on SA1960.203.B9.[11] *An Anthology of Scottish Women Poets* (1992), edited by Catherine Kerrigan and Meg Bateman, features, alongside established published poets, various female ballad singers or reciters in a section called 'The Ballad Tradition'. They are portrayed as representatives of a poetic, anonymous ballad culture, from Andrew Crawfurd's Meg Walker, to Mrs Brown of Falkland, singers collected by Greig and Duncan, through to Jeannie Robertson and her daughter Lizzie Higgins. Aside from the curious fact that the singers' items are published absent of their music, (harking back to bad habits of old), alongside the expected Child ballads of 'The Twa Brothers' and 'The Trooper and the Maid' we find Jeannie's rendition of 'The Hobo Song'[12]:

> Riding on a east-bound freight train
> Speeding through the night
> Hobo Bill, a railroad bum
> Was fighting for his life
> The sadness of his eyes revealed
> The torture of his soul
> He raised a weak and wearied hand
> To brush away the cold
> Bo-ho, ho, bo-ho, Billy.[13]

Whilst presenting a related paper on items from the *Kist*, I played this to a mixed audience of Scots and Americans; there was much shrugging of shoulders from the Scots, including noted academics, but American arms shot straight up: 'Jimmie Rodgers!'. It is, indeed,

Jimmie Rodgers' 'Hobo Bill's Last Ride', written by Waldo O'Neal around 1929. From the many songs that could have been chosen from Jeannie's vast repertoire, quite why this features in Kerrigan and Bateman's collection is something of a mystery in terms of its value as a representation of Scottishness or Scottish poetry.

While the book is hardly intended as a definitive bible of *folksong*, it *does* attempt to appear as a comprehensive anthology of Scottish female poets, from Gaelic scribes as far back as the fifteenth century up to modern writers like Liz Lochhead. Its introduction sets up the inclusion of the ballad singers as,

> the strongest continuing influence in Scottish poetry... in the work of traditional singers like Jeannie Robertson and Lizzie Higgins, the ballad in performance continued to find a place in modern life... the influence of the ballad on women poets has been singular... for many women poets the home of their history.[14]

Clearly, what we do *not* have here is a ballad. One wonders whether the selection had been made from print sources lacking much in the way of annotation, or without hearing the conversation immediately following on the tape:

> **HH**: When did ye first hear 'The Hobo Song', Jeannie?
> **JR**: Well, I learnt it aboot 37 years ago Hamish, or 36 years ago.
> **HH**: Aye. And who was it who sang it?
> **JR**: Well I jist heard it sung by several of the older ones... an I liked it an learnt it
> **HH**: Aye. Was it somebody that had been in the States or just somebody that spent all their life in Scotland?
> **JR**: No... it was jist somebody spent all their life in Scotland, Hamish.[15]

Hamish clearly knows what he is collecting here, but through the mists of time, possibly incomplete indexing or records in the School's archive, and some notion that everything emanating from the great Jeannie Robertson's mouth must be valid as Scots folksong, the entirety of Jeannie's highly-varied repertoire, drawn from several genres, is overlooked.

This is further demonstrated on the tape of Jeannie's 'The Braes o Killiecrankie', collected by Hamish:

> For on the thistle I sat doon
> I nearly jumpit tae the moon
> I nearly jumpit tae the moon
> For the lass that stole ma hankie
>
> O tooral ooral ooral ay,
> O fal da doodle i-doo-ay
> O fal da doodle i-doo-ay
> On the braes o Killiecrankie
>
> Oh Jean MacNeil she's fair and fat,
> She wears her hair below her hat
> She wears her hair below her hat
> On the braes o Killiecrankie
>
> Her feet is big and her face tis flat,
> And her curly locks hing doon her back
> Her curly locks hing doon her back
> On the braes o Killiecrankie
>
> Oh Jean she began to curse,
> Her bloomers fell doon, and her stays it burst
> She gied her aul erse a twist
> And she ca'd it through a windae
>   (SA1954.088, transcribed by Steve Byrne)

In their seminal book, *Jeannie Robertson: Emergent Singer, Transformative Voice*, James Porter and Herschel Gower claim that they have excised all Harry Lauder songs from their selections illustrating her repertoire, in favour of giving a 'full representation of traditional, orally transmitted items'.[16] They then proceed to give a highly hypothesised commentary on the above song:

> A parody of Hogg's 'Killiecrankie,' this comic squib was part of Maria [Jeannie's mother]'s legacy... The overall tone is one of caricaturing sexual mishap (simulated orgasm suggested in verse 1).[17]

Thanks to the internet, we can show that what we actually have here is a conflation of two Harry Lauder songs, 'The Lass o Killiecrankie' (Jeannie's verse 1) and 'Jean McNeil' (Jeannie's verse 2), from 1911 and 1927 respectively, with probably a bit of Jeannie Robertson original or embellishment in the mix.

It is unclear as to whether Hamish necessarily knew this to be a Lauder legacy, but prior to the emergence of the internet, wherein cylinders and gramophone records such as the Lauder examples are now being digitised and are widely available for the first time,[18] it would be understandable that he may not have known. This was not an unusual occurrence either, by any means; Belle Stewart's repertoire contained the Harry Lauder piece 'Piper Macfarlane', long misidentified as 'The Bonnie Wee Lassie Frae Gourock' in a variety of sources such as the MacColl and Seeger study of the Stewarts of Blair.[19]

Anyone familiar with Richard Thompson's 'Don't Sit on My Jimmy Shands!' will be well-used to the fragility of 78rpm gramophone records, as well as wax cylinders invariably shaved and reused. In spite of recent digitisation efforts, it may well prove that a complete physical legacy of the late nineteenth and early twentieth-century Scottish music recording industry will be impossible to reconstruct. As such, several other music-hall style pieces may end up as 'traditional' pieces. Interestingly, Hamish seemed to be somewhat dismissive of what he called 'the occasional 'Scotch' item deriving from Harry Lauder or Will Fyffe,' when commenting on an anticipated pub singsong arranged with a contact in Edinburgh (c. 1953), 'frankly I didn't look forward to the evening with any particular pleasure.'[20]

What does this tell us in terms of tradition bearers' sources? In part the answer has been there all along. Within the School's archive, there are several recordings of renowned singers discussing the advent of the gramophone; on SA1960.167, Lucy Stewart tells Kenneth Goldstein that her family got a gramophone in 1907 and had Harry Lauder and Scott Skinner records. On SA1960.144.B7, she is recorded singing Lauder's 'The Wedding o Lauchie McGraw'. On SA1962.47, Jeannie Robertson says her family acquired a horn gramophone when she was five or six and going to school in Blairgowrie (c. 1913-1914) and listened to Harry Lauder records.[21] On SA1963.083, Jeannie sings a version of Lauder's 'The Weddin' o' Sandy MacNab', saying 'I used tae sing a lot o that Harry Lauder sangs.'[22] Admittedly, Hamish did not seem particularly worried about the trend, noting:

> Almost invariably... singers have 'collected' folk-songs from the
> wireless and gramophone records too, but the versions taken from
> these sources begin to get modified and transformed in exactly
> the same way as many of the old broadsheet ballads did which
> entered folk currency from printed copies hawked at fairs or feeing
> markets.[23]

While it is impossible to form a generalisation about perceptions of
songs collected in the field from such a small group of examples, we
should see this as some indication of over-willingness to believe in
the intrinsic 'orality' of everything proffered by informants. It may
be a signal of the need to listen to items in their full context, with
the conversation before and after, or indeed the recording session
as a whole, to gain a fuller understanding of many songs, instead of
what can often be the case in anthologies in print or on CD, the songs
largely in isolation.

But what of the worth of such songs themselves as a part of Jeannie's
repertoire? Well, as Norman Buchan wrote of Hamish Henderson,

> he knew the task was to dredge, was to trawl, and you took
> everything up... whether they mattered a good deal or not, the
> body was incomplete without them... He had both the quality
> approach... understanding the importance of a big ballad... but
> also knowing that the squibs were part of the process.[24]

However, is Norman Buchan's description of these *non-exotic, taken-
for-granted* songs as 'squibs' a value judgement on the singers' own
choice of repertoire? I would suggest that we have perhaps developed
a tendency to be slightly selective in our understanding in order to
create a definable 'Scottishness' in the repertoires of the established
'tradition bearers', when in truth their repertoires were every bit
the proud mongrel hybrid Scotland—'A' the bairns o Adam'—that
Hamish himself revelled in, in his own song and poetry.

So what purpose does this serve? Well, far from seeking to say I got
one over on *this* scholar or that, I am keen to demonstrate the immense
power of the internet and ongoing digitisation in terms of gaining
a truer picture about items in the archive and, by extension, our

folksong culture. Porter and Gower omitted the Lauder, music hall and American songs from their study of Jeannie, but they themselves say that such unfashionable songs made up some 10 per cent of her repertoire.[25] That is a significant number in my view, and one of several areas for further research. Secondly, I believe that the work begun through *Tobar/ Kist* is the starting point for us to reconsider our view of such songs in the context of the overall repertoires of our most famed folk singers, and, crucially, the collecting of Hamish Henderson.

Now that we are fortunate enough to have such resources at our disposal, before we dismiss these kinds of songs too readily, we should consider what Hamish wrote when referring to The Corries, in his *Times* obituary of Roy Williamson:

> If a few purists could occasionally be heard at the bar complaining that this was more music hall than folk-song, they were invariably countered by aficionados who pointed to the honourable folk tradition represented by Scots music hall itself.[26]

Consider also Willie Mathieson of Ellon's 'Hey Donal' on SA1952.001, which is essentially Lauder's 'Hey Donal!', recorded for Edison in 1908. The 'Hey Donal' chorus element itself builds on a fine tradition of refrains stretching back to Robert Tannahill[27] and David Herd[28] in the eighteenth century, and many of Lauder's songs themselves built on existing popular melodies and song fragments.

Gems in the *Kist*

In spite of the handful of items of surprising or 'disappointingly recent' provenance, there are still hundreds of items of undoubted pedigree and rarity within the archive. Whether Hamish really knew the precise heritage of everything he was collecting is an unanswerable question, though in many cases I am sure he did. With the advent of the internet, we are able to conclusively show just *how* old some of the items are, and give further weight to Hamish's strong belief in the power and long heritage of the tradition. It also bears out his awareness, often forgotten by folkie 'punters' in romantic 'pure oral tradition' searches, of the strong print tradition from which many songs came into the repertoires of singers, even if they turned out to be minimally literate Traveller singers; lines in the songs of Jeannie Robertson's uncle, Geordie Robertson, prove his songs clearly had eighteenth and nineteenth-century printed parallels,[29] which could conceivably also be their sources.

A prime example is from 1958, when Hamish collected the song 'Kate MacLaren' from Bella Higgins in Blairgowrie:

> Oh Kate MacLaren it is my name
> I brought myself to both grief and shame
> For the murder of my baby dear
> I gots [sic] transported for seven long year
>
> [tape break]
>
> Him bein a baby both meek an mild
> Where are you goin my baby cried
> Oh me no answer to him did pay
> I threw my baby in without delay
>
> For two or three minutes he struggled sore
> His cries were heard far from the shore
> O mammy mammy let me on shore
> And I'll wander where you'll never find me more
>
> Oh me bein tempit all with the same
> I kicked my baby back in again
> For two or three minutes he struggled sore
> His cries were heard far from the shore
>
> He got a hold of a bunch of grass
> He got a hold and he held it fast
> Cried mammy mammy let me on shore
> And I'll wander where you'll never find me more
>
> So me bein tempit all with the same
> I kicked my baby back in again
> For two or three minutes he struggled sore
> He sunk to the bottom never to rise no more

So early early by the break of day
Two fishermen they had come that way
They spied his little corpse upon the shore
And her guilt was revealed now for ever more[30]

This song was very difficult to find trace of, and only appears to have been collected from Bella and her husband Jock. Many of the cataloguing song searches of obscure material were solved through the ability to type parts of lines in quotation marks into Google, in the hope of hitting a match. Often this could mean seeking out the most distinctive parts of the narrative and trying variants thereof. In this case, it was the phrase "For the murder of my baby dear", yielding a single result in Google leading to the mudcat.org folksong discussion website and resource.

It transpired that this song appeared as a broadside in Cork, Ireland, around 1860, called 'The Lamen[ta]tion of Jane M'Cullen for the Murder of Her Child'.[31] While parts are in fairly stock broadside language, indicating a relationship with the Yorkshire or Lincolnshire broadside 'Betsy Watson', there is a strong indication of the print influence upon Bella Higgins' rendition at some point in its life.

A copy of 'Jane M'Cullen' is held in the National Library of Ireland, an institution yet

Fig. 2–Bodleian Library Broadside collection, Shelfmarks: 2806c.8(94), Harding B 26(328)

Fig. 3 – Text of the Cork 'Jane M'Cullen' broadside with cognate lines from Bella Higgins' version highlighted.

to digitise its broadsides as far as I know, and it is also in the online Bodleian Library broadsides resource.[32]

The search has barely begun on this particular example, but it gives us pause for thought as to how a Cork-printed broadside ends up in the mouth of a Scottish Traveller some 90 years later, when the song appears to have little remaining currency elsewhere, in Scotland or Ireland.

One further example is 'My Wee Doggie' found in the repertoires of Jeannie Robertson and Jane Turriff of Mintlaw, although Jeannie's version is more fragmentary:

> For it's my wee dog learnt me a trick,
> To go out a-hountin when it was late;
> When it was late and thae roads bein dry
> For a-hountin we went, my wee dog and I
>
> But aye she whistled and aye she sang
> And the sang she sang bein a thread o blue,
> 'Go away young man because I don't love you.'[33]

Once again, through the power of the internet, searching threw up a broadside ballad printed in the period between 1674-1679, in the Bodleian Library broadsides collection called 'My Dog and I', stanza 5 of which reads:

> My Dog and I have got a trick
> It is to cure maids when they are sick
> When the'r sick and like to die,
> Then thither goes my Dog and I.[34]

Fig. 4 Bodleian Library Broadsides Collection, Shelfmark: 4o Rawl. 566(108)

Not overly close to Jeannie's per se, but closer inspection of the broadside along with Bell Robertson's (no relation) version in the *Greig-Duncan Folksong Collection*, song no. 254, version G, reveals that the sixth stanza of the broadside is startlingly close to the second stanza of Bell's, and possibly indicates a considerable currency for variants of the song in Aberdeenshire at some point in the late nineteenth and early twentieth centuries:

A Greig-Duncan (254)

My dog and I hae learned a trade,
To go a-hunting when it is late,
When it is late and there's none to spy,
To the hunting goes my dog and I.

In winter when the weather's wet,
My dog and I we warm our feet,
In summer when the weather's dry,
To the hunting goes my dog and I.
My dog and I will catch some hare,
For geese and gazelle will not be there,
They'll not be caught, they fly so high,
To the hunting goes my dog and I.

B 'My Dog and I' (c.1675), verses 5 & 6

My Dog and I have got a trick,
It is to cure maids when they are sick,
When the'r sick and like to die,
Then thither goes my Dog and I.
  My Dog and I, my Dog and I,
Then thither goes my Dog and I.

But if the weather prove foul and wet,
My Dog he shall not wet his feet;
But if the weather prove fair and dry,
Then a [whissing?] goes my Dog and I.
  My Dog, &c.

This is strong evidence, I believe, of the continued influence of three-centuries-old print upon lowland song culture right into the heart of the twentieth century. The songs may well have come through the singers' families orally, but they have at one time or another had a pronounced print heritage.

These examples clearly show that, with the public launch of the full *Tobar/ Kist* website imminent, this is but a starting point. There is much to be done in the years ahead in terms of examining the riches in *Tobar/ Kist* more closely, to reassess the material and its origins, and the cultural perceptions we draw from it.

Hamish as a fieldworker

We have looked at ideas of how not absolutely everything Hamish recorded can be viewed as culturally 'pure' or valid as oral tradition, if indeed such a thing exists. We should also consider briefly Hamish's methodology as a fieldworker, namely the way in which some of the material was obtained. It has not been widely stated before, though it may have been privately acknowledged, but it is my view, from experience of listening extensively to the tapes, and reference to my own training as a fieldworker at the School of Scottish Studies, that Hamish himself occasionally overstepped the role of the fieldworker in terms of his involvement with his informants, in relation to conventional or 'proper' fieldwork methodology.

In several cases Hamish actively took part in creating or recreating the 'tradition' he was recording whether it was by providing prompts to aged informants for certain songs, or stopping and starting the tape until he had helped the informant recall an item, often with knowledge from his own repertoire. Hamish was also, as Norman Buchan called him, 'a collector who was interested in the living thing, that also songs had to be made, who wrote songs himself',[35] and in some cases suggested lines for songs to the likes of Jeannie Robertson, such as 'I'll Lay Ye Doon Love', discussed by Ailie Munro.[36] In recording a young Jean Redpath on SA1960.205, Hamish encourages her to make a new medley from two separate songs, from her mother's repertoire, both sung to the tune of the Gaelic song 'Brochan Lom'. Cutting such a clip and listening in isolation, in the style of some commercially-released compilations, could easily make one think that there was such a song in a 'traditional' form. In such cases, working on *Tobar/ Kist* has been invaluable in terms of listening to tapes in their entirety, and gauging the context in which items came about being recorded. We also can get a feel for the level of 'self-editing' that went on during the tapes, the amount of 'click-clunking' of the stop and record buttons, partly through a need to conserve scarce and expensive tape space, but one suspects for other reasons too, not least to elicit more complete performances.[37]

This may seem obvious, as Hamish was indeed a working songwriter and a folk process within himself, and as such it would not seem unusual that he was giving people songs to sing, or recording them singing his songs and so forth. However, strictly speaking, that is not what many collectors would consider to comprise ethically-sound, objective fieldwork. We should hardly be surprised though, for as Timothy Neat notes, 'Hamish knew he had a life-story well worth the telling. He started a personal archive at the age of eight!'.[38] Whether or not this is strictly accurate, we must be careful to bear this in mind when listening to Hamish's tapes, given this highly personalised collecting method. A key question is, how much does the nature of an archive collection owe to the individual idiosyncracies of the collector?

No boundary between folk culture old and new

One could consider Hamish's unorthodox methodology as being the very energy that propelled his collecting forward. His view of folk culture seemed to follow similar blurred lines between material old and new as it did between informant and collector. Many hands are still wrung across internet discussion boards and elsewhere to this day about what 'folk' and 'traditional' means, as if some hard and fast definition would somehow solve a wheen of problems. This ignores the very fact of what Hamish appeared to advocate, of the constant ebb and flow and fluidity of folk culture, including the poet and the songwriter, the bard as well as the source singer. He saw no paradox or contradiction in recording a traveller's generations-old Child ballad one minute, then a budding Edinburgh songwriter's topical ditty about the Portobello sewage works and its effect on the local bathing habits the next. Herein lies a key factor in Hamish's importance for Scotland. He could easily have been another dusty antiquarian fascinated by, but despairing of, the 'last leaves' of a tradition to be captured before the twentieth century overtook it. But his linking of old and new, of renewing his carrying stream and not shying away from the stench of the Portobello sewer—whether that be literally or as a metaphor for the bawdy underbelly of Scottish folk culture![39]—has been a major catalyst in the continuing folk revivals in Scotland. It seems as if he knew that, as the Italian artist Maurizio Nannucci proffered in his 1999 work, 'All Art has been Contemporary' at some point in its life,[40] and that notions of tradition are far from static. Such ideas are borne out by the examples earlier in this chapter, of the once-contemporary Harry Lauder being recycled in the mouths of (by and large 'source') singers in the 1950s and '60s.

As we have already seen, there was also no universal method or great royal lineage to be followed in terms of how songs were learned by such tradition bearers. Contrast that with the modern way that singers today often seek approval from their peers, or 'the scene', by listing their close connections to tradition bearers (in many cases, people recorded by Hamish!). It is, at times, a rather self-aggrandising, self-fulfilling prophecy of 'the scene' that seems to crave authenticity and a real link with the tradition bearers of the past that often pays no heed to the fact that in many cases songs were in fact learned from records of the day or from far less cast-iron sources than 'oral disciples' might have us believe.

Alongside Hamish's unorthodox methodology was his attitude towards access to the School's archive holdings. As previously mentioned, this is discussed in greater detail by Ailie Munro.[41] In contrast to some of his colleagues, in particular the School's archivist at one point, Alan Bruford, Hamish's view was more flexible in terms of wider public access to materials being collected in order for young singers to hear material and learn it to carry on the stream:

> Traditional material gleaned from archives or other sources is subject to potential misuse by unethical performers; this is a risk that Hamish Henderson felt it is necessary to take. Additionally, Henderson has felt since the beginning of the School that copyright should not prevent the dissemination of traditional songs to revival singers, as we have noted. The ambivalence of the School's archivist [Alan Bruford] toward this practice is clear in the following remark: 'I would be a bit reluctant to let somebody have... free access to the School's archives for material that they wanted to perform

themselves, without having a good idea how they were likely to perform it.'[42]

Hamish's championing of the likes of Blanche Wood, Isla St Clair and Flora MacNeil, (two of whom appeared in the seminal 1951 Edinburgh People's Festival Ceilidh), all teenage singers when first recorded and put on the concert stage, demonstrates clearly that he did not believe in a delineated, museum-like approach to preserving the tradition, but adhered firmly to replenishing the carrying stream. Take Jeannie Robertson's performance of 'Mattie Groves', Child 81 'Little Musgrave and Lady Barnard', on SA1960.203, as transcribed in Bronson's *Traditional Tunes*.[43] Although it is a weighty Child ballad, the performance should, in my view, be judged on musical and performance merits alone, rather than given instant kudos as a part of an ancient 'oral' tradition because of the weight of the rest of Jeannie's repertoire. The reason being because—as far as is known—this was a song Jeannie learned from contemporary sources, including the late Sandy Paton, of the US Folkways record label, as a woman who was by then an active stage performer, keen to improve and enhance her repertoire within an evolving professional career. This would seem to have been nothing unusual, as Jeannie's career developed:

> The idea of folklore as a continuum is a relatively new idea promoted by the Americans. Here is an example of how the tradition continues to create itself. At a sing-song in a pub… in Edinburgh, I heard 'King Fareweel'… Jeannie Robertson then heard it and liked it, and… sought and learned another 'stronger' version in Aberdeen. One day she sang it to a group of Glasgow school children amongst whom was Andy Hunter… he created his own version… what, I believe, is the finest Jacobite song of all… written not in 1745 but in 1964! That… shows you the working of the folk-process, like nothing else.[44]

However, within that approach, Hamish sounded a cautionary note about 'having to steer the Scottish folksong revival between the shoals of dusty archivism on the one hand and commercial prostitution on the other'.[45]

Where is Hamish in the folk revival today?

A s I sat at the Scottish Trad Music Awards in December 2009, Hamish's words regarding Maurice Fleming's misgivings about the newly-evolving folk scene of the 1950s and '60s came into my mind:

> What is anyone of intuitive sensibility and intelligence going to think and feel when he hears a song that has achieved beauty and character on the lips of a singer such as Jeannie Robertson, or John Strachan of Fyvie, being pop-folked up by some boneheaded sod whose ideas are centred exclusively on the spondulicks? His reaction will probably be... that the entire folk-song revival must be 'the biggest confidence trick since the Sermon on the Mount'.[46]

The music I heard that night was so widely different from the music on the archive tapes, that I really began to wonder whether mine and subsequent generations have also started, like their 1960s counterparts before them, to chase the spondulicks in this internet age of YouTube and *The X-Factor*. Has an almost *überpositive* encouragement of young people into courses to study traditional music led to an endless conveyer belt of samey, carbon-copy soundalike twenty-somethings, crowding an already crowded marketplace more akin to the pop world, with little to choose between largely 'ok' performers? Between 'dusty archivism' and 'commercial prostitution', are we beginning to lean towards the latter? Does the clamour of the internet age mean people rely on other non-musical advantages like significant marketing budgets or media publicists more akin to the pop world? It is a somewhat understandable approach in this day and age, as the current folk revival wave peaks with a plethora of eager performers emerging from traditional music courses, that some kinds of hooks are needed to help filter through the barrage. Perhaps this is as much a generic twenty-first century issue as purely a folk one.

While Hamish's entire raison d'être in his collecting efforts, aside from the political aspect, would seem to aim precisely at the concerns expressed by Alan Lomax, namely that traditional, local culture was at risk of being lost, largely through mainstream society abandoning it,[47] Hamish nonetheless recognised that the media age also holds advantages for marginal cultures, as he wrote:

And what about the influence of radio and TV? Well, here again, I think the tendency has tended to be too pessimistic by half. The coming of print and the broadsheet did not kill folksong; it merely meant that another less assimilable strain entered it, leaving gobbets of material which might take decades even centuries to dissolve. The radio and TV are by comparison much more fluent media— they are (or can be) in fact, a powerful ally of culture, and offer immense possibilities for the diffusion of... our national culture... 48

In the even further developed internet age in which we find ourselves, the same near-paradox continues apace. While the internet is a homogenising force, and millions of us are all seeing the same YouTube clip disseminated via Facebook, it also provides small, accessible and punchy platforms for marginal cultures to have a place, and in some cases thrive.

But, that said—where are the Jeannie Robertsons and John Strachans? Where is Hamish in all this? An unanswerable question within the bounds of this essay, but perhaps Hamish gives us something of an answer in his own writing; he may not have found the current scene anything to worry about:

As for the songs I collected and put into circulation, I did this in the context of a definite cultural strategy... My hope... has been to encourage young folk to approach their cultural heritage with creative élan.[49]

However, one of my own misgivings focuses on one word in the above quote—'songs'. Instrumental music is yet again in rude health. It will not be answered within these pages, and I cannot speak for the Gaidhealtachd, but regarding my own lowland hameland, where are the young singers? In this internet age, with the *Tobar/ Kist* website as the major portal, it seems obvious to me that a major next stage is to seek ways to encourage young people to engage with the project, 'dig where they stand' and connect with, revive and take ownership of their local songs.

The 'normalisation' of Scottish culture?

It is now nearly a decade since Hamish's passing, and as this current book demonstrates, the time is ripe for a reappraisal of his collecting activities and legitimate questioning of its net worth in twenty-first-century, SNP-governed Scotland.

What I have tried to depict so far is Hamish's all-encompassing yet complex approach to a fluid folk culture within his collecting that did not seem to differentiate between seemingly less valuable and invaluable material, between orally-transmitted or newly-created, did not separate experienced performer from young singer interpreting old material anew, or songwriter reinterpreting a local incident that may well have repeated itself, unwittingly, over cycles in different guises from Child ballad to penny broadsheet to folk club ditty. Hamish's recording of the 'squibs', as Norman Buchan put it, was testament to the man. With this in mind we also have to consider his collecting and cultural energising in relation to Scotland's political and cultural outlook today, a very different place indeed to that which Hamish collected in. Or is it?

I have suggested that Hamish's collecting illustrates an almost forgotten or unacknowledged Scotland, one rich in folk (sub-)culture, knowledge of which has dissipated gradually through the twentieth century. Culture carried by a community described by Timothy Neat as being 'outside the loop of Church, State and Property'.[50] This is for a complex number of reasons, not least amongst them politics, and this is something I have experienced first hand. At the 2009 Hamish Henderson Memorial Lecture in Edinburgh's City Chambers, the then Culture Minister Michael Russell spoke of the 'normalisation' of Scottish culture. While this may have been meant partly as a nod to cultural and linguistic projects in Catalonia, it was a reference I had heard before, not long after the 2007 Scottish Parliament election which gave Scotland its first SNP government. At an arts event launch, an SNP MSP told me that, as far as Scottish culture was concerned, they were now just 'getting on with it'. There was no longer a stuttering debate about what it was or who was entitled to what, and the government did not have to think tactically or politically about how far it should go in acknowledging or associating with it. The implication was that for some years, successive Labour/Lib Dem — and thereby unionist — devolved governments had failed to grasp the drunk man's thistle of Scottish culture for fear that it appeared all too Scottish, and as such fuel to the separatist fire. I also recall that the initial reaction from members of the Labour administration at the City of Edinburgh Council to supporting the Hamish Henderson lecture and the Carrying Stream festival, the former which I helped instigate through my post as Traditional Arts Officer, was far from instantly warm. This probably had as much to do with Hamish's particular brand of politics—a bit too leftie for the New Labourites of the day perhaps—as anything else, but I could not help feeling there was an issue with the Scottishness of the traditionally 'uncool' folk culture he represented. It certainly was not of the ilk of Edinburgh's established festivals which are more the kind of places at which Cooncillors like to be seen! It should be said, of course, that an SNP government doth not a happy traditional arts community make! This is as much to do with the revolving door at the culture brief, as with looming spending cuts and the painful uncertainty surrounding the protracted transition to Creative Scotland. While my experience of contact with the administration has been largely positive relating to Scottish arts, the SNP government has yet to come up with the goods to earn its traddy credentials.

But this of course emphasises the fact that culture and politics are not always easy bedfellows. Anecdotally regarded as the best Minister for the Arts we never had, Norman Buchan MP (who recommended Jeannie Roberston for the MBE), was a Labour die-hard who dismissed separatism. Whether Hamish particularly attached his collecting and dissemination cultural strategy to the nationalist cause is up for debate. For all his particularly partisan approach at the time of Sky-High Joe and the EIIR postbox bombings in the 1950s,[51] going so far as to pen 'The Mains o Rhynie' in praise of the embryonic SRA,[52] Hamish seemed to have mellowed in his latter years. As a half-Dub on my father's side, I have, however, often wondered at Hamish's association with that most nationalist of Irish families, the Behans of Dublin. A keen supporter of Dominic Behan,[53] with whom he perhaps found something of a common bond, given Dominic's habit of reworking older songs under several pseudonyms, I would be interested to see if further research might reveal more in regard to Hamish's approach to the Irish question, and whether he transplanted any of that to his political and cultural thinking on Scotland. I have in my possession two songbook pamphlets which belonged to Hamish, one entitled

The 1916 Song Book, published by the Irish Book Bureau, and the other entitled *Songs, Ballads and Poems by Famous Irishmen*, by Peadar Kearney, Dominic Behan's uncle and author of the Irish national anthem. It is inscribed, 'If you did NOT get the letter with words of Boy from Wexford write and let me know/Dom'. Presumably Dominic? Whether Hamish had such items in his library purely out of folkloric, academic interest, or for more political reasons (perhaps as inspiration for contributions to the *Rebel's Ceilidh Songbook, Sangs o' the Stane* et al?), or kept them purely because they were gifts is difficult to tell. They are hardly innocuous tomes by any stretch of the imagination. Of course, the Irish brand of nationalism is a socialist republicanism which ideologically would not have been a million miles away from the author of 'The John MacLean March'. While Hamish was too much of an individual to be claimed by any one particular political party, at one time in his life it would seem the nationalist cause was a place in which he felt rather comfortable.

Leaving political debates aside, what role has the lack of 'normalisation' of Scottish culture had on the seemingly unavoidable Scottish cultural cringe? Although not writing expressly about folk culture, the *Herald* journalist Alan Taylor's words could easily be transposed onto such matters:

It is hard to think of another nation which would treat its cultural heritage so cavalierly. Hard, too, to think of another nation that would not want to champion its culture, not least to its own citizens. Scotland, though, is not like other countries. For whatever reason it has lamentably been the case for longer than one cares to think that so many of those charged with maintaining our culture have often been the ones who do their utmost to undermine it, for who knows what motives and leading to who knows what damage to the national psyche... there has never been a nation so receptive to other cultures that has treated its own with such disdain.[54]

Hamish, a remembrancer by his own definition,[55] armed with his cultural vision and drive, unabashed, tenacious, relentless and deeply politicised, his schooling and army training matched with natural ability—as Alec Finlay has described, managing to cross borders and 'cut through people's differences'[56]—set out to redress such a pitiful state of affairs, with the sorry notion that, 'very few Scots ever have a chance of hearing the old songs given in the authentic manner.'[57] It is something we should make a priority to continue to try to rectify. Part of this lamentable scenario is likely attributable to Hamish having discovered he had been kept 'off the air for ten years' by the BBC.[58] Some might also argue that the educational curriculum in Scotland in the twentieth century has resulted in whole generations having no knowledge of Allan Ramsay, Robert Tannahill, Robert Fergusson, Hugh MacDiarmid or indeed Hamish Henderson himself, meanwhile existing on a tabloid diet of myths of the Braveheart ilk.

From my own standpoint, as a former local authority officer involved in promoting the traditional arts, I have studied the evolution of a new attitude towards the traditional arts from British and Scottish administrations since the 1970s. It can be argued that Hamish's work has had a considerable role to play in this. Without the weight of the work that Hamish led on, not only as a collector but as someone who actively participated in the folk revival since the 1950s, we could still be dealing with a near-invisible subculture. Ailie Munro comments in detail on Hamish's unique role in this as one of the few members of the School of Scottish Studies staff who attended events, engaged with the revival and encouraged and recorded young performers.[59] Other staff seem to have shown a snobbery towards 'revivalists' as not being the 'real deal', evidenced by the fact that even until 1988, the School's archive card index did not have a subject heading for 'revival'.[60] Without Hamish as the go-between, the original folk scene networker, an intelligence officer of sorts once again, with a nose for marginal cultures under the surface, like tracing the old drove roads, engaging with and being trusted by Travellers, being allowed in on The Horseman's Word and things of that ilk, in a country not traditionally disposed to folkloric studies, we might still be struggling for acknowledgement. That is not to say that there is not more to do to widen knowledge of our traditional cultures to the Scottish public; there most certainly is. But we have been given an almighty push start by Seumas Mòr.

Two, or more, Scotlands?

There are two histories of every land and people, the written
history that tells what is considered politic to tell and the
unwritten history that tells everything.

Calum MacLean, 1957.

As I touched upon at the beginning of this chapter, an overview
of Hamish's collecting and the country it represents has been
in some respects difficult to obtain, for a variety of reasons, political,
practical and sentimental. I would venture that, with the examples
given thus far, we are but at the start of what needs to be a revisiting
of not only the material itself, but ideas of the wholeness of Scottish
culture. Looked at in its entirety, (although I confess my current
interpretation is biased towards the lowland Scots side; Hamish also
did considerable work in the Gaidhealtachd), Hamish's collecting
presents us with an image of a different Scotland than we are used
to in these demarcated, categorisation-dependent times. Henderson's
vision, nay his personal experience, was of a Scotland where the
supposed twa cultures lived cheek by jowl, more often than not being
happy bedfellows and producing—sometimes incestuous!—offspring.
In recent years, imbalances in government funding for cultures defined
on linguistic terms has opened up rifts between Scots and Gaelic, or
lowland and highland (however one wishes to style it), that seem
somehow anathema to Hamish's own background, experience and
vision, as evidenced by items from his collecting heyday. Consider
Hamish's interview in 1954 with 83-year-old Geordie Robertson,
Jeannie Robertson's uncle. In a largely Scots-language-dominated
session, Hamish asks Geordie about some of Geordie's relatives from
Struan in Perthshire, in amongst various other queries about Gaelic
terms for particular items:

HH: If I said tae ye 'A bheil gàidhlig agad?' [Do you have Gaelic?]
GR: 'Ye're speirin if I have the Gaelic! Chan eil gàidhlig…' [I haven't
got Gaelic…tape cuts off][61]

A beautiful juxtaposition of Scots and Gaelic, unusual and probably
uncomfortable for those central-belters of a them-and-us mindset.
Geordie Robertson switches with little thought or apprehension. In
its own way, without overstating the case, it represents what was

particularly Hamish. What this shows, I believe, is a glimpse into a gentler, more culturally-intertwined Scotland than is readily thought to be the case these days by a painfully ignorant majority of the Scottish populus. This shows vital information on social attitudes towards Gaelic amongst older sections of society, a world away from the divisive attitudes I have occasionally encountered in the course of my arts administration career. To my mind, this does away with that most frequent of central-belt monoglot internet bulletin board posts, 'this was never a Gaelic area!'[62] — perhaps written from Balerno (Baile Àirneach, 'hawthorn farm'), or Craigentinny (Creag an t-Sionnaich, 'rock of the fox').[63] It also undermines any preconceived ideas about Jeannie as a great doyen of pure lowland Scots folksong — firstly she was already trilingual, in Scots, English and Cant — as here is her uncle in reach of a Perthshire Gaelic heritage. There are occasional tapes throughout the archive of primarily Scots-language informants with mixtures of language across the highland line, or with contact to Gaelic through their close family, though it may not have been passed down to them.

Such attitudes did and do not necessarily apply to Gaelic alone but, as Hamish has suggested in his personal notes, to wider folk culture, describing modern Scotland's attitude towards the poet as being 'one of amused contempt, mixed sometimes with hostility — particularly in Edinburgh — the only town I know where the bourgeois mental attitude... has soaked down to the entire working class.'[64] A man of languages and letters, a true Weltenbürger — literally 'a citizen of many worlds' — Hamish railed at such divisive attitudes, and through his work and writing proved the facileness and futility of seeking to artificially compartmentalise Scotland into separate linguistic and cultural camps, like trying to carry the Niagara — the carrying stream — in a tin can full of holes. He knew full well that the lines were far from thick, black and rigid, but rather more like intermingling tributaries crossing the centuries through the Perthshire hills. As Alec Finlay states in the introduction to *Alias MacAlias*:

Hamish revelled in this polyglot oral tradition, which made such a nonsense of the ascendancy of any single tongue. He took delight in demonstrating that all languages are... 'bastard' affairs. He insists there is to be no standard language; no orthography should ever become a question of race or blood; even the orthodoxy of a single homogenous nation is repudiated.[65]

Perhaps all of this shows us a glimmer of an even older past described by 0Professor Thomas Owen Clancy, Chair of Celtic at the University of Glasgow:

...the divide between Gael and lowlander was never a chasm. Throughout the early modern period, individuals and families moved between both zones and both cultures. Towns like Perth, Stirling, Aberdeen had long-standing relationships with Gaelic-speaking hinterlands which were close at hand. In the 15th century the lords of the isles were as often in their seats in Inverness and Dingwall as in Islay. The family whose hands scribed the most important manuscript of the Gaelic middle ages, the 16th century Book of the Dean of Lismore, boasted notary publics; in this manuscript, Gaelic poems are rendered in the spelling conventions of lowland Scots.[66]

Linked to this is the idea of the proud mongrel hybrid, described by Fred Freeman in his inaugural Hamish Henderson memorial lecture in 2002,[67] and Hamish's apparent delight in exposing the bundle of contradictions we are, firstly as a country, and as individuals. One of the best examples of this is Jock Cameron, originally from Fife, latterly from Granton, Edinburgh, a tape of whom I catalogued for *Tobar/ Kist* on SA1953.262. A proud Orangeman, and from a long line thereof, he also sang, oddly, some might venture, the Jacobite 'King Farweel'. Hamish attributed this partly to Jock wishing to 'honour the memory of another breed of 'Loyalists' who had fought for a different cause... he recognised the Jacobites as having been in their own way Scottish patriots.'[68] On the tape, Jock says he got the song from his grandfather, a Black Watch soldier from near Inverness. Therein also lies a simpler reason often overlooked by eager folklorists seeking weighty reasons behind a song appearing in a singer's repertoire which appears again and again on the tapes—its currency within the singer's own family.

Hamish's work therefore illustrates a Scotland that is piob mhòr and Aberdeenshire fiddle, bothy ballad and waulking song, well-travelled broadside and psalm, muckle sang and silly Jack tale, traveller cant, beurla reagaird, Gàidhlig agus Scots, fisher toon and Glenlivet fairm,

Lewis machair and Kintyre village, Edinburgh schoolyaird and Glasgow howff, Orange and Green and Red, and many colours in between.

The Kist is rich

Hamish is rightly revered for his overarching omnipresence in the cycle of folk revivals since the 1950s, and, well-complemented by many illustrious fellow collectors, colleagues and compatriots, he was the key figure in the profile of the School of Scottish Studies since its inception. It is very easy to idolise and mythologise him, given the very nature of the gregarious man he was, and the way in which the natural romanticism of the folk scene has helped cultivate his image. But the cold, hard facts remain. His contribution to the field of Scottish folklore, in the way in which he acted as a focal point and fulcrum, not only for collecting but for propagating songs, writing of new material and re-energising the folk process, is unrivalled.

For all of Hamish's belief in and advocacy of the value of Scottish traditional culture, it needs to be seen through the prism of the man, who was far from one-dimensional. The expanded 2004 edition of *Alias MacAlias* deserves to be more fully read. A full reading, in between the lines, and in conjunction with the tapes, gives a broader and multi-faceted picture of a culturally-rich Scotland across all its geography and communities; not only that but also a Scotland removed from insular soul-searching isolation, and positioned easily within *Weltkultur*. Hamish quite readily juxtaposed items from his fieldwork with the likes of Hölderlin, Lorca and Gramsci, and never in an effort at intellectual superiority, but in validation, like Calum MacLean, 'lifting the humble/ Whom our age put aside'.[69]

If we are truly to 'normalise' Scottish culture, perhaps it is time to steer ourselves away from idealistic notions of cultural nationalism and distinctiveness, towards a more Hendersonian *Weltkultur,* or a Lomaxian cultural equity.[70] The evidence in the archive, as far as Scots song goes, suggests that we need to become more informed and honest about the common folksong culture we share—through the well-travelled ballads and the cheap printing press—with our Anglic-speaking neighbours south of the border, in Ireland and across the Atlantic, and unhinge ourselves from from over-obsessing about the 'oral' and 'authentic'.

While understandably seen as primarily Scoto-centric, Hamish's work is permeated with a constant Weltanschauung, with 'aa the bairns o Adam' in his 'hoose', and therein lies the nub of the man; he was as much 'Rhynie' as 'Rivonia'. The ad-libbed farewell given at the end of a 1979 ceilidh at the School of Scottish Studies is proof eneuch. (Duncan Williamson and Stanley Robertson had just sung songs describing discrimination against the Travellers, including how Travellers fought for their country but were shunned by the authorities at home):

A few weeks ago I was in the desert, I saw the burial ground at Alamein, which is a... sight that would stay in my mind for a long long time. And among the graves there, I saw among Gordons, Argylls, Camerons and Seaforths... names like Stewart, and Williamson, and Kelbie, that reminded me of many folk that I knew at home. I also saw the graves of the people that were in the 1st South African division that I was attached to. Dutch and British South Afrikaaners and South Africans with names like [Ngoulouleme?] and one or two other African names. These were cape coloured lads, all these are lying together, there is NO Apartheid in that graveyard. And that is the last wish, last thought rather, linking to Stanley [Robertson]'s song and Duncan [Williamson]'s song, that I would leave with you. If it is a sober and thoughtful thought, then it's none the worse for that. But we have enjoyed ourselves, once again, good nicht.[71]

In a conversation in Sandy Bell's, after the launch of the second volume of Timothy Neat's Hamish biography in November 2009, I got involved with two friends who shared my own part-Irish heritage, one of whom had been one of Hamish's helpers in the latter years of his life. We shared many funny tales about Hamish and ourselves (although the tales of Hamish were exclusively theirs; I can never pretend to have known the man in person), and our shared conclusion was that, away from all the academic theorising, Hamish's greatest ability, from the pulpit of Sandy Bell's, was in encouraging us to be ourselves. To take gentle pride in the culture that is ours, to not shy away from it, nor feel that we ever have to apologise for it or hold it in disdain. It was his belief that our own individual cultures, Scots and Gaelic, however pure or mongrel hybrid, were all valid parts of the shared human experience, and could stand shoulder to shoulder with the greatest world literary and cultural figures, and that we were simply fooling ourselves and taking things for granted if we believed otherwise. As if almost to echo the more progressive arguments in favour of Scottish self-determination, in terms of our own culture Hamish taught us to dig where we stand, that the shovel is our own, it is already in our hands, and the digging is ours to do. He has plooed the soil for us and sown the seeds; we must cultivate the crop year on year, and bring in the hairst.

Now, for the first time, we have widespread access to these endless riches from the Tober/ Kist project. Hopefully, the material therein will, in the spirit of Hamish, renew the cultural life of Scotland through reconnecting communities with the riches many may have never known they had. The clamour of the internet-powered early twenty-first century is of course arguably much greater than the entire clamour of the twentieth century, but we must persist, and use the power of newfangled tools to whittle it down, to re-create and re-energise from within, à la Hamish. We must find a way to educate sometimes glaikit Scots in a meaningful way about the culture they have been missing, that has been kept from them—whether for reasons of politics, cultural cringe or pure economy of scale—and insist that in our society, grandad's old songs are worth something more than being simply New Year party pieces. And it is with a proper presentation, dissemination and honest, objective and well-informed reinterpretation of Hamish Henderson's collecting legacy, and Hamish's personal archives, that we must begin.

References:

1 Annual Hamish Henderson memorial lecture, on 7 November 2009, at the City Chambers of Edinburgh, as part of the eighth Carrying Stream Festival.

2 *Folk Music Journal*, Vol. 6, no. 2 (1991), pp. 132-168.

3 See http://www.tobarandualchais.co.uk / www.kistoriches.co.uk

4 Due to funding shortfalls at the time of writing, the work of *Tobar/Kist* may not manage to catalogue all the School's material as envisaged, but will still achieve several thousand valuable hours' worth of catalogued recordings for public access.

5 Hamish Henderson, *Alias MacAlias*, edited by Alec Finlay (Edinburgh: Polygon, 2004), p. xxvii.

6 Hamish writing in 1956, quoted in Timothy Neat, *Hamish Henderson, A*

Biography: Volume 2 (Edinburgh: Polygon, 2009), p. 121.

7   *Ibid*, p. 21.

8   *Songs of a Scots Tinker Lady*, Riverside Records RLP 12-633.

9   James Porter and Herschel Gower,   *Jeannie Robertson, Emerging Singer, Transformative Voice* (Phantassie: Tuckwell Press, 1997), p. 4.

10 Hamish Henderson, *The Armstrong Nose: Selected Letters of Hamish Henderson*, edited by Alec Finlay (Edinburgh: Polygon, 1996), pp. 76-78.

11 The School of Scottish Studies archive system uses SA for 'Sound Archive', 19XX.xxx for the year and tape number. Specific item numbers are also given in most cases, eg, SA1960.203.B9, with A usually referring to side one of the tape, B to side 2.

12 Catherine Kerrigan & Meg Bateman (ed.), *An Anthology of Scottish Women Poets* (Edinburgh: Edinburgh University Press, 1992), p. 150.

13 Published by Peer International Corp/ Peermusic (UK) Ltd.

14 Kerrigan & Bateman, p. 5.

15 SA1960.203, transcribed by Steve Byrne.

16 Porter & Gower, p. 150.

17 *Ibid.*, pp. 201-202.

18 Particularly through the Internet Archive, archive.org, and the University of California Santa Barbara Cylinder Preservation and Digitization project (http://cylinders.library.ucsb.edu/).

19 Ewan MacColl & Peggy Seeger, *Till Doomsday in the Afternoon: Folklore of a Family of Scots Travellers, the Stewarts of Blairgowrie* (Manchester: Manchester University Press, 1986). As far as I know, this song does not exist digitally and does not appear on modern CD re-releases of Lauder discs. The sheet music for the song was copyrighted in 1906, printed in 'Francis & Day's 2nd Album of Harry Lauder's Popular Songs', London, c.1909-1912.

20 Alias MacAlias, p. 32, quoting from 'The Underground of Song', in *The Scots Magazine* (Feb 1963).

21 SA1962.74.B14-17.

22 SA1963.83.A15.

23 Alias MacAlias, p. 20, quoting from 'Rock and Reel', in *Scotland* (November 1958).

24 See *Tocher* 43 (1991), p. 21.

25 Porter & Gower, p. 282.

26 Alias MacAlias, p. 209.

27 See 'Hey Donald! How Donald!' in *Complete Songs and Poems of Robert Tannahill* (1877), p. 21.

28 'Donald Cowper' in Hans Hecht, *Songs from David Herd's Manuscripts*,

(Edinburgh: W J Hay, 1904), p. 172.

29 Such as 'King James and the Tinker' and 'William and Nancy, or The Two Hearts', both on SA1954.091, with broadside versions in the Bodleian Library as far back as 1796. The former possibly has a traceable lineage to the 1560s, as a relation of Child 273, 'King Edward the Fourth and a Tanner of Tamworth'.

30 SA1958.064, transcribed by Steve Byrne.

31 Bodleian Library broadsides collection, shelfmarks: 2806 c.8(94), Harding B 26(328).

32 http://www.bodley.ox.ac.uk/ballads/ballads.htm

33 SA1960.203, transcribed by Steve Byrne.

34 Bodleian Library Broadsides Collection Coles, F (London); Vere, T (London); Wright, J (London); Clarke, J (London), Date: between 1674 and 1679 – Shelfmark: 4o Rawl. 566(108).

35 Alias MacAlias, p. xxiii.

36 Ailie Munro, The Folk Music Revival in Scotland (London: Kahn & Averill, 1984), p. 96.

37 In some cases it is only through careful listening to the enhanced digital versions of the tapes that recording breaks within song performances can be detected. This may imply that sessions have been stopped in order for a contributor to remember or to locate a verse, perhaps from a printed source, (or perhaps with the assistance of the fieldworker?). Additionally, although this is nothing to do with the propriety of Hamish's collecting style, the tapes reveal that a considerable number of informants sang from books or manuscripts. Again, this is only clear from being able to enhance the digitised versions of the tapes and listen to pages being turned.

38 Neat (2009), p. xv.

39 Hamish performed an important role in his collecting of bawdy material, so often eschewed by earlier collectors; in fact, he seemed to revel in it, transmitting a great swathe of it into his own works such as 'Auld Reekie's Roses'.

40 Nannucci's art installation – All Art has been Contemporary in neon letters – famously graced the entrance of the Altes Museum in Berlin.

41 Ailie Munro, 'The Role of the School of Scottish Studies in the Folk Music Revival', Folk Music Journal, Vol. 6, no. 2 (1991), pp. 132-68.

42 Ibid., p. 148.

43 Bertrand H Bronson, Traditional Tunes of the Child Ballads (Princeton: Princeton University Press), 4 volumes, 1959-1972.

44 Neat (2009), pp. 128-129, quoting from Henderson archive.

45 Ibid., p. 139, quoting from the Henderson archive.

46 Alias MacAlias, p. 15.

47 Alan Lomax, 'Saga of a Folksong Hunter – A Twenty-year Odyssey with Cylinder, Disc and Tape', *HiFi Stereo Review* (May 1960).

48 Neat (2009), p. 126, quoting from Hamish Henderson, 'Rock and Reel', *Scotland* (November 1958).

49 Neat (2009), p. 138, quoting from a letter to Jimmie MacGregor, 10 Feb 1967.

50 Neat (2009), p. 340.

51 *Ibid.*, pp. 313-337.

52 SRA = Scottish Republican Army. See Neat (2009), pp. 315-317.

53 Dominic was invited by Hamish to appear at the 1954 People's Festival Ceilidh. See SA1954.105.

54 Alan Taylor, 'What is art?', *The Herald* (7 Feb 2010).

55 Hamish calls himself and fellow folklorists from the early days of the School of Scottish Studies this in his commentary in Timothy Neat's film *Journey to a Kingdom*, 1992.

56 Alias MacAlias, p. xxiii.

57 Neat (2009), p. 307.

58 Hamish writes of meeting an associate of BBC 'high-heid yins' sometime after 1957, who told him as much, in, 'It was in you that it a' began', in *The People's Past*, edited by Edward J Cowan (Edinburgh: EUSPB, 1980), p. 12.

59 Munro, pp. 154-155.

60 *Ibid.*, pp. 150-151.

61 SA1954.091.

62 See <<http://thescotsman.scotsman.com/scotland/Mike-Russell-Attack-on-Gaelic.5891248.jp>> and <<http://edinburghnews.scotsman.com/topstories/Critics-pan-plan-to-put.5788975.jp>>, accessed Sep 2010.

63 City of Edinburgh Council Gaelic Language Plan Draft, 2009, p. 13. Edinburgh has a long Gaelic lineage—as the Plan also states, 'The first printed Gaelic book was published in Edinburgh in 1567, as were the first secular Gaelic book (1741) and the first collection of Gaelic poetry (1751). The Highland Society of Edinburgh, a leading academic and cultural body, was set up in 1784. The University of Edinburgh was the first in Scotland to establish a Chair of Celtic, in 1882. A bilingual plaque in Johnston Terrace marks the site of the first Gaelic Chapel in the city, established in 1767.'

64 Quoted in Neat (2009), p. 139.

65 Alias MacAlias, pp. xxvi-xxvii.

66 Professor T O Clancy, 'Gaelic Scotland: a brief history', quoted on the Bòrd na Gàidhlig website, <http://www.gaidhlig.org.uk/a-ghaidhlig/about-gaelic/history.html>>, accessed Sept 2010.

67 Initiated by Edinburgh Folk Club with the support of the City of Edinburgh

Council. At the time I was the Council's Traditional Arts Development Officer, one of the few posts of its kind in Scotland at the time. A version of the lecture is published in the sleeve notes to 'A' the Bairns o Adam' tribute CD, Greentrax CDTRAX244.

68 Alias MacAlias, p. 191.

69 From 'Cumha Chaluim Iain MhicGill-Eain'/ Elegy for Calum I. MacLean', by his brother Sorley.

70 See 'Appeal for Cultural Equity', in Alan Lomax, *Selected Writings 1934-1997*, edited by Ronald Cohen (New York/London: Routledge, 2005), pp. 285-99.

71 SA1979.019.8. Whether there really are people of those Traveller names at Alamein is not clear; not all of these appear on the Commonwealth War Graves Commission records for Alamein. Nonetheless, the power of Hamish's point, in equating the Travellers' plight with the apartheid regime, remains.

CONTRIBUTORS

MARGARET BENNETT worked closely with Hamish Henderson in the School of Scottish Studies at the University of Edinburgh. She is an internationally renowned singer, folklorist and prize-winning author. Her books include *Scottish Customs from the Cradle to the Grave*; *Oatmeal and the Catechism: Scottish Gaelic Settlers in Quebec*; and in 2009, *Dìleab Ailein: Newfoundland Traditions Across Four Generations*. Her latest book: *In Our Day ...Reminiscence & Songs from Rural Perthshire* in press, Grace Note Publications, 2010.

EBERHARD 'PADDY' BORT works at the Institute of Governance at the University of Edinburgh. He is also chair of Edinburgh Folk Club who have, since 2002, organised the annual Carrying Stream Festival—a celebration of he life and legacy of Hamish Henderson (www.carryingstreamfestival.co.uk).

STEVE BYRNE is a folksinger and folklorist from Arbroath. A graduate of the School of Scottish Studies, he plays with one of Scotland's leading folksong groups, Malinky, as well as being an established solo artist. For five years from 2002-2007, he was Traditional Arts Officer for the City of Edinburgh Council, before departing to work on Tobar an Dualchais / Kist o Riches as a Scots Song cataloguer.

COREY GIBSON is, at the time of writing, a PhD candidate with the English Literature Department of the University of Edinburgh. His thesis explores the formulation and implications of Hamish Henderson's cultural-politics.

ROB GIBSON has been a long time SNP activist and former District Councillor in Ross and Cromarty. He is currently a Member of the Scottish Parliament. Scots, Gaelic and Traditional Arts are core interests as are nuclear disarmament, affordable housing and saving consultant led services in the NHS.

GEORGE GUNN was born in Thurso, Caithness, where in 1996 he returned to live and work with the Grey Coast Theatre Company, of which he is the artistic director. He is well-known for his stage plays, and has had several collections of poems published, the latest being *The Atlantic Forest*.

JOY HENDRY is the editor of Scotland's finest literary journal, *Chapman*, and has published widely on Scottish poetry and literature for many years.

TOM HUBBARD's most recent book is the novel *Marie B.* (Ravenscraig Press), based on the life of the Ukrainian-French painter Marie Bashkirtseff. In the Spring Semester of 2011, he is Lynn Wood Neag Distinguished Visiting Professor of British Literature at the University of Connecticut.

GEORDIE MCINTYRE is a Glaswegian of Highland and Irish descent. His lifelong involvement in traditional song and poetry is reflected in his singing, collecting and song-writing. He has recorded four joint albums with his wife Alison McMorland, the latest being *Where Ravens Reel*—launched at the 2010 Carrying Stream Festival.

BRIAN MCNEILL is a Scottish folk multi-instrumentalist, songwriter, record producer and musical director. He was a founding member of the groundbreaking Battlefield Band and Director of traditional Music at the Royal Scottish Academy for Music and Drama in Glasgow.

EWAN MCVICAR was born in Inverness in 1941. As a singer, songwriter, collector of children's lore and one of Scotland's best known storytellers, Ewan has visited over 200 schools in Scotland and six other countries. Ewan has written or co-written several books on aspects of Scots traditional song.

PINO MEREU is an Italian scholar, translator and folklorist, born in Sardinia, and the organiser of the Hamish Henderson Folk Club in Rome.

TIMOTHY NEAT is an art historian, writer and film-maker. His two-volume biography of Hamish Henderson was published by Polygon in 2007 and 2009. Other books include *Part Seen, Part Imagined, The Summer Walkers, The Voice of the Bard*; Films include *Hallaig, The Tree of Liberty, Play Me Something* (winner of the Europa Prize, Barcelona 1989).

TESSA RANSFORD (www.wisdomfield.com) is a poet, translator, literary editor and cultural activist, having also worked as founder and director of the Scottish Poetry Library. Tessa initiated the annual Callum Macdonald Memorial Award for publishers of pamphlet poetry in Scotland, with the attendant fairs (www.scottish-pamphlet-poetry.com). Her *Not Just Moonshine: New and Selected Poems* (Luath) was published in 2008.

MARIO RELICH is an Associate Lecturer in English and Postcolonial Literature at the Open University. He is on the Board of the Scottish Poetry Library and Secretary of the Poetry Association of Scotland.

DONALD SMITH is founding director of the Scottish Storytelling Centre, and was artistic director of its predecessor, the Netherbow. As playwright, novelist, storyteller, teacher and commentator he operates on the cultural frontline, and counts Hamish Henderson as a formative influence. He is currently a visiting professor at Napier University, and a long-term associate of the School of Celtic and Scottish Studies at Edinburgh University.

SHEILA STEWART MBE is the last in the line of the Stewarts o' Blair, a travelling family who have made a unique contribution to the musical and oral traditions of Scotland. Her mother was the legendary 'Queen amang the Heather', the singer and storyteller Belle Stewart, and her father, Willie Stewart, was a noted piper. Her books include *Pilgrims of the Mist: The Stories of Scotland's Travelling People* (Birlinn), *Queen Amang the Heather: The Life of Belle Stewart* (Birlinn), and her *A Traveller's Life: The Autobiography of Sheila Stewart* wilkl be out from Birlinn in March 2011.

GARY WEST is head of the School of Celtic and Scottish Studies at the University of Edinburgh. Originally from Perthshire, he became a student of Hamish Henderson at the School of Scottish Studies at the age of 18. He is also a distinguished piper and broadcaster.

Printed in Great Britain
by Amazon.co.uk, Ltd.,
Marston Gate.